This book examines a question generally neglected in the study of
international relations: why does a militarily and economically less
powerful state initiate war against a relatively strong state? Thazha
Varkey Paul analyzes this phenomenon by focusing on the strategic
and political factors which influence a weaker state's decision for war.
The key argument of deterrence theory is that the military superiority
of the status quo power, coupled with a credible retaliatory threat,
will prevent attack by challengers. The author questions this notion
by examining six twentieth-century asymmetric wars: the Japanese
offensive against Russia in 1904; the Japanese attack on Pearl Harbor
in 1941; the Chinese intervention in Korea in 1950; the Pakistani
offensive in Kashmir in 1965; the Egyptian offensive in the Sinai in
1973; and the Argentine invasion of the Falkland Islands in 1982. The
book's findings have wide implications for the study of war, power,
deterrence, coercive diplomacy, strategy, arms races, and alliances.

ASYMMETRIC CONFLICTS: WAR INITIATION BY WEAKER POWERS

Cambridge Studies in International Relations is a joint initiative of Cambridge University Press and the British International Studies Association (BISA). The series will include a wide range of material, from undergraduate textbooks and surveys to research-based monographs and collaborative volumes. The aim of the series is to publish the best new scholarship in International Studies from Europe, North America and the rest of the world.

CAMBRIDGE STUDIES IN INTERNATIONAL RELATIONS

Series list continues after index

ASYMMETRIC CONFLICTS: WAR INITIATION BY WEAKER POWERS

T. V. PAUL

Assistant Professor, Department of Political Science
McGill University

CAMBRIDGE
UNIVERSITY PRESS

Published by the Press Syndicate of the University of Cambridge
The Pitt Building, Trumpington Street, Cambridge CB2 1RP
40 West 20th Street, New York, NY 10011-4211, USA
10 Stamford Road, Oakleigh, Melbourne 3166, Australia

First published 1994

A catalogue record for this book is available from the British Library

Library of Congress cataloguing in publication data

Paul, Thazha Varkey
Asymmetric conflicts: war initiation by weaker powers /
Thazha Varkey Paul.
     p.   cm. – (Cambridge studies in international relations: 33)
Includes bibliographical references and index.
ISBN 0 521 45117 5 (hardback)   0 521 46621 0 (paperback)
1. War (International law) 2. Great powers. 3. States, Small.
4. International relations. I. Title. II. Series.
JX4511.P38 1994
355.02–dc20 93–1794 CIP

ISBN 0 521 45117 5 hardback
ISBN 0 521 46621 0 paperback

Transferred to digital printing 1999

CONTENTS

TABLES

PREFACE

Events in the Persian Gulf during 1990–91 brought back fears of large-scale conventional wars suddenly erupting in theaters of perpetual tension such as the Middle East. Although predictions of obsolescence of major wars among advanced industrialized countries hold for the time being, war still seems the *ultima ratio* for resolving conflict, at least among some states. The Persian Gulf War generated debates, especially in the United States, on the advantages of air power and short wars and the virtue of high spending for sophisticated weaponry, even during a period of relative economic decline. In January 1991, the US decision-makers abandoned their earlier adopted strategies of deterrence and coercive diplomacy against Iraq in favor of "compellence" or active use of military force.

The American deterrence strategy was aimed at preventing Iraq from undertaking further attacks on other states in the region, especially Saudi Arabia, while the compellence strategy was meant to pressure the Iraqi leadership into backing down from its annexation of Kuwait. The behavior of the challenging smaller power during both the crisis and the subsequent war raised doubts about the notion that when confronted with overwhelming force, states would modify their recalcitrant positions. To a certain extent, the Iraqi willingness to suffer incalculable damage at the hands of a multinational force headed by a super power, possessing several times superior technological prowess, military capability, and economic power, showed the limits of applying coercive diplomacy against a determined opponent.

History has witnessed over and again challengers and defenders, both strong and weak, pitted against each other on the battlefield. Traditional schools of power politics, such as balance of power, view the outbreak of war among equal powers as less likely because power parity neutralizes both states' chances for victory. Attacks by weaker powers against stronger opponents are seen as improbable given the notion that rational decision-makers would not engage in such risky ventures that they are likely to lose. More modern schools of conflict behavior such as deterrence also view war initiation by weaker powers as unlikely, especially if the superior power has the capability to deny the challenger battlefield success.

This book looks at the empirical question of why, repeatedly in history, weaker powers have engaged in wars against stronger adversaries. I argue that a state inferior in overall power capabilities, even after assessing its disadvantages vis-à-vis the opponent, may still go to war against its stronger adversary by making choices that are within the realm of rational calculations. These choices depend largely on the particular strategy, weapons, and great power alliance support that the weaker state holds and domestic configurations in these states prior to war initiation. This contention is examined in the light of several historic cases and by looking at the decision-making process before the outbreak of war.

The work on this study has been greatly assisted by a number of senior scholars, colleagues, and friends, primarily at the University of California, Los Angeles (UCLA) and McGill University, Montreal, and family members. My deep and sincere gratitude goes to Richard Rosecrance who provided several valuable theoretical and empirical insights as well as moral support from the very outset. Several of my colleagues and friends at UCLA, McGill University, and elsewhere provided excellent assistance, especially by way of commenting on earlier chapter versions. They include: Alexander George, John Mueller, Kal Holsti, Richard Smoke, Michael Intriligator, Richard Sisson, Cherie Steele, John Hall, David Lake, John Kroll, Ajit Jha, and Jennifer Tow. I am particularly grateful to Professors George, Mueller, and Smoke and Cherie Steele for making extensive theoretical and methodological comments on earlier chapter versions. The UCLA Workshop on International Security was a great arena for intellectual exchange, constructive criticism, and re-evaluation of my arguments. A number of students who took my graduate seminar on international conflict and cooperation at McGill University also helped me refine some of the arguments.

George Quester, John Vasquez, Bennett Ramburg, Edward Laurance, Robert Glasser, and Lars Skalans read the extensive research proposal and made useful suggestions. Others who helped me in one way or other include: Michael Brecher, Baldev Raj Nayar, Arthur Stein, Robert Dallek, Damodar Sar Desai, Patrick James, Paul Noble, Jerome Black, Mark Brawley, Bahgat Korany, Vendulka Kubalkova, William Potter, Samuel Noumoff, Hudson Meadwell, R. Venu, T.T. Poulose, B. Vivekanandan, and Mustapha El-Seyed. Christian Dinwoodie and Mark Peranson provided excellent research assistance. Professor Zhu

Chun and interpreter Zhu Liu of the Beijing Institute for International Strategic Studies hosted my visit to China in August 1992 and extended generous hospitality. I am also thankful to my brother, T.V. Mathew and my in-laws, Anna and P.O. Varghese for their constant encouragement. My wife, Rachel deserves special praise for her unfailing support and assistance during the undertaking. She showed great enthusiasm for the project by way of editing and proofreading several drafts as well as by bearing with my occasional absences during field trips abroad. Thanks also goes to my little daughter, Kavya, for being a great source of joy and inspiration.

Generous financial assistance was provided by fellowships and travel assistance from the University of California's Institute on Global Conflict and Cooperation (IGCC); US Institute of Peace, Washington DC, through its Randolph Jennings Peace Scholar Award; Institute for the Study of World Politics, Washington DC; UCLA's Center for International and Strategic Affairs (CISA) and the Department of Political Science; and McGill University, through a social science research grant. The travel supports facilitated my undertaking useful field research trips to Japan, China, India, Pakistan, Argentina, and Egypt and conducting extensive interviews with scholars and decision-makers in these countries who have knowledge of the cases. These interviews undoubtedly provided me with greater insight into the wars, their variations and commonalities as well as the specific contexts in which they were fought. In these countries several individuals helped me to make the trips fruitful by arranging interviews and other facilities and I thank them all.

I THE THEORETICAL FRAMEWORK

1 INTRODUCTION: WAR INITIATION IN INTERNATIONAL RELATIONS THEORY

This book addresses the question of war initiation in asymmetric conflicts – a conflict in which two states with unequal power resources confront each other on the battlefield. In most theoretical discussions on war, not much attention has been paid to the basic question under investigation here: *Why does a militarily and economically less powerful state initiate war against a relatively strong state?* Examples of asymmetric wars in which the weaker side attacked its stronger opponent abound. Prominent ancient cases include the Spartan attack on a coalition of Athens, Corinth, and Argos in 394 BC, Pyrrus' attack on Italy in 275 BC, the several Gallic, Gothic, and Heruli invasions of the Roman Empire in the third century AD,[1] and the Muslim invasion of Persia in AD 636.[2]

In the modern era, a number of such wars have occurred. For instance, Frederick the Great possessed an inferior force level when he waged the Seven Years' War against Austria. In fact, his 30,000-strong Prussian Army beat an Austrian force of 80,000 at Leuthen.[3] The Hungarian attack on Turkey in 1747 is another case of this nature. The initiators of the First Balkan War in 1912 – Bulgaria, Serbia, and Greece – possessed a combined force smaller than that of their target state, Turkey, and yet were able to defeat their superior adversary.[4] The Paraguayan attack on the allied forces of Argentina, Brazil, and Uruguay in 1866, the Japanese attack on Russia in 1904, the Polish–Ukrainian attack on the USSR in 1920, the Finnish attack on the USSR in 1941, and the Japanese attack on Pearl Harbor in 1941 are other prominent examples of relatively weak states initiating wars in the modern era.

In the post-World War II period, several wars have been initiated by weaker states against their more powerful adversaries. The Chinese intervention in Korea (1950), the Pakistani offensive in Kashmir (1965), the Israeli attack on the Arab states (1967), the Egyptian offensive against Israel in the Sinai (1973), the Syrian offensive against Israel in the Golan Heights (1973), the Cambodian military incursions against Vietnam (1977), the Somali attack on Ethiopia (1977), the Ugandan attack on Tanzania (1978), the Argentine invasion of the Falklands (1982), and the Croatian offensives against Serbia (1993) all stand out as important cases in which the relatively weak side launched war against a state with more overall power capability.[5]

Although it is not the focus of this study, a number of brinkmanship crises have also been initiated by weaker states.[6] Iraq's brinkmanship behavior during the Persian Gulf Crisis of 1990–91 is such a case. The Iraqi regime's annexation of Kuwait in August 1990 and its unwillingness to defuse the crisis by withdrawing from the occupied nation led to a militarily disastrous situation vis-à-vis a superior US-led coalition. The ensuing military confrontation virtually threatened the very survival of the Iraqi state, suggesting that a weaker nation even under threat of annihilation need not bow down to the enormous military power arrayed against it. In addition, several wars of independence in Asia, Africa, and Latin America have been initiated and won against colonial and imperial powers by weaker liberation forces. In the post-war era, many powerful countries had to withdraw their interventionist armies without achieving their objectives against less powerful guerrilla forces.[7]

The rationale for this study thus springs from a realization that these cases neither comprise a negligible number of inter-state wars in the modern age, nor are merely inconsequential outliers in the overall incidence of international warfare. Although there have been significant attempts to define and theorize global wars, asymmetric wars initiated by weaker states still elude serious attention from the field of international politics. Major systemic explanations of war tend to focus upon long-term changes in hegemonic leadership and control associated with structural conditions in the international system.[8] Other theorists have attempted to find causes of wars in the growth and changes in population, technology, resources, markets, and national expansion.[9] Although these explanations provide broad theoretical bases for understanding international conflict, especially the underlying causes resulting from anarchy and other structural properties, they tend to be of limited use in explaining proximate or contextual factors that lead to the outbreak of asymmetric wars, in particular their timing. As A.J.P. Taylor observes, the general causes of wars may be found in systemic properties such as anarchy, but for particular causes that resulted in specific wars one has to look deeper into situational or contextual factors.[10]

Crucial studies on systemic and sub-systemic wars have also focused upon separate long-run and short-run variables that have correlations to war initiation.[11] One of the central debates among theorists who study long-term variables has been whether power parity among opposing states or preponderance of the status quo power preserves peace at the systemic as well as the sub-systemic level.[12] This debate is largely derived from the conception of classical balance of power theory which contends that the power preponderance of one state or a coalition of states is so unstable that wars are bound to occur as such a state or a coalition is tempted to indulge in aggressive behavior.

Power parity and war initiation

Notwithstanding the disagreement among scholars and statesmen on the precise meaning of balance of power, it can reasonably be stated that the theory is predicated on the argument that peace is preserved only when an equilibrium of power exists among great powers as otherwise the strong may attack the weak.[13] The initiators of wars generally are stronger states who, if not balanced by countervailing power, would be tempted to upset the status quo in order to change the system in their favor. If an equal distribution of power exists, no single state or coalition of states will possess overwhelming preponderant power and thereby the incentives to launch war against weaker states. In other words, power parity prevents war since no state can expect victory in such a situation. The potential initiator, who is deterred by a realization that its chances of military victory are limited because of high uncertainty, will prudently avoid engaging in war.[14]

The theory's contention that "parity preserves peace" is based on a notion that an aggressive state will not go to war if it perceives that its power (or the power of its coalition) is less than that of the opponent.[15] Thus the theory assumes that states engage in wars only when they have superior capability, which in turn allows them to win. On the contrary, if their existing capabilities do not allow military victory, states will not engage in war initiation. Although a preventive war is not ruled out, the best way to achieve an equilibrium or an optimum level of power and security is through the alignment of small states among themselves and with the opponents of the hegemonic power.[16] Structural realists contend that secondary states flock to the weaker side in order to form coalitions that may achieve defensive or deterrent strength sufficient to dissuade adversaries who are usually the stronger states.[17]

Despite its strengths in explaining war initiations by dominant powers, the preceding discussion suggests that the balance of power theory and its main hypothesis, "parity preserves peace," cannot fully account for wars begun by weaker states. Although preventive wars by

5

weaker states are included in the theory as a means to balance a stronger potential aggressor, this category forms only one type of asymmetric war. As per the theory, minor powers generally should not launch wars on their own as they are conceived as objects of major power politics. They are at times considered as states that can produce troublesome situations which can be exploited by major powers.[18] The "parity leads to peace" hypothesis would thus predict that weaker states should not be the initiators of major inter-state conflicts. Yet a number of historical examples show that these states do engage in war initiations on their own against more powerful adversaries. The contention here is that although balance of power theory has strong merits in explaining war initiations by dominant powers, it needs further qualification as well as the inclusion of additional variables if asymmetric war initiation by weaker states is to be explained more accurately.

Preponderance and war initiation

The alternate hypothesis to "parity preserves peace," i.e. "preponderance deters war," is put forward by, among others, power transition theorists.[19] According to this theory, peace is maintained when satisfied great powers are in preponderance, while war is more likely when dissatisfied challengers begin to approximate their capabilities with the preponderant power. Other theorists who subscribe to this hypothesis agree that preponderance is a pacifying condition. To Claude, a potential aggressor is more likely to be deterred by confrontation with a preponderant rather than a merely equal power[20]. Knorr considers war by a state confronting a preponderant power unlikely, as weak states "do not even consider certain courses of action, because it is obvious that they are likely to incur the displeasure of a militarily very superior state ..."[21] Some theorists have applied the "preponderance deters war" hypothesis to regional sub-systems where the superiority in capability of one or more status quo powers is deemed to have prevented war by relatively weak challenging states[22]. In the policy realm, many national leaders follow the "peace through strength," dictum without question. The rationale for high military spending has been that peace can be ensured only by preparing for war. Scholars and policy makers tend to cite historical examples to show "how failure to maintain adequate armed forces strength has led to an aggressive war."[23]

Although the "preponderance deters war" hypothesis seems to have some merits, our discussion so far suggests that it cannot fully account for asymmetric wars initiated by weaker states. Notwithstanding the possibility that overwhelming preponderance may exert some influence on the calculations of potential war initiators, it is not apparent how the presence of a general preponderance in capabilities of a stronger power deters attack by a weaker challenger. Additionally, the theorists who use this hypothesis tend not to specify the type of preponderance, i.e. offensive, defensive, or deterrent, that can result in preventing weaker powers from undertaking asymmetric war initiations. Moreover, in some of the cases I study, the overall military and economic dominance of the status quo power was neither a pacifying condition nor a deterring factor against a weaker state attacking.

War initiation in decision level theories

Unlike systems level theories such as balance of power and power transition, decision level theories focus specifically on the cost/benefit calculations that initiators make prior to launching wars. For instance, deterrence theory considers retaliatory military threats and their impact on the choices for or against war by decision-makers. The expected utility model of Bueno de Mesquita also looks at the on-the-eve calculations of war initiators. Although deterrence theory has many systems level attributes, the concern here is how it treats decision-making by an initiator who is about to launch an attack.

War initiation in deterrence theory

Deterrence is largely a decision level theory that considers short-term factors as critical in war initiation and war prevention. The mainstream deterrence theory contends that the possession and deployment of adequate weapons (whether conventional or nuclear) and the credible communication of their use would deter an aggressor from challenging the status quo militarily.[24] This conception could be applied to both general deterrence and immediate deterrence. In the former, opponents maintain armed forces with an expectation that the implicit threat of resorting to force deters the potential attacker. Immediate deterrence is likely to obtain when one state seriously considers an attack and the defender mounts a successful retaliatory threat in order to prevent it. General deterrence focuses on the deployment and implicit threat of using military power to prevent military and diplomatic crises from erupting in an adversarial relationship, while immediate deterrence deals with war prevention once a crisis begins.[25]

Theorists have classified deterrence into deterrence by punishment and deterrence by denial. As regards the former, states in adversarial relationships maintain adequate amounts of forces, especially of nuclear nature, to maintain a credible retaliatory capability. The potential initiator is deterred because of the threat of retaliation or punishment that makes the benefits from the attack of lesser value than its costs. In a deterrence by denial relationship, adversaries maintain military forces, especially conventional, ground, sea, and tactical air forces, with the purpose of denying battlefield success to their opponents. As war initiation does not promise gaining one's objectives on the battlefield, the potential initiator is deterred from engaging in an attack.[26] Denial type deterrence is most significant in the conventional realm. And for this study, the most relevant deterrence version is deterrence by denial, as embodied in theories on conventional deterrence. Deterrence in the conventional sphere has been defined as a function of the capability of denying an aggressor its battlefield objectives with conventional forces.[27]

According to the deterrence logic, especially as presented by the first and second wave (or classical deterrence) theorists, the attacker will be more likely to fight (deterrence failing) to the degree that the attacker's overall existing and potential military and economic capabilities exceed those of the defender.[28] A key embedded argument in deterrence theory is that decision-makers of a given nation will rationally calculate the military balance with its adversary and will decide (1) to attack if the balance is favorable, or (2) not to attack if it is unfavorable.[29] The theory treats decision-makers as value maximizers who choose war only if its benefits exceed costs. They are also expected to make calculations on the probability of success and the likely response of their adversary if they initiate a war. Accordingly, if the probability of success is remote because of the threat of retaliation by the adversary, the would-be initiator refrains from launching an attack.

Deterrence theorists, especially those who subscribe to the deterrence by denial approach, thus pay a great amount of attention to balance of military forces between the attacker and the defender in the correct deterrence force equation, as without sufficient capability a potential aggressor would not contemplate an attack. It is generally assumed that a state will not initiate a war that it expects to lose, so that the defender's possession of superior military capability (besides the adversary's recognition of the superiority) is a sufficient condition for successful deterrence.[30] The initiator must calculate whether it has the required military capability to win a war with the defender, and the cost of such an action. This calculation affects the attacker's raw utility of fighting the defender, and also its estimate of the probability that

8

the defender will retaliate.[31] Deterrence by punishment also gives prominence to the capability factor in the war calculations of likely initiators. According to this approach, if the potential initiator believes that the defender has the capability and the willingness to retaliate, it is deterred by a conviction that the threatened punishment exceeds the benefits of attacking and that the attack will make it worse off than not attacking. However, if the initiator believes either that the defender is incapable or that its threat is incredible, then it will attack.[32]

From this discussion it is apparent that deterrence theory has constraints in explaining war initiation by a weaker state. A weaker power may engage in war without expecting a major military victory, contrary to the expectations of deterrence theory.[33] In some asymmetric wars, the initiators' expectations in terms of military victory were less pronounced than the calculations in terms of political victory. As I will show through the case studies, in some instances these calculations were based on expectations that war might bring political changes that could help alter an unfavorable status quo. Among other political motives, a challenger may view war as a means to get sympathy for a cause, or if defeated, to lose honorably rather than give up without a fight. A related second dimension of war initiation that is not given full consideration in the theory pertains to different options and strategies that an initiator may have. Thus a weaker challenger with a "controlled pressure" strategy may not be deterred when the defending power is exclusively concerned with major attacks.[34] In other words, a weaker challenger can pursue particular strategies that do not involve an all-out war in order to achieve its objectives. Finally, most often the theory does not adequately consider the influence of time pressure on decision-making. Challengers under serious time pressure may attack, despite the theory's prediction that rational decision-makers will be prevented from attacking by the defender's deterrent threat. Decision-makers who experience time pressure may view an opponent's deterrence policy as offensive and aggressive and may therefore resort to arms in order to prevent such presumed aggression that could occur in the future.

A problem with deterrence theory is that its focus is rather narrowly predicated on the defender's capability for denial and credibility of threat for punishment purposes. The absence of these conditions could be important in the calculations of states that initiate wars, but they are inadequate to explain several wars started by weaker challengers. The theory leaves out other variables that can play crucial role in an initiator's calculations as well as conditions that could spark war at particular junctures in an enduring conflict relationship involving two unequal powers. The third wave deterrence theorists have attempted to rectify some of the problems associated with the theory. Psychological studies during the 1970s and the 1980s have brought forth some key problems in the theory.[35] Case studies have cited several instances of deterrence failures. Some such case study authors have highlighted the lack of political content in deterrence as well as the problems associated with the deductive logic of the theory.[36] Yet deterrence still largely remains a capability and threat-oriented strategic theory that gives scant attention to political variables that impinge upon the calculations of initiators and defenders.

War initiation in an expected utility model

The BDM model, as described in Bueno de Mesquita's *The War Trap*, attempts to explain war initiations by the strong and the weak alike on the basis of the theory of expected utility. It contends that national leaders make deliberate choices based on their estimation of costs and benefits that are equivalent to losing and winning a war. These choices depend on: (a) the relative strengths of the attacker and the defender, (b) the value that the attacker places on changing the defender's policies, relative to the possible changes in policies that the attacker may be forced to accept if it loses; and (c) the relative strengths and interests of all other states that might intervene in the war.[37] The gains and losses are multiplied by the respective probabilities of their occurrence, in order to arrive at the expected positive utility of war initiation. War initiation also depends on how risk-acceptant or risk-averse a decision-maker is and what the expected response of third nations would be in the event of war. The leader who contemplates war is assumed to make assessments about the relative value that the third states may contribute to his nation as compared to his adversary.[38]

As the first major attempt to explain war initiations by the weak and the strong alike, using a broad expected utility framework, this model is significant. The prominence it gives to responses by third states and the risk-taking propensities of decision-makers as crucial variables makes it more valuable than systems level theories in explaining asymmetric wars. However, the model seems incomplete for understanding war initiations by weaker states as it ignores key variables such as strategic calculations and domestic power changes. In most of the cases I study, relative gross capability in its abstract form does not appear as a sufficient indicator as to when war initiation occurs. For some states, the expected utility of war can be positive even when relative gross capabilities are not.

10

Further, as Bueno de Mesquita uses only cases of war occurrence, it is not apparent what the state of the independent variables are when decision-makers fail to initiate wars. A constraint of the model is thus its static nature. A more dynamic theory would explain why wars occur at particular times and not at others.[39] Additionally, the model tells little about the stakes in a conflict, the nature of the deteriorating status quo, or the state of other political and military conditions that generate war decisions. A more complete theory would explain how utilities are shaped, from where they are derived, who shapes them and how external and internal changes affect them in decision-makers' choosing between war and peace.[40] The model also does not take into account the effect of limited choices under time pressure on decision-making. These criticisms do not imply that the model is entirely inappropriate to explain asymmetric wars. The contention is that it can be made more effective by incorporating factors such as strategic and domestic calculations of initiators that may in turn help explain asymmetric war initiations more accurately. The additional variables that can account for changes over time seem crucial in explaining why asymmetric wars are initiated during some periods of time and not others.[41]

Why study asymmetric wars?

A variety of war initiation theories has been discussed in this chapter. The alternative theories bring forth the limited consensus among scholars on the causes of wars, the role of the initiator, and the role of power in the war initiation process. Furthermore, despite the extensive attention devoted to war in international relations theory, we still lack a systematic explanation of the factors and conditions that allow war initiations by weaker powers.[42] The discussion reveals that the mainstream theories incline to make us believe there is little sense for the weaker side to go to war. Broader systemic theories such as balance of power and power transition view asymmetric war initiation as unlikely to occur. They leave out the specific short-term and medium-term determinants that affect the preferences of initiators and therefore seem to be of limited help in explaining the timing of war in particular asymmetric conflict situations.

Decision level theories such as deterrence and expected utility are only partially useful for this purpose because they pay inadequate attention to factors such as strategic considerations and domestic calculations of initiators. Therefore, additional inputs are needed to make them sufficiently strong to explain asymmetric war initiations.

11

We need to know what political and strategic conditions can account for war initiations by weaker states at particular junctures in order to have a comprehensive understanding of the international conflict process in its manifold dimensions. An important objective of a study on asymmetric war should therefore be explaining not just the question "Why?" but also "Why now?" i.e. the timing of war initiations.

The significance of understanding asymmetric wars is reinforced by the fact that, with the demise of the Cold War, the chances of a global war breaking out may be low, but wars among medium and small powers may continue.[43] If historic trends are any indication, the initiators of some future wars will be weaker challengers. This study is an attempt to fill this gap in conflict research, i.e., explaining the dynamics of asymmetric war initiations. In this process, I attempt to answer the research question "Why do conditions of neither parity nor preponderance avert war at all times and in all historical contexts?" In seeking an explanation the study draws hypotheses from theories on strategy, arms races, alliances, and domestic politics. Four critical variables pertaining to the initiator are teased out from this literature: the politico-military strategy, fluctuations in short-term offensive capability, great power defensive support, and changes in decision-making structure. The hypotheses are tested in light of six historic cases of asymmetric war initiations in an effort to bring forth the major determinants of a relatively weak state's decision to start a war.

The main objective of this study is thus to investigate the political and strategic considerations and expectations a relatively weak state may hold while initiating war against a more powerful adversary. It thus goes beyond the standard state-centric explanations by looking at what goes into the calculus of decision-makers. For this purpose, I link domestic and international factors that may influence the war initiation process. The rationale for such an endeavor is rooted in a conviction that decision-makers' preferences for war and peace are shaped by domestic and international considerations, much more than the military factors that many contemporary strategic theories tend to consider. Only by linking domestic political processes and international power rivalry will we be able to understand deterrence process in general and war initiation by weaker challengers in particular. By paying more attention to the four variables applied in this study, theories of wars may be made richer and more accurate. The "process tracing" method of this study allows one to investigate deeper into the calculations and motivations of decision-makers prior to going to war.

The book argues that in an intense rivalry between two unequal

12

powers, despite the possession of superior gross military and economic power capability by a defending state, a motivated weaker adversary can employ military force if its key decision-makers perceive that they can achieve their limited objectives in a short war. The significance of these initiations is that they occur even when the initiator knows that the balance of overall capability favors the defender. The policy relevance of this study is that it challenges the "peace through strength" belief held by many states, that the possession of superior military power by itself will prevent wars. It argues that deterrence and war prevention may not be achieved merely by the possession of gross military and economic power. An understanding of the motivational dynamics of challengers can be beneficial in explaining deterrence failures, especially in the conventional realm. This may also help us determine how political factors shape the conflict behavior of states so that methods to strengthen deterrence in its multi-faceted dimensions can be devised.

The book's outline is as follows. The second chapter presents the key arguments of the study. Four major factors and their linkages to the outcome variable are provided in order to explain the war initiation process of relatively weak challengers and to identify the key factors that may generate asymmetric wars. Definitions of important concepts and the methodology applied in the study are also presented in this chapter. The study follows a comparative case study and a comparative time frame method. Under this methodological scheme, the time when an attack took place is compared with periods in which an attack was considered but did not materialize. Such a method allows us to see the absence of which factor or factors prevented war in the cases concerned and the arrival of which particular factor or constellation of factors made war possible. The objective is to identify the relative importance of variables, singularly or additively, that have a bearing on war decisions in different cases. The rank ordering based on the relative weight of these factors would assist us to evaluate what is more vital in explaining war initiations at critical points in time.

In chapters 3 to 8, six case studies of asymmetric war initiations, drawn from the twentieth century, are undertaken in order to test the propositions advanced in chapter 2. These cases are: (1) The Japanese attack on Russia (1904), (2) the Japanese attack on Pearl Harbor (1941), (3) the Chinese intervention in Korea (1950), (4) the Pakistani offensive in Kashmir (1965), (5) the Egyptian offensive in the Sinai (1973),[44] and (6) the Argentine invasion of the Falklands (1982).[45]

The similarity of these cases is that in all of them, the initiators of wars were the relatively weak belligerent powers, in terms of overall power capability. By examining these cases, we can test theoretically valuable propositions and generalizable observations. Data for the cases are collected from historical accounts, memoirs, interviews, and other primary and secondary sources dealing with these wars and the decision-making process by key actors prior to war initiation. I have conducted extensive interviews with decision-makers and scholars wherever it was possible. Their accounts are corroborated or discounted by comparing them with several historical sources. The concluding chapter summarizes the theoretical findings of the study and presents the implications of the findings for future research, especially their relevance to theories such as deterrence, expected utility, polarity, and balance of power.

2 EXPLAINING WAR INITIATION BY WEAKER POWERS IN ASYMMETRIC CONFLICTS

Introduction

The preceding chapter raises the point that the question of relatively weak states initiating wars has received insufficient attention in international relations theory and conflict analysis. Although some theories touch on asymmetric wars, they consider in detail neither the factors and conditions that generate them, nor the process through which this type of war initiation occurs compared to other forms of dyadic or general wars. Therefore, the need to explain and connect key variables that can have a causal effect on the decision to initiate war is all the more imperative. To begin with, I accept the notion that there are profound and general causes for the outbreak of wars, such as conflicts resulting from the anarchic and self help nature of the international system. These general causes, however, can be elucidated as well as complemented if we can trace the proximate or more immediate causes that recur from case to case in a particular type of war. A simple analogy might help clarify this point. There is a constant possibility of fire breaking out in many forests. But, like wars, wildfires do not necessarily break out all the time. What ignites fire at a given point in time may depend on several factors and conditions, such as the temperature level and the direction of the wind. Likewise, there are proximate factors that can explain what sparks war at a given point in time in an enduring conflictual relationship even though the anarchic and competitive nature of the international system allows these wars to occur. This study is an effort to elucidate these proximate factors that permit the outbreak of war at critical junctures in asymmetric conflict relationships.

Some assumptions

This study assumes that decision-makers make cost/benefit calculations prior to launching a war, consistent with the instrumentalist

15

conception of rationality.[1] This notion of rationality is somewhat similar to the Bayesian conception of "subjective rationality." According to the Bayesian model, the values, beliefs, and expectations of a decision-maker are important factors that determine his probabilistic assessment before he undertakes a course of action. As per this notion, a particular course of action has merit as long as it makes the best consequences the most probable. In such a conception, "the goodness and probabilities of the consequences are the agent's subjective assessment," while "how true, reasonable or otherwise objectively or morally sound these assessments are, is regarded as a separate question."[2] The implicit notion here is that "whether or not a given course of action in a given decision-making situation is rational is not an absolute kind of thing: A course of action is rational only relative to a possessed body of information (beliefs and desires) in terms of which the merits of the available courses of action can be rationally evaluated."[3]

This study further assumes that decisions to pursue war and peace are made by decision-making groups with particular external and internal motives. It also views war decisions as conditional, perception-dependent, and time-dependent, i.e., wars are initiated when favorable conditions are perceived by decision-makers who may pursue the war path for attaining their domestic or international goals. This assumption entails some modifications in a strictly rational-choice decision-making approach. As Allison states, this approach incorporates the decision-making group's characteristics and it locates its choices by taking into account the group's "weighting of goals and objectives," as well as "tendencies to perceive (and to exclude) particular ranges of alternatives ..."[4] Chief executives may declare war and may make important decisions, but they need not be the only decision-making unit. It is assumed that power groups surrounding them play significant roles in war decisions.

I assume the existence of at least four requisite conditions prior to war initiation by a weaker state in the type of asymmetric conflicts covered in this study. They are: (1) the presence of serious conflict of interests; (2) the weaker side values higher the issue in dispute; (3) the weaker side is dissatisfied with the status quo; and (4) the weaker side fears a deterioration from, or no change in, the status quo in the future. To begin with, it is assumed that a major conflict of interests exists between the initiator and the defender over a substantive issue of contention which each values in varying degree. The conflict generally becomes more intense as attempts at a negotiated settlement fail, or a chain of actions and reactions between the parties escalate it into a crisis. The initiator is assumed to attach greater value to the object in contention and is willing to demonstrate its resolve through the use of military force. The defender in this context is the stronger power that wants to preserve the benefits that the status quo provides if it is a status quo state.[5] The attacker is the relatively weak state that intensely desires to alter the status quo to a favorable state which may, in some cases, be the restoration of the status quo ante.

The relative value of the issue in dispute as well as the unwillingness of the status quo power to concede ground could increase the resolve of the weaker side on the basis of what Rosen calls, "the willingness to suffer," especially when the weaker power may have more at stake in the dispute than its stronger adversary. The militarily inferior side in a conflict may compensate for such an inferiority by exhibiting greater interest and stronger resolve.[6] The relatively weaker side may gain more from a stronger opponent as the former may have a greater rational incentive to fight harder.[7] Furthermore, in a bargaining situation, a state that demonstrates an irrevocable commitment may succeed in bringing the range of indeterminacy down to a point that is most favorable to it.[8]

If there is a great disparity in power, negotiations on an issue of intrinsic or strategic value may not yield much by way of results.[9] The more powerful may perceive that there is no great need to concede. The weaker side can view this as intransigence, forcing its decision-makers to take drastic steps that may ultimately change the perceptions of the adversary on the need for a negotiated settlement. Status quo powers tend to be reluctant in yielding major concessions, especially to weaker challengers. This is largely due to two factors. First, such powers tend to develop confidence in their military and political advantages and can believe that the weaker side will behave irrationally if it engages in a war that it is expected to lose. Second, they may feel that concessions can be viewed as a sign of weakness by other states – allies and adversaries alike. A status quo power may thus view tough posturing as essential for the purposes of signalling intentions to both enemies and friends as well as deterring potential adversaries. Their decision-makers may also view standing firm attractive for reasons of reputation.[10] These reputations are often generated in the perceptions of others in light of how steadfast a state is in its willingness to honor its commitments or threats or both, and in standing by once-declared principles or policies.

In some situations, the stronger side may also contemplate an imposed solution, especially if it holds greater power capabilities and bargaining advantages. Solutions of this nature are attractive to some

17

such states, as they preclude long, drawn-out negotiations that often require a willingness to extend concessions. Snyder and Diesing present the dilemma that a challenger faces in an asymmetric conflict situation. The status quo power may use the threat of no agreement to get a better outcome for itself. In order to arrive at an agreement, a weaker challenger state may have to give more concessions or employ coercive tactics such as war.[11] There is an additional advantage that the defender possesses: the legitimacy that status quo brings over a period of time. A state with a clear and long-established status quo tends to have an edge in the perceived balance of legitimacy.[12] Therefore, status quo powers generally attempt to prolong their control over the issue in dispute with the expectation that as more time passes, they will increase the legitimacy of their position in the dispute.

The continuation of a status quo that is unfavorable to the weaker power has implications for the outbreak of war. One of these is with respect to preventive war. The leadership of a weaker nation might decide to go to war if it perceives that the long-term prospects for resolving the issue are slim, and therefore finds the status quo intolerable because the existing trends may define the long-term developments.[13] A fear that the status quo will deteriorate even further in the future and that waiting will not make a substantial difference in the state of the conflict may give an added incentive for a weaker state to engage in a preventive war.[14] The initiator can perceive that if it does not strike it may suffer serious long-term political and economic disadvantages. Thus a major reason for Germany's decision to go to war in 1914 was its fear that with the completion of the rail system and the re-armament program, Russia would have an additional 40 percent military strength and that waiting would have made Germany's prospects for victory very slim.[15]

Bargaining theorists support these arguments on time pressure. According to Cross, the effect of time on bargaining is three-fold. First, actors may discount future benefits on the basis that they should be enjoyed now rather than later. This is because the passage of time has costs, in terms of resources expended and sacrifices made as a result of the postponement. Second, the utility of an agreement may change with the passage of time. Finally, bargaining costs can recur at each time period, resulting in an increase in the total costs over time. The consequence of these three factors is that the more distant the agreement, the less its present value.[16] This bargaining logic can be applied to asymmetric war initiations as most such wars are attempts at bargaining through coercive means. The effect of time pressure on a weaker state's decision-makers may be that as time passes the perceived value of the issue in contention may change in favor of the defender, and it may become difficult for a country with limited resources to challenge the status quo state militarily or diplomatically.

The deteriorating status quo, the unyielding position of the stronger power, and preventive motivation are all underlying factors that affect the overall calculations of states in conflict situations. However, one may argue that the mere existence of a conflict of interests or the unyielding position of the status quo state need not always lead to war. This contention is based on a realization that many sub-systemic disputes, with the status quo favoring the stronger state, have been in existence for decades with wars erupting only occasionally. For instance, the Arabs and the Israelis, and the Indians and the Pakistanis have been in conflict over questions of intrinsic and strategic value ever since their states became independent. Although the sub-systems of the Middle East and South Asia experienced many crises that were on the verge of outbreak of major hostilities, large-scale wars among these states broke out only on a few occasions.[17] War seems more like an exception than the norm even within highly adversarial dyads. In many instances, the potential initiators, for some reason or other, refused to escalate the crises into military hostilities. When it comes to asymmetric conflicts, weaker states with long-standing disputes, exploit some crisis situations by initiating wars, while ignoring others. The significant question for this study is why during some specific times did the relatively weak state attack the stronger side? What prompted the decision to attack in some instances, and, conversely, the decision not to attack in other instances even when there were strong political or military pressures to pursue a military course of action?

In an effort to generate the most relevant explanatory variables relating to asymmetric war initiation, I raise the following preliminary questions. Under what conditions, when, and why does a state in conflict with a more powerful adversary decide to commit itself to war, even when the overall balance of military and economic power is unfavorable to it? Does the possession of limited quantities of offensive weaponry and the expected defensive support of a great power encourage a weaker state to attempt to use military means to alter an unacceptable status quo? What roles do particular strategies of war play in the decision process? Do the emergence of insecure regimes and powerful domestic groups that propose offensive policies increase the chances of war?

To provide a plausible explanation, theoretical arguments are drawn from the literature on strategy, arms races, alliances, and domestic

19

politics. Four different variables pertaining to the initiator are deduced from the above stated questions and applied to the cases in order to explain asymmetric war initiations. Although these variables may also be applicable to a stronger power's war initiation against a weaker opponent, they are considered to be of greater importance to asymmetric war initiations by weaker powers, as I will subsequently seek to show. These variables that pertain to the initiator are:

(1) *The politico-military strategy.*
(2) *The possession of offensive weapon systems.*
(3) *Great power defensive support.*
(4) *Changing domestic power structure.*

Time pressure is the intervening variable that links these four factors and the outcome variable, war initiation. "Now or never" may be the pressure that the decision-makers of a relatively weak state can experience in periods prior to war initiation.

Defining concepts

Before stating the hypothesized relationships between the above-stated variables and war initiation, the definitions of the major concepts used in this study are essential for the proper application of the theoretical framework and a systematic analysis of the case studies. An "asymmetric conflict" is defined as a conflict involving two states with unequal overall military and economic power resources.[18] The main target of explanation of this study, however, is not conflicts involving an extremely strong and a very weak power, but relatively unequal powers. The discrepancy ratio between the initiator and the defender in power terms is generally 1:2 or more. An "initiator" is the state that first launches a military attack. For the sake of consistency, this definition holds regardless that the dispute or crisis that generally precedes the war may have been initiated or precipitated by the target state; in this case, the stronger power. The rationale here is that an initiator, even under time pressure, generally tends to have at least a few options prior to launching an attack. It may assume a defensive or deterrent posture, attempt negotiations with the opponent, seek good offices of other states or international organizations, or do nothing and wait for another opportune time for attaining its objectives. In other words, an initiator of war in this study is the state that makes a conscious decision to escalate a dispute or crisis into an armed conflict.

The term, "strategy" is applied in the sense of both Clausewitz's definition: "The employment of battle as the means toward the attainment of the objective of war," and Liddell Hart's definition: "The art of distributing and applying military means to fulfil the ends of policy."[19] Thus strategy is conceived as the application of military force on the battlefield in order to achieve specific policy goals.[20] A "limited aims/ fait accompli strategy" refers to the employment of military forces in battle in order to achieve limited goals (such as taking portions of a territory) that are not equivalent to the decisive defeat and surrender of the enemy. The latter goals often characterize attrition and blitzkrieg strategies. The objective of a limited aims strategy is to create a political or military fait accompli, or an irreversible condition, which may not be altered following the conclusion of the war, although the defender may prefer maintenance of the condition prior to war.

In this study, "alliance commitment" refers to the defensive support of one state by another in either one or some combination of military, economic, and political terms. The support considered here is confined to non-combative, defensive roles and is not in the form of large-scale participation in actual fighting. "Great power alliance support" is used instead of any third party alliance, as historically great powers have been more forthcoming and effective in supporting their weaker allies.[21] "Offensive weapons" refer to those systems that are useful for offensive attack and tactical advancement (e.g. tanks, deep penetration aircraft), as opposed to defensive weapons (e.g. anti-aircraft guns) that are useful for holding one's forces and territory against invading troops.[22] Some defensive weapons may also come under the offensive category if they can be employed for offensive purposes. I recognize that the distinction between offensive and defensive weapons is often unclear. A weapon that may have offensive application in a particular theater may be of defensive value in another context. However, for consistency, in this study offensive arms denote weapons that facilitate tactical advancement, although some such weapons may have been classified by countries and manufacturers as defensive systems.

"Domestic power structure" refers to the chief executive and the decision-making group surrounding him or her who are in power, and the key interest groups that support them. "Militaristic groups" refer to decision-making units that have an explicit preference for war as the most favored option to settle a dispute when there are choices such as resorting to diplomacy or doing nothing. These preferences might be expressed prior to the war. If they were not clearly articulated, one can deduce the preferences from activities of the concerned decision-maker over a period of time.

This study uses "power" as synonymous with overall power defined in terms of resources. It follows the commonly used "power as resources" conception in defining relative power capabilities of states.[23] The state with more resources is assumed to have greater holding power and is expected to inflict greater harm on a state with less capability in a long war if it is willing to use all its capabilities and if everything else remains the same.[24] In other words, the long-term mobilization potential may be higher for those states with more holding power. The sources of power in this study are demographic, economic, and military, i.e., active population, gross national product, per capita income, industrial capability, technological prowess, the total strength of the armed forces, and weapons systems, in both their quantitative and qualitative dimensions. While attempting to define power, one may also have to look at its structural, relational, and behavioral aspects. It is recognized that intangible and subjective factors such as leadership, morale, resolve etc. can form significant determinants of national power. Yet convincing measures for these factors are unavailable and therefore they are not taken into account in this study. However, it is recognized that these factors can play an important role in the calculation of initiators, weaker in overall material capability.

Yet another dimension of power that needs to be addressed is the loss-of-strength gradient problem. According to Boulding, a state is at its maximum competitive power at home, but its ability to dominate another state declines the farther it operates from home.[25] Although this is a valid problem in some circumstances, especially before the advent of aircraft and large cargo ships, I would argue that it is no longer the determining factor in power equations, with the development of new technologies, large numbers of aircraft carriers, rapid deployment capabilities, self-sufficient overseas bases, and above all with the arrival of deep penetration aircraft, and tactical, medium-range and long-range missile systems. To one analyst, even in olden days this problem was not as determining as geopolitics analysts feared since logistics support by water has been generally cheaper and easier than over land.[26] In some historic instances of asymmetric wars such as the Russo-Japanese War, this factor did play a role in hindering an effective Russian defense against Japan's surprise attack. Even in this case, one could contend that the loss-of-strength gradient mattered only in the short run, as the materially strong Russia was slowly bringing in more forces and supplies while the weaker Japan was draining out its capabilities and feared defeat in a long, drawn-out war.[27]

Conditions and causes

A brief note on the distinctions between necessary and sufficient conditions, and conditions and causes is appropriate at this stage. A necessary condition has been defined as a "circumstance in whose absence a given event could not occur," and a sufficient condition a "circumstance such that whenever it exists, a given event occurs."[28] Some philosophers of science have argued that in historical explanations, the most feasible strategy is to identify key necessary conditions that may have causal attributes, as sufficient conditions are more difficult to specify.[29] The causal attributes of conditions are a matter of dispute in the philosophy of science. To some philosophers of history, citing necessary conditions by itself constitutes explanations for the occurrence of an event. W.B. Gallie, Arthur C. Danto, and William Dray fall under this category of scholars who argue that the presentation of necessary conditions itself has causal equivalence. To Gallie, a historical event could be explained by way of referring to "one or a number of their temporally prior necessary conditions," and then indicate that "some one of a disjunction of describable conditions is necessary to its occurrence; and the explanation consists in elucidating which one of this disjunctive set is applicable, in the sense of being necessary, to the event in question."[30]

Although in this study, the arrival of particular conditions and factors is hypothesized to have resulted in wars, the sheer presence of these factors is not sufficient to explain war initiation in all historical contexts. However, their arrival in different configurations in asymmetric conflict situations may increase the probability of war initiation by the weaker belligerent state, and therefore may have attributes of sufficient as well as necessary conditions. Additionally, the more these conditions are present, the more likely that war would occur in an asymmetric conflict relationship. It may be added that general historical patterns may be elucidated with some predictability, if the same conditions recur in several historic cases of a particular type of phenomenon, across time periods and regions. In such instances, one may argue that the causal attributes of these conditions are stronger than if they simply appear in only one historic event of this nature. They may thus be treated as having attributes of sufficient conditions.

Why asymmetric war initiations occur

In this section, the relationships between the previously stated four major variables and asymmetric wars are hypothesized in an effort to find an explanation for war initiation by weaker powers. First, the initiator's strategic calculations are hypothesized to have linkages to the choice for war and its timing. In subsequent sections, the hypothesized relationships between war and changes in short-term offensive capability, great power support and domestic power structures are presented.

The strategic factor in asymmetric war initiation

A potential war initiator may employ three strategies – attrition/ maneuver, blitzkrieg (lightning strike), and limited aims/fait accompli – while pursuing its objectives through military means. An attrition/ maneuver strategy is one in which the attacker's main concern is defeating the defender in a series of set piece battles.[31] As Luttwak states, under the attrition/maneuver strategy an attacker treats an opponent's forces as an array of targets to be destroyed unless it retreats or surrenders. The strategic objectives may be realized owing to the attacker's superior firepower and material strength.[32] By following the blitzkrieg strategy, an attacker attempts to defeat the opponent's army by achieving strategic penetration during which the former may "pierce the defender's front and then drive deep into the defender's rear, severing his lines of communication and destroying key junctures in the network."[33] Concentration of forces, especially of tanks and aircraft at decisive fronts so as to achieve strategic penetration, is a key characteristic of this strategy. Under a limited aims/fait accompli strategy, an attacker is only interested in capturing a portion of the enemy's territory or the attainment of some political objective which is not tantamount to a complete defeat of the adversary.[34]

The key argument on war initiation in this study is derived from these three strategic choices that a potential initiator may adopt prior to going to war. The probability of asymmetric war initiation is high if the weaker state's decision-makers believe in the efficacy of a successful limited aims/fait accompli strategy. The expectation that a limited aims/fait accompli strategy would help attain the objectives at stake gives a weaker state incentive to strike, as decision-makers may fear that with the passage of time such a strategy would fail to produce successful outcomes. However, if a weaker initiator expects that the attack would turn into a long, drawn-out attrition warfare, it may desist from engaging in war. This is because its decision-makers may be cognizant of the danger that an indecisive, long war of attrition can wear out their military and economic strength, affecting the morale of

24

the people and soldiers alike that can result in military and political catastrophes.

A limited aims/fait accompli strategy envisions neither total victory nor unconditional surrender of the opponent's forces. Seizing portions of territory for future negotiations is the main characteristic of this strategy which entails the achievement of quick "faits accomplis."[35] As Liddell Hart suggests, a limited aims strategy does not seek to overthrow the enemy's military power. Such a strategy is adopted by a weaker state when it perceives that it does not have the necessary superiority for a successful, decisive operation.[36] Weaker initiators may face constraints in employing a strategy of attrition/maneuver in inter-state war situations as in an attrition battle, and the chances of a weaker force becoming exhausted or marooned are higher as a result of the cumulative destruction of forces.[37] An attrition/maneuver strategy entails wearing down an opponent in numerous set piece battles, which generally requires great material and human strength. Such a strategy entails protracted warfare which if adopted by a weaker side may fail to attain its objectives.[38] Along with Mearsheimer, I argue that deterrence or the chances of war prevention are more likely when a weaker potential initiator expects that it will have to fight a prolonged attrition war with a stronger opponent.

This does not mean that attrition strategy is not useful for weaker states that are on the defensive. If the stronger opponent is sensitive to taking casualties – as most advanced industrialized states are – the initiator can gain its objectives by following a strategy of attrition by inflicting maximum casualties on the opponent, after assuming a defensive posture. This posture should, however, avoid static or fixed defenses and the aim of the guerrilla is to evade direct battle with stronger enemy forces. An attrition strategy, relying on guerrilla tactics, may thus bear fruit in achieving an outcome favorable to a weaker army which is on the defensive. Terrain covered with forests or mountains provides adequate cover and hiding places for the guerrilla fighters who are engaging in attrition style warfare. For a successful guerrilla campaign, the guerrilla forces should have the support of the local population, by way of providing material replenishments and hiding places.[39] In such a situation, the cost tolerance of the stronger side can be tested by a weaker foe through prolonged guerrilla resistance. The experience of the US in Vietnam, the USSR in Afghanistan, France in Algeria, India in Sri Lanka, and Israel in Lebanon lend support to this contention. The argument here is that attrition has limitations as an offensive strategy for a weaker initiator while it may be effective as a defensive or defensive–offensive strategy. In the latter situation, a weaker belligerent assumes a defensive position initially, but as the war progresses, it launches counteroffensives so as to wear down the adversary and thereby deny the latter strategic as well as tactical gains.

Although blitzkrieg is a strategy that a relatively weaker state with a powerful armored force can employ, it still requires heavy reliance on mobility, speed, and decisive advantage at key points. The terrain should permit the employment of this strategy. The strategic objective of blitzkrieg, the decisive destruction of an opponent's forces, may also be difficult for a weaker state to achieve.[40] If a weaker state can expect successful employment of a blitzkrieg strategy, it may also provide incentive to the state to initiate an asymmetric war. Thus, in particular conflict situations, a weaker state can employ blitzkrieg or attrition tactically in order to obtain limited gains. Elements of blitzkrieg have tactical utility if the capability in armor and aircraft and the terrain allow the weaker side to concentrate its forces at decisive points and achieve strategic penetration. The Israeli strategy in 1967 was of this nature. A weaker side may also pursue attrition at the tactical level if manpower and terrain allow it. Some tactical elements of guerrilla warfare may be employed in such operations.

However, for weaker initiators, both attrition and blitzkrieg strategies have limitations at the higher operational–strategic level. A weaker state can rarely achieve the objective of complete destruction of its stronger adversary and hold on to the military and political gains for a long period of time. The case of Israel in 1967 again can be cited in this respect. Although Israel was able to destroy a great number of the Arab forces, it would have been highly unlikely for it to achieve total destruction or complete occupation of the opponents' territories and hold on to them as the Allied powers were able to vis-à-vis Germany and Japan in World War II. Likewise, although attrition strategy has been successfully used to wear down stronger adversaries by weaker revolutionary guerrilla forces, in the inter-state contexts, weaker initiators have rarely been successful in using the strategy for the same objective. This is because attrition generally does not allow short wars fought for the purpose of achieving limited goals.

Within a limited aims/fait accompli strategy, offensive–defensive military doctrines would dominate the war plans of weaker powers. Such doctrines presuppose quick offensive military thrusts followed by a defensive posture to create a fait accompli situation in order to preserve the limited gains until political settlements can be achieved, mostly through third party intervention. The adoption of offensive–

defensive doctrines is based on an assumption that the defense can stand up in the short run and that the stronger status quo power may not be able to use its offensive power successfully to overwhelm a deeply entrenched defensive force. The weaker initiator may expect that the political and military costs of overcoming its defensive position are likely to dissuade the stronger side from undertaking a counter-offensive, sufficient in strength to overwhelm the defender. A weaker initiator's limited aims strategy can help avoid a massive military mobilization and an all-out retaliation by the adversary. Stronger states tend to exhibit higher confidence in their overall capacity and in their fighting forces' ability to deter smaller powers and therefore may not take the weaker side too seriously, at least in the initial phases of the conflict. If the asymmetry in gross capabilities is too large, the stronger state may feel assured of victory without a major fight.[41]

The weaker state's limited aims strategy as well as limited offensive capability can help prevent the total commitment of military forces by the stronger state. Its deployment of massive forces may also be prevented by internal opposition. On the other side, however, the weaker state may be employing all it can at decisive points in order that its objectives can be achieved in a short span of time. A limited aims strategy can also provide advantages to the initiator because the defender's war plans may not envision such contingencies adequately, as larger powers tend to focus on bigger threats to their security. By the time the defender develops a strategy to deal with the situation and decides to mobilize, the war may have come to a close, resulting in the freezing of the fait accompli situation.

Victory, measured in military terms, may not describe all the tangible and intangible strategic goals a war-initiating nation may have in asymmetric conflicts. A weaker state may also gain political victory from a situation of military stalemate, or even defeat, if it can reduce the political capability of the stronger state to wage a war over time.[42] The possibility of political victory thus can increase the weaker state's incentives to strike, employing a limited aims strategy. Losing honorably, after a bold fight may also strengthen a weaker state's bargaining position vis-à-vis the stronger opponent. This can be in the form of post-war negotiations and third party support, sympathy, and recognition of the weaker side's cause. Additionally, war may bring to world attention an otherwise moribund issue and help increase the domestic support of the ruling elite.

The adoption of limited aims strategy by the initiator is generally based on the expectation that the war will remain limited. A limited war, by definition, entails a battle confined to a local geographical area, directed against selected military targets and with restricted objectives.[43] Such an expectation can spring from a conviction that the stronger power would neither escalate the war into larger operations, nor fight with all its resources. Therefore, a massive retaliation by the defender is improbable. The total obliteration of one nation by another one is unlikely to happen, especially in a war in which combatants fight for limited stakes. The limitations on the stronger power in this respect may be due to technological constraints, third party pressures, or moral restraints.[44] In extreme situations, a weaker side may believe that the stronger state would not respond militarily at all to its limited military venture. The initiators of asymmetric wars would assume that they could limit the area of operation to specific points where they have advantage and can bear the costs of a counter-attack. Additionally, decision-makers of the weaker initiator may believe that the stronger side would not fight long wars and that a diplomatic settlement could be reached without incurring major political and military costs. The expectation could be that the stronger side would not be able to bear the political costs of engaging in a long war although it has the capability to do so. Alternatively, an objective such as bringing the issue to international attention may be achieved through a short war in a limited area of operation. All these expectations can arise even after the defender communicates its determination to deter any military challenge designed to upset the status quo.

Limited war expectations may originate from the past behavior of the stronger side in its response to crises and challenges by other states.[45] The stronger power's behavior during a preceding crisis can have a major effect on an initiator's strategic calculations regarding the credibility of the defender's military and political commitments to protect the status quo. Limited war expectations can also result from a conviction that international opinion, especially the possible responses by great powers, may restrain a stronger adversary from using all its retaliatory capability. Decision-makers of the weaker state may also believe that public opinion within the stronger state would be against sending forces in a war that is of relatively low value to the defender, especially if it involves territory that is under the stronger state's extended deterrence domain.[46] A conviction that striking first entails certain strategic and military advantages for the initiator may give incentives to the leaders of the weaker state to go on the offensive. Superior strategy and strong resolve become crucial factors in an asymmetric war, waged for limited aims, in which the power disparity between the belligerents – in terms of force-in-being – is not very large.

28

Thus the long-term military capability of the defender rarely plays a significant role in the strategic calculations of an initiator who expects to fight a limited, fait accompli war and not a war of attrition.[47]

A key element of a limited aims/fait accompli strategy may be surprise, which, if properly employed, can destroy a good portion of the defender's unalerted forces. This can result in the defender being unable to use its forces efficiently and effectively, while the attacker maximizes its own capabilities and firepower.[48] Therefore, in most instances, surprise has been an instrument in the hands of a weaker state, providing the initiator with an advantage that it may not otherwise enjoy.[49] Surprise can sometimes not only work as a means to balance the numerical inferiority but also to destroy the morale of the opponent's forces.[50] The important characteristic of a surprise attack is that it allows the initiator the choice of time, place, and method of engagement, while denying all these to the opponent. As it may make possible a quick victory at relatively low costs, surprise attack is the most important means through which a weaker initiator can expect to defeat (or avoid defeat in an encounter with) an adversary who holds more power resources.[51]

An additional factor in a weaker state's strategic calculations may be greater force mobility, which reduces the time element in the military equation and thereby increases its ability to control the spots where fighting takes place. Much of the offensive capability the weaker side holds may depend on its ability to exploit the weak or blind spots of the adversary's standing force and to choose the time and place of the battle. This also helps to reduce the force attrition rate as the weaker side has a higher probability of suffering more casualties in a long war.[52] The materially weaker side can also reap limited victory by employing all its forces at decisive points, especially when the stronger side's forces are dispersed on different fronts. A key factor that facilitates surprise attack is secrecy. Greater secrecy presupposes a smaller force level which otherwise may be detected and destroyed prior to the attack. Such force levels call for a limited aims strategy and a short war, as longer wars require greater preparation and thereby increase the possibility of being detected.

Although a stronger state may also possess all the aforementioned strategic calculations when it launches an attack against a weaker adversary, the contention here is that they are of greater applicability to a weaker initiator. A stronger power can afford to use strategies such as attrition/maneuver, due to its larger resource base and ability to wage longer wars. If the stronger power has greater advantage in armor and aircraft it can also wage a blitzkrieg attack. Although surprise attack can help both stronger and weaker initiators strategically, it is more critical for the latter in order to compensate for some of its disadvantages in capability.

Offensive weapons, limited capability and war initiation

A second key factor that is hypothesized to have relationship to war initiation by a weaker state is the possession of short-term offensive capability by such states. More specifically, the availability of short-term offensive capability can provide incentive to a weaker state that is dissatisfied with the status quo to initiate war against a stronger opponent, especially when it expects that striking first promises quick success. The initiating state's decision-makers may realize that the potency of such weapons is only of short duration and that the enemy might acquire more of similar or superior weapon systems.[53] The stronger power may also devise counter-measures in the long run, that can offset the weaker state's temporary advantage. Thus a weaker state that is in serious conflict with a stronger opponent may experience intense time pressure to exploit a temporary window of opportunity, believing that a particular weapon system may have only a short-term offensive advantage, in the immediate theater of operations. Therefore, it is better to strike when these weapons can make a difference rather than to wait, when that advantage may be lost. A stronger power may not feel the same pressure to make use of a short-term advantage, especially if the status quo is favorable to it. Waiting can also be helpful to a stronger state because it may increase its capability as more time passes.[54]

Offensive weapons can serve dual purposes: They can increase the initiator's ability to injure the enemy, while decreasing the power of the defender to injure the initiator.[55] Furthermore, they may make it easier to destroy an opponent's forces and occupy territory. Thus short-run stability could be greatly determined by the kind of weapons that belligerents possess.[56] A weaker initiator's ability to harm its relatively strong adversary may result from the latter, having had no chance to adapt to the new weapon, producing only a "suboptimal response." The short-term disparity in offensive capability can also inflict negative psychological effects on the defending side's armed forces. As Axelrod suggests, a weapon's value is discounted over time as the secret weapon may be uncovered and can thus become ineffective if not used immediately.[57]

The above contention on short-term offensive capability and war initiations does not preclude the possibility of arms races having a

30

stabilizing effect in some situations.[58] However, nascent arms races are vulnerable to exploitation, especially by weaker challengers who may intend to make use of short-term military opportunities provided by offensive weapons acquisition. This argument is fairly consistent with some major studies on the linkage between arms races and war. For instance, Huntington argues that war is more likely to occur in the early phases of an arms race.[59] This is when the relatively weak state attempts to catch up with the stronger power. The probability of war is higher at a time when the stronger side's short-term window of vulnerability is about to close. The weaker challenger's decision-makers may believe that if not attacked at this time, the stronger power may become overwhelmingly superior and the window may be closed for ever.

Alliance support and war calculations

Shifts in alliances involving great powers can be a third major factor in a weaker state's timing of attack and its calculations regarding the enemy's ability to retaliate. There is a clear advantage in striking when the opponent has few alliance partners as it will have less retaliatory power whereas the weaker state's alliance partnership with a great power assures it support in terms of both tangible material assistance and a defensive shield against massive retaliation by the stronger adversary. The great power's defensive support can help ensure that the defender does not escalate the conflict beyond the weaker state's capability limits. The great power need not have concluded a formal alliance relationship with the weaker initiator. All that matters is that there is a relationship which provides the weaker state expectations regarding politico-military support in the event of war.[60]

The possibility of war initiation may be higher if the alliance relationship is new, when policies and responsibilities are not clearly defined. A weaker state may expect political and military support from the great power ally under these circumstances. Ambiguous signals such as verbal support by the officials of the great power ally, especially in an early alliance relationship, can raise the expectations of a weaker initiator with respect to possible support. Once an alliance relationship is institutionalized, such expectations may become more realistic with respect to the partners' roles and responsibilities in war.

These arguments are consistent with many theoretical findings on the alliance–war nexus. Singer and Small find that a strong relationship exists between war and alliance, especially at the early stages of an alliance commitment.[61] Ostrom and Hoole find that alliance commitment led to more wars during the initial two to seven years of their existence.[62] Siverson and King's research also supports the argument that the chances of allies fighting are stronger in the early stages of an alliance relationship.[63] Bueno de Mesquita and Singer conclude that between 1815 and 1965, the life span of average defense pacts was ninety-four months and of ententes, sixty-eight months, suggesting that few alliances last over a long period of time.[64] As these studies point out, great power alliance support fluctuates with the passage of time. Minor powers contemplating wars often take into account the factor of fluctuating alliance commitment when making choices for war. Hence time pressure, in terms of when one has defensive support from a great power, can be a major factor that a weaker state's decision-makers may consider before going to war. Such a conviction could arise from a realization that alliance commitments may change in the future and that the probability of success in the war may decrease as time lapses.

The level of great power alliance support for weaker challengers is dependent on systemic polarity. Thus, when acute bipolar or multipolar competition exists, smaller powers can expect support from their great power allies. Under conditions of intense bipolar or multipolar competition, a smaller state can engage in war with its stronger opponent with the expectation that its great power ally will provide support, especially if the adversary belongs to the other side of the bipolar or multipolar equation. A great power's support in the war greatly depends on the value it attaches to the smaller ally and the value it gives to defensive commitments. Although the smaller ally is engaging in an offensive action, great powers can provide support with defensive coloration if the tides of war turn against their smaller ally. Thus weaker allies tend to exhibit a tendency to exploit the great power security umbrella in order to enhance their own national interests.

Although support from a great power can be a factor in the calculations of a stronger power contemplating war against a weaker opponent, this condition may be more critical for a weaker initiator. A stronger power can generally fight a war with a weaker enemy alone and need not be overly concerned about escalation especially if the asymmetry in power resources is very large. A weaker initiator, on the other hand, is indeed taking a bigger risk than its stronger counterpart because escalation may have a more adverse effect on the former. The defensive support of a great power can provide assurance to the weaker state that its stronger opponent will practice restraint in the war. The observance of such restraints on the part of a weaker defender need not be critical in the calculations of a stronger initiator.

Domestic structure and asymmetric war initiation

The fourth critical variable that is hypothesized to have a relationship with asymmetric war initiations is changes in domestic power structure. Specifically, I argue that the chances of war initiation by a weaker state are greater when the power structure changes in that state and when an insecure, militaristic group assumes control of the decision-making process. Such a group may view a limited war as an attractive option for the attainment of their domestic and international goals. They could view military pressure as the best route to change the policies of an otherwise recalcitrant adversary under the expectation that the opponent would not cooperate in the resolution of the conflict through peaceful means. Changes in decision-making structure can occur as a result of regime changes through coups or transfer of power via internal power struggles, or changes within an existing regime through alteration of personnel.[65] In fluid internal situations, military or civilian groups that value the use of force may gain control of a state and thereby the foreign policy decision-making process. They may obtain support of pressure groups that demand militaristic solutions to their dispute with the more powerful adversary.[66] The political orientation of these groups, especially their preferences for military solutions, can be inferred by studying their declared positions on similar questions and their political activities prior to assuming power.

If a regime's legitimacy and popularity are low, particularly at the early stages of its inception, diversionary wars can be an effective means to attain popular support. A newly installed regime may also view the successful removal of external threats as a prerequisite for establishing its internal control and legitimacy. Such regimes, similar to newly established states, are more likely to face political and economic instability and worry about their longevity of tenure. Therefore, they are more likely to engage in foreign crisis and conflict behavior.[67] The intransigence of the stronger power or the continued failure of negotiations in resolving the dispute may be used by such decision-makers as pretexts for offensive military action. Militaristic decision-making groups may perceive grievances more intensely and may therefore exhibit a greater willingness to utilize opportunities provided by the acquisition of offensive weapon systems and by changes in alliance and strategic configurations. Such decision-making groups may feel intense time pressure to find a military solution to a

33

dispute for predominantly internal reasons of legitimacy and political control.

This factor may also be relevant to a stronger initiator who launches an attack against a weaker or an equally powerful state. However, I argue that its pertinence is greater for a weaker power as war initiation entails greater external and internal risks and costs for a weaker state. Changes in domestic power structure could be the precursor of war initiation by a weaker power whose survival as a state itself may be under challenge if it goes to war. This is because there is generally more at stake for a weaker power than a stronger power in an asymmetric war. Therefore, decision-making groups which are willing to take more risks and which value negotiated solutions less favorably tend to generate conditions for war with their stronger adversaries.

The relationship between decision-making structures and international conflict has attracted a good amount of scholarly attention. Mayer argues that decision-makers are political actors with tangible political, ideological, and economic interests. While making decisions for or against war, they are influenced by a mixture of external and internal considerations.[68] Rosecrance contends that the directional ethos of the elites has an important relationship to international stability. He links the most violent forms of international conflict to wide divergences in elite ethos. Accordingly, decisive changes in the international system have been correlated with fluctuations in the internal positions of elites[69]. Hermann finds that particular decision structures exert powerful impact on foreign policy behavior as different structures and processes produce different results.[70] The "operational code" approach also considers the beliefs of decision-makers as having significant effect on what choices countries make with regard to war and peace.[71]

The hypothesis presented here suggests that domestic leadership structures may have significant explanatory power as to why some states pursue war-like policies while others seek negotiations, even when the objective systemic conditions facing them may be the same. Different leadership structures can lead decision-makers to respond to various crises differently. Thus a group of militaristic decision-makers, with little legitimacy and with specific political, economic, and military objectives, may behave differently from their counterparts who may be inclined to pursue negotiations. Changes in individual actors may bring changes in motivations and responses to various stimuli. As a historian puts it, a number of historic crises never ended up in wars, due to a great extent to political decisions by "actors who preferred drawing back from the brink by resorting to diplomacy."[72]

Summarizing the argument

The main contention of this study is that in contexts of military and economic asymmetry between two antagonistic states engaged in conflict, the weaker challenger can initiate war against the relatively strong adversary if its key decision-makers believe that they can achieve their political and military objectives through the employment of a limited aims/fait accompli strategy. Conversely, if a weaker power expects to fight an offensive, attrition-style warfare, it may desist from engaging in war initiation. Superior aggregate military and economic power of the defender need not deter a challenger if its decision-makers expect a limited war and perceive political and military advantages accruing from a fait accompli attack. The support of a great power ally and the possession of short-term offensive capabilities can increase the probability of such war initiations. Short-term offensive capability and windows of opportunity may be exploited if the weaker state comes under the control of militaristic decision-making groups that lack political legitimacy. Such decision-making groups, with the support of interest groups and organizations such as the military, can opt for war when they perceive that certain existing advantages in weaponry and political conditions may never return and that an attack can bring political and economic changes in the status quo that are advantageous to their nation in general and to the decision-making group in particular.

A methodological note

The method adopted in this study is that of comparative case study.[73] More concretely, the study employs the method of structured, focused, and controlled comparison by systematically differentiating a number of critical factors in a relatively weak state's war-initiation decisions from six major wars of the twentieth century.[74] In recent years, the method has been criticized by formal theorists as less rigorous than, and therefore failing to meet the "scientific" standards of, "theory construction and verification."[75] But as George contends, this "process tracing ... historical method is not simply descriptive, but one that identifies cause and effect link between independent and dependent variables by formulating theoretically relevant questions" on each of the cases as well as by establishing "provisional" but valuable generalizations.[76] In that sense this method is a definitive advancement over many descriptive historic accounts that do not look for generalizable patterns. The method also has advantages vis-à-vis many deductive and quantitative approaches that often lack historical depth and veri-fiability.

The criteria for case selection are:

(1)   They occurred in different geographical regions during differ-ent time periods of the twentieth century, but share many characteristics and exhibit adequate variations that allow con-trolled comparison.
(2)   In all these instances, the initiator possessed inferior overall military and economic power, in terms of a majority of indica-tors of power capability. The overall power ratio between the initiator and the defender was generally 1:2 or more. Battle-field outcome was not a factor in choosing the cases or in determining relative power capability of the belligerents, as the weaker states in some cases did win or manage to end the war in stalemate.
(3)   The parties were nation states. This study excludes civil wars or colonial wars.
(4)   The wars involved major use of military force and not border skirmishes.
(5)   The battle deaths in each case were 1,000 or more.

Despite the apparent uniqueness of each war and the variations in the contexts in which they were fought, by raising similar questions about each of these cases, one can draw valuable causal inferences on asymmetric war initiations that may have predictive value. The ques-tions are:

(1)   What was the comparative military and economic strength of the belligerents?
(2)   What was the nature of the issue at stake?
(3)   What was the perceived balance of interests between the initiator and the defender?
(4)   What motives did the relatively weak state have in initiating war against a stronger adversary?
(5)   What were the expectations regarding the defender's likely response?
(6)   What was the state of the four variables pertaining to the initiator (i.e., military strategy adopted, great power support available, possession of offensive weapon systems, and dom-estic power structure) when the war occurred?
(7)   The arrival of what specific condition or combination of con-ditions favored war initiation in a given case?

36

Additionally, the period during which the war took place is compared with previous periods when war was seriously considered by decision-makers in order to see why the weaker challenger initiated the war at a certain time but not others. The effort is to determine whether they failed to attack because of the absence of these factors or for some other reasons. This method of testing will enable us to distinguish the most critical factors that can account for the weaker state's war initiation at a particular juncture.

II THE CASE STUDIES

3 THE JAPANESE OFFENSIVE
AGAINST RUSSIA, 1904

The Russo-Japanese War began with Japan's surprise torpedo attack on the Russian Fleet at Port Arthur on February 8, 1904. The causes of this war have hitherto been generally sought in the long-run political factors such as the aggressive policies of Russia and the Japanese compulsion to resist its adversary's expansionist moves in the Far East.[1] Military historians and practitioners of war have studied this conflict with keen interest for its lessons in strategy, tactics, and performance of weapon systems, but not necessarily attributing prior changes in these factors as having much causal effect on the Japanese decision to go to war in 1904 against an opponent with more aggregate power resources.[2]

A major objective of this chapter is to fill this gap in the study of the first important war of the twentieth century, i.e., to explain why the Japanese oligarchic rulers decided to commit their nation to the war path in February 1904 after years of hesitation characterized by intense hostility towards Russia and several unsuccessful attempts at a negotiated solution. More importantly, why did the Japanese Army, after assessing Japan's overall relative inferiority and after concluding that Japan only held a fifty-fifty chance of victory, recommend an offensive? Likewise, the Japanese Navy had estimated that Japan would lose at least half of its ships in the effort to control the surrounding seas of the theater of operations.[3] Although the long-run causes of the war are also explored here, the chief purpose of this chapter is to see what specific short and middle-term conditions arose by February 1904 that provided Japan incentive to take the drastic step of fighting a declining but still colossal Russian Empire.

The balance of capabilities

As regards comparative force level in 1904, Russia enjoyed an overall preponderance. In most indicators of aggregate power capability – population, economic strength, and military prowess (in both qualitative and quantitative senses) – Russia was far superior to Japan.[4] In naval strength (tonnage), the Russian Fleet was the fourth largest in the world, following those of Britain, France, and Germany. In number of ships, it was world's third largest, with 272 ships, of which 19 were battleships.[5] At the time of war, the Russian Army consisted of over a million men, in addition to a strong reserve force, 345,000 cossacks, and a militia. Altogether Russia could mobilize a force of 4.5 million.[6] The Japanese Army numbered 850,000, of which only 180,000 constituted regular soldiers, while the rest, 670,000, were reserves, a force much smaller than the total Russian troop strength. However, the greatest advantage that Japan possessed was in its ability to mobilize and deploy forces in the theater of hostilities faster than Russia. But this advantage was of short run, because once the Russian replenishments arrived the Japanese forces would become inferior in quality and quantity. As proven at the end, despite several battlefield successes, Japan could not completely dislodge Russia from Manchuria. Had the war continued beyond August 1905, indications were that Japan could have been defeated in a war of attrition.[7]

The Japanese offensive capability at sea was also of short-run nature. Although Japan's combined squadrons possessed a total tonnage of 260,000, compared with the Russian Pacific squadron of 190,000, the latter retained over 320,000 tons in its Baltic and Black Sea Fleets.[8] Russia also possessed major advantages in ship building and ship repair. Four major ship-building facilities – the Baltic Emergency Works, the Nevsky Works, the Putiloff Armaments Concern, and the Kolpino Steel Works – provided Russia with sufficient capability to build several ships and repair the damaged ones. On the contrary, Japan's ship-building industry was in its infancy, forcing it to conserve all its largely foreign-made ships. Japan had no capability to replace any of the capital ships and first-class cruisers if they were destroyed in the war.[9] With regards to reserves of armed ships, Japan only had two armored cruisers, *Nisshin* and *Kasuya*, and had no shipyards to build more.[10]

Considering this major discrepancy in overall power capability, one would expect that the sheer might of the Russian Empire would have deterred Japan from taking the military initiative. The Russian expectation indeed was that Japan would not dare to launch an attack against a far superior European power. Before analyzing the key conditions and factors that allowed war in 1904, I will trace the background of the conflict, especially how the incompatible strategic objectives and territorial policies of the defender and the challenger interacted.

42

The Russo-Japanese conflict: an imperial rivalry

The roots of the Far Eastern conflict were derived from the dispute over possession of territories that both Japan and Russia perceived as legitimate for their economic and security objectives and political ambitions. In the Japanese point of view, the continued presence of Russia in the region would have spelled the weakening of Tokyo's influence and the curtailment of its imperial goals. According to this perspective, had the Russians succeeded in permanently establishing their control over China and Korea, the security of the Japanese mainland itself would have been endangered.[11] Korea thus formed a forward defense and a buffer zone for Japan against potential threats from Russia. In the eyes of the Japanese decision-makers, therefore, the removal of the Russian presence from Manchuria and Korea dovetailed the very survival of the imperial state and its further expansion.

For Russia, the control over Manchuria and Korea was a logical conclusion of its eastward push for the attainment of cheap resources and easy markets. However, from the perceived balance of interests, the stake for Russia was described as nothing more than dominance over a territory, adjunct to its Siberian possessions, driven largely by the imperial ambitions of overzealous bureaucratic actors, with and occasionally without the connivance of the Tsar.[12] Additionally, a defeat in the war would have spelled a deathblow to the existence of Japan as a nation, let alone its imperial ambitions. For Russia, a defeat would have been a local event, confined to the outer fringes of a vast empire.[13] In a general sense, when these irreconcilable strategic and military objectives clashed, the side which perceived a higher stake in the dispute and an advantage in taking military action, i.e. Japan, decided to strike, even after realizing the possibility of defeat. The decision thus showed that in many respects the weaker side perceived a higher stake, largely deriving from its strategic and intrinsic interests, and exhibited a higher willingness to bear the costs of war.

Although the broader, long-term political and economic rivalry that led to the outbreak of the war seems important, it does not explain fully why Japan waited so long, even though it had every reason to fight Russia and had made contingency plans to do so. More specifically, why did it fail to attack in 1895 when Japan was deprived of reaping the fruits from the Sino-Japanese War by the Triple Intervention of Russia, Germany, and France? The Russians were the chief protagonists of this move, and the Japanese ire was all the more directed against them. Although the April 1895 Shimonoseki Treaty between Russia and China that ended the Sino-Japanese War provided substantial concessions from China to Japan, the Russian-led intervention compelled Japan to give up or reduce most of those claims.[14] Again in 1901, Japan had made preparations for war as a result of serious ruptures in diplomatic relations. The attempt here is to explain why war did not break out during those two previous occasions and why it did erupt in February 1904.

In an effort to find a plausible explanation, this chapter tests the major hypotheses advanced in chapter 2. Do the four key factors of asymmetric wars presented, individually or additively, account for Japan's decision to initiate war in February 1904? By translating these factors into the Japanese context, I ask the following questions: First, did the Japanese decision-makers perceive a successful limited aims/ fait accompli strategy in achieving their politico-military objectives while taking the decision for war? Second, what role did short-term offensive capability play in the Japanese calculations regarding the timing of operations? Third, did the defensive alliance support from Britain give Japan incentives to go to war? Finally, did domestic changes in Japan result in the coming into power of an insecure regime, dominated by a group of militaristic leaders bent on pursuing war as the ideal policy vis-à-vis Russia? The arrival of which one or more of these factors made the crucial difference in the decision to launch an attack? To begin with, what were the adversaries' strategic calculations on the eve of war in February 1904? Did the conflicting strategic objectives of the defender and the challenger and their interaction contribute in any way to the outbreak of a major armed conflict between the antagonists?

Russia's diplomatic and political posture

First, what was Russia's grand strategy, especially with respect to the Far East, prior to the war? Examining the political as well as the military aspects of this strategy seems necessary in order to see how they interacted and clashed with those of Japan. The key to Russia's expansionist policies in the Far East at the turn of the century was the occupation of Manchuria and the eventual domination of Korea. The forceful evacuation of Japan from the Liaotung Peninsula at the close of the nineteenth century greatly facilitated Russia's penetration into Manchuria. In 1896, Russia acquired the rights to build the Trans-Siberian Railway through Eastern Manchuria. Officials in the Russian Government considered the Siberian Railway as an instrument to strengthen the Russian Navy's position in the Pacific and to facilitate

Russia's "control over the entire movement of international commerce in Pacific waters."[15] The Russian rulers had couched the railway construction in a mutually beneficial fashion for both China and Russia, but it was in fact meant for them to achieve permanent dominance in the region. By 1898, the Russian penetration received another boost with the granting of a lease to Port Arthur and the recognition of its special position in Manchuria by China.[16]

The Tsarist regime refused to withdraw from the Liaotung Peninsula, despite a promise given to China to do so by October 1903. Under the April 1902 agreement, the Russians were to evacuate completely in eighteen months in a three-phased operation. The first phase of the withdrawal was conducted as promised. However, the second phase, due to be completed by April 1903, never took place largely due to internal power struggle among factions of Tsar Nicholas II's advisers. One of these factions, headed by Privy Counselor Ivan Bezobrazov, wanted Russia to expand aggressively to Korea and Manchuria and ultimately succeeded in gaining the upper hand over its rival group, led by Foreign Minister Vladimir Lamsdorff and Finance Minister Sergei Witte, which was willing to provide some concessions to Japan.

The Tsar held a conference on February 7, 1903 to decide the question of withdrawal at which Witte, Lamsdorff, and the War Minister, General Alexei Kuropatkin advocated a conciliatory posture towards Japan by agreeing to withdraw the Russian claims over Korea and South Manchuria. However, the Tsar, siding with the expansionists, decided not to proceed with the promised evacuation.[17] In addition, in July 1903, the Tsar appointed Admiral Eugene Alexeyev, an avowed advocate of Russian expansion to Manchuria, as the Viceroy to the Far East. Then onward, Alexeyev and Bezobrazov took complete control of the Far Eastern policy and began to develop plans for the economic expansion of Russia in the newly occupied territories.[18] The group's thinking was summarized in a 1903 statement by one of its prominent members, the Minister of the Interior Vyacheslav Plehve, in these words: "Bayonets, not diplomats, have made Russia; by bayonets and not by diplomatic pens must the Far Eastern problem be solved."[19]

Along with their penetration into Manchuria, the Russians also began to show an active interest in Korea. Their rejection of the Japanese negotiating position – exchange of Manchuria for Korea – signalled to the latter that they were bent on total control of both the territories. In 1902, a Russian company began to cut timber from the Yalu banks on the Korean side and Russian troops eventually occupied this region by the summer of 1903. Several rounds of unsuccessful negotiations were held to try to resolve the dispute between Russia and Japan on the Far Eastern territories. The Japanese ire reached its zenith when the Russians rejected Japan's final proposal to leave Korea to its dominance in exchange for Manchuria to the Russians.[20]

Russia's military strategy: dominance of defense

Although the political and strategic goals of Russia in the Far East were on a grand scale, its military strategy was inadequate for confronting an enemy that was bent on launching a surprise attack and a short war. The Russian strategy, on the eve of the war, relied heavily on deterrence at the general level and on assuming a defensive posture if war occurred. Although at the immediate deterrence level, in early 1903 the Russian leaders had made a limited move when they ordered the Russian ships in the Mediterranean to proceed to the Far East, no serious retaliatory threat in response to an attack by Japan was made prior to the war.[21] Russia was caught unaware when the attack took place on February 8, 1904. The Russian troops in the Far East were not under mobilization orders as the rearmament and reorganization of the forces were going on during that time.[22] The Port Arthur Fleet had been ordered not to make any moves that would be interpreted by Japan as provocative, which resulted in the ships lying off the port, unprepared for defending against a major attack. The Russian ships were sent out to anchor in the open instead of being positioned at the port, battle-ready. Additionally, the Russians neither darkened their ships, nor put out any torpedo nets. They also made no arrangements for patrolling the adjacent waters.[23]

Even after the outbreak of the war, for almost two months, the naval squadron at Port Arthur remained strictly on the defensive, a mere anchored "fortress fleet," thus sacrificing the mobility greatly needed in naval warfare.[24] One may argue that in terms of an immediate deterrence strategy, the Russian ship movements did not signal a sufficient retaliatory threat to Japan. Part of the reasons for the Russian unpreparedness and defensive posture may be attributed to the conviction among senior Russian leaders and officers that Japan would not dare to attack because in order to do so it had to deploy troops in Korea. A prerequisite of this was the neutralization of Russian sea power itself in the adjoining waters.[25] The Russian leadership, especially the Bezobrazov group was convinced that merely demonstrating a will to stand firm and defending Manchuria along the Korean border would keep Japan at bay.[26] The Russians seemed to have taken the Japanese threat lightheartedly, as most big states tend to do in asymmetric conflict situations. The Russians also thought their overall superiority in capability would work as a sufficient general deterrent threat and thereby would prevent Japan from engaging in an offensive.

On the eve of the war, the bigger defending power thus showed overconfidence in its ability to deter and defend, without taking adequate precautions against a possible surprise attack by a relatively weak challenger that held an intense desire to alter the status quo. The Tsarist regime also thought waiting could be in the interests of Russia, as every passing month saw Russia's military position in the Far East improving steadily.[27] The Russian overconfidence was again manifested in the Tsarist regime's failure to dispatch the Baltic Fleet promptly after the outbreak of hostilities. The arrival of this fleet early on would have altered the course of the war to the benefit of Russia. The fleet was ordered for service in the Far East only on April 30, 1904 and could leave the port only on October 15, 1904. The Russians thus lost the determining first few months of the war, inadvertently giving Japan a decisive advantage on the battlefield. Eventually the Baltic Fleet arrived at the Sea of Japan towards the end of the war to be confronted by Admiral Togo's fleet (inferior in both number and tonnage), and was defeated at the Battle of Tsushima on May 27, 1905.[28] During this battle, Togo applied his famous "T" tactics by suddenly changing course and bearing down diagonally on Admiral Zinovy Rozhdestvensky's fleet, thereby forming a "T." The Japanese admiral fought with superior speed and fired more shots than the numerically superior enemy could, and defeated the Russian fleet in a decisive battle that lasted for only a few hours.[29]

The Russian unpreparedness was also manifested on the ground. Their forces in Manchuria were scattered, allowing the Japanese to engage in concentrated attacks. The Russians attempted to cover all strategic spots and in that process allowed Japan to take the initiative, especially at the latter's strong points.[30] Even after the Japanese ground attack gained momentum, the Russian strategy remained essentially defensive and counter-offensive while Japan pushed forward with its offense-dominant strategy. To the Russians' dismay, in the Manchurian theater, battlefield successes were greatly determined by offense.[31] The Russian strategy, especially immediately prior to and during the early phase of the war, was based on an expectation that the army units in Manchuria could stand on the defensive until reinforcements arrived by the Trans-Siberian Railway. Simultaneously, the besieged Port Arthur was expected to hold out, to be

47

defended by its garrison and the Pacific Fleet. Once the Baltic Fleet arrived, the combined fleet was expected to defeat Togo's force and sever the Japanese Army's communications links. The anticipation was that seeing this formidable Russian military might, Japan would surrender after some fight, and accordingly preparations were made for the military occupation of the vanquished.[32] Decision-makers in St. Petersburg also believed that Japan would eventually exhaust its resources and that the Russian Navy would show its superior strength.[33]

A long war and a war of attrition were thus in the strategic calculations of Russia. Many high-ranking officials, both in St. Petersburg and in Manchuria, as well as the general Russian public, regarded Japan's armed forces with contempt. The Russian defeats in various battlefields were regarded as temporary, reversible setbacks.[34] The Russian decision-makers also underestimated Japan's military strength and the willingness to employ all it could in order to achieve its objectives. The Russian military attaché in Tokyo, Colonel Vannovski, sarcastically reported that it would take hundreds of years for Japan to achieve the naval capability sufficient to challenge the Russian forces. He also recommended that a strong cavalry regiment equipped with artillery could defeat the Japanese without confronting any major resistance.[35] The Russians believed that their overall power position would deter a Japanese attack. They could comprehend neither the logic of a possible Japanese surprise attack, nor that the enemy was determined to alter the status quo through a limited, fait accompli operation. General Kuropatkin confides that the Russian leaders were ignorant of Japan's readiness for war and thought that the Japanese had no intention of using military force to achieve their demands. They felt that the outbreak of war would depend upon their decisions, as opposed to those of Japan.[36]

During the preceding years, the Russian leaders had, however, made some efforts to strengthen their military position in the region. Between 1898 and 1902 the Russian force deployments had increased by thirty-one battalions, fifteen squadrons, thirty-two guns, and three battalions of fortress artillery – consisting of 37,000 men. The long-term Russian plan consisted of bringing into the Far East 172 battalions of which at least 100 would be readily available. These plans were heavily dependent on the availability of railway transportation.[37] War Minister, Alexei Kuropatkin, anticipated that by 1906–7 Russia would have brought a sufficient number of forces to deter and defend any attacks from Japan.[38] Clearly, the Russian leadership was preparing for larger threats and longer wars, as manifested in their troop deployments and

48

long-term plans for the domination of Manchuria and Korea. As the bigger power, Russia was convinced that it could afford to be stubborn and that granting Japan any concessions would lead to more concessions. The Russians thought flexibility would result in war, and a tough posture would preserve peace.

Japan's strategic calculations

While the Russian strategy relied on an implicit general deterrent threat and a belief that a possible attrition war would prevent an offensive by the challenger, Japan was preparing for a surprise attack that would compensate for its inferiority in overall power capability and help achieve its limited strategic and tactical objectives in a quick, fait accompli war. The Japanese expectation was that once some tactical gains were made in Korea and Manchuria the enemy would not be willing to pay the cost of removing a well entrenched defensive force. A timely peace settlement would transform the military successes of Japan into permanent political gains. Even before launching their offensive, the Japanese decision-makers thought about a peace settlement with the help of third party intervention so that Japan would be able to preserve its limited gains from the war. They were also aware of Japan's inability to wage a protracted, attrition style war which would suit the stronger Russia and would hurt the strategic and political goals of a weaker Japan.

Japan's war plan envisioned three phases: The torpedo attack on ships at Port Arthur, the destruction of the Russian Fleet off Port Arthur, and the landing of troops at the Chemulpo harbor in Seoul, Korea.[39] The initial Japanese strategic objective was to impose unrecoverable damage on the Russian Fleet at Port Arthur and the surrounding waters by attacking through the interior lines of operations at sea. After this attack, the Japanese strategy called for a quick landing of ground forces on the Korean peninsula and driving the Russians out of Korea and Manchuria. The major aim of Admiral Heihachiro Togo's night attack on February 8, 1904 on Russia's Pacific squadron at Port Arthur was to inflict a fatal immobilizing blow so that it would not risk a battle with the Japanese fleet in the future.[40]

In Admiral Togo's calculations, without such destruction the Japanese Army would not be in a position to dispatch its troops to Manchuria and Korea. The objective of capturing Port Arthur required Japan to transport four army corps to nearby Pitzu-wo, sixty miles east of the city. Three of these corps would engage the Russian forces, stationed between Hai-cheng, Mukden, and Liao-yang, while the fourth one would fight its way down the Manchurian peninsula in order to reach the outskirts of Port Arthur. Once the Russian field armies were pushed back or held at bay, the advancing Japanese troops could reinforce their positions.[41] The operational plan also entailed minimum damage to the Japanese Fleet, as Japan would have fewer replacements (unlike Russia, which could afford to bring in more ships from its European Fleet).[42]

Superior tactical concepts and their application in battle formed a key part of the Japanese war plans. In naval warfare, Japan had perceived early on the value of the column and the broadside fire which they successfully employed against the Russian Fleet. Quick concentrations of ground as well as naval forces under the command of semi-independent divisions for flexible operations, limited battle-field gains, and conservation of ships, formed the other key tactical approaches of Japan.[43] On the ground, the Japanese tactic was to utilize their guns as a unit and fire en masse on enemy concentrations.[44] The Japanese planners estimated that replenishments from Russia would take months to arrive and that they could achieve their military objectives before that. The strategy was one of high risk, because if the Japanese Fleet did not succeed in accomplishing the task of making the Russian Far Eastern Fleet ineffective, the latter could pose a formidable threat to Japan's plans to land in Korea and Man-churia. Besides, if the battle was not concluded quickly, the Russians could send additional naval reinforcements from their Baltic Fleet and dispatch army reinforcements via the Trans-Siberian Railway when the winter months were over. However, the single-track Siberian Railway meant that the Russians would take months to bring in a large number of forces. A quick war would, however, incapacitate the relatively smaller force stationed in the Far East.[45] Additionally, the Russian Black Sea Fleet was forbidden to pass through Bosphorus, as per the Treaty of Berlin. Both Turkey and Britain refused to waive this Treaty clause for Russia.[46]

The Japanese leaders were fully cognizant that they could not defeat Russia in a long, attrition war and that a short, fait accompli war, localized in the Far Eastern theater, offered the best chance to attain their objectives. The eve-of-war deliberations, held on February 4, 1904 at the Imperial Palace, revealed a consensus among the decision-makers on the absolute necessity to make the war short in order for Japan to make any headway. They even thought a defeat was not improbable, but were confident that Japan could survive that too. In such a contingency, "Japan might lose Formosa and be forced to pay a war indemnity, but she would survive and after 100 years could tackle

Russia once again."[47] The oligarchic decision-makers made a unanimous decision that their country "however poorly prepared, should go to war at once, because further delay could only be detrimental to Japan."[48] War could be shortened by the expected intervention of President Theodore Roosevelt to help conclude an armistice agreement. At this Imperial Conference, the Japanese decision-makers had already agreed to ask the US to intervene in order to conclude the war.[49]

Decision-makers in Tokyo were aware that their inferior industrial and economic capability meant fighting and winning a protracted war almost impossible. This expectation was evident in Field Marshal Oyama's statement to Navy Minister Yamamoto in July 1904 before he left for Manchuria to command the forces there: "I will take care of the fighting in Manchuria, but I am counting on you as the man to decide when to stop."[50] Four decades later, in the Tokyo trials after World War II, Prince Kanoye was quoted from his diary: "In other words, they were thinking of ending the war at the time of beginning it."[51] The Japanese decision-makers were thus from the very beginning concerned with bringing the war to a "satisfactory conclusion" as it was clear that Japan could not conquer Russia. All they could envision was a war "fought for limited gains."[52] The Russian weakness in mobilizing quickly meant that Japan possessed a short-term advantage in the theater of operations. Thus neither the large Russian forces on the European front nor the greater mobilizational potential of Russia deterred Japan which viewed those forces as being unavailable in the first few decisive months of the war.

A limited aims strategy was clearly evident in the initial Japanese war plans. In the summer of 1904, Japan's objectives were to obtain a completely free hand in the affairs of Korea and a war indemnity from Russia. Japan was even willing to return Port Arthur to China and to keep the Manchurian Railways under international control. After January 1905, the Japanese objectives changed slightly as they now wanted to retain Port Arthur which they had occupied after a long battle.[53] Although pursuing a limited aims strategy was clear in the Japanese intentions all through the war, it became more apparent as the war progressed toward its first year. After few major victories, especially the one in the Battle of Liao-yang in August 1904, the Japanese commanders began to feel the crunch of resource scarcity, especially in supplying the troops with proper ammunition. As the Russians began to bring in more and more troops from Europe in preparation for an attrition war, the Japanese military pressured the political leadership for a diplomatic solution through the good offices of the US. Although Japan won an indecisive victory in the Battle of Mukden in March 1905, the Russians had brought to Manchuria an army three times the size of Japan's, under the new commander, General Linievitch. The Japanese Army commanders in Manchuria estimated that in order to defeat the Russians decisively, Japan would have had to reinforce its forces by six additional divisions and needed another one billion yen.[54] On March 8, 1905, War Minister Terauchi made a request to Lloyd C. Griscom, the American Minister in Tokyo, to convey to President Roosevelt: "Time had come when the war should cease" and that he was "quite ready to stop fighting."[55]

After the Battle of Mukden, Field Marshal Marquis Oyama, the Commander of the Manchurian Army, wrote to the imperial head-quarters: "whether we decide to advance further in pursuit of the enemy or to take a course of positional warfare, unless our military operations are in accord with the national policy, the struggle perhaps costing several tens of thousands of lives, will be in vain."[56] This message from the field commander was passed on to the political leadership by Yamagata Aritomo. In his memorandum to the Prime Minister, Yamagata warned that the Russians would never sue for peace and that the war would turn into an attrition battle lasting many years. In his words, Russia would not request for peace unless Japan invaded Moscow and St. Petersburg. "First, while the enemy still has powerful forces in its home country, we have already exhausted ours. Second, while the enemy still does not run short of officers, we have lost a great number since the opening of the war and cannot easily replace them."[57] The Chief of Staff of the Manchurian Army, Kodama Gentaro, told the Cabinet on March 31, 1905 that "the country that starts a war should know how to stop it, and that a poor country such as Japan had nothing to gain from a protracted war."[58] Clearly, the Japanese decision-makers desired an early termination of hostilities as they could neither plan on subduing Russia completely, nor wage a protracted war, chiefly due to Japan's economic and military weaknesses. A favorable peace settlement was thus high on the agenda of the Japanese diplomatic parleys from the very outset of the war.[59]

The expectation of a successful limited aims/fait accompli strategy was a key determining factor that led to the Japanese offensive against Russia in 1904. The decision-makers in Tokyo anticipated that a surprise attack would enable them to engage in a short, fait accompli war that would remove the Russian presence from Korea and Manchuria and provide Japan with territorial gains. The Russian inability to bring in a substantial number of forces and its failure to formulate a clear-cut deterrent strategy also encouraged Japan to go for an offensive. In strategic interaction terms, the strategic choices of the weaker initiator depended heavily on how the stronger defender would respond in a prospective war. The Russian inability to retaliate massively meant Japan enjoyed a short-term window of opportunity which could be exploited if it engaged in a limited aims/fait accompli war.

Offense dominance

Japan's strategic choices in 1904 reflected a second dimension of Tokyo's military calculations; its short-run offensive advantage in the theater of operations. While the Russians were making long-term plans for a slow but steady expansion of their military position in the Far East, by 1904 Japan had acquired sufficient short-term offensive capability for a limited war confined to the Far East. For the Japanese decision-makers, it became apparent that time was running out and that Japan should strike without delay to make the maximum use of its newly acquired weapon systems, lest their military position should become increasingly tenuous.[60] By 1904, Japan had acquired some powerful weapons of the time, enabling it to engage in a short war with a more powerful adversary. Japan's humiliation in the 1895 Triple Intervention gave its leadership a strong determination to build an offensive capability. In 1896, six more divisions were added to the standing army, making its total strength thirteen. In 1898, Japan organized its cavalry and artillery as independent brigades and provided them with more advanced rifles and quick-firing guns. All these programs were completed by 1904. Japan had also acquired another powerful weapon of the times, the whitehead torpedoes.[61]

By the end of 1903, the Japanese Navy had procured six first-class battleships and eight armored cruisers. In quality, four were superior to Russia's comparable ships in the Far East, while two were of the same caliber. Japan's military and strategic calculations relied heavily on the survival and efficiency of these ships.[62] Japan's naval building program, begun in 1896–97, had envisioned the additional acquisition of sixteen cruisers and twenty-three destroyers, bringing its total naval capacity up to seventy-six vessels, with a total of 258,000 tons.[63] As this acquisition reached its zenith, Japan's leaders became increasingly concerned about Russia's plans for a massive naval buildup in the Far East. They were under intense time pressure to strike while their limited advantage in the local theater persisted, or else a favorable political or military outcome in the future would be hard to come by. The Russian naval program, that was in progress at the end of the nineteenth century, would have made its navy more powerful than even the British Navy in the east of the Mediterranean.[64] The Russian Navy was building five new warships, to be added to the Far Eastern Fleet. By 1905, Russia's Far Eastern Fleet would have had at least twelve modern battleships at its command, as compared to seven that Japan possessed at the time of the war. Additionally, the Japanese Fleet was not expected to receive any new ships before 1905.[65]

The long-term Russian military plan was clearly to make a formidable presence in the waters surrounding Port Arthur in support of its territorial advancements in Manchuria and Korea. In 1899, in addition to the naval expansion program, the Russian leadership had decided to establish an army comprising ninety-six battalions, fifty-seven squadrons, twenty-six guns, and three and three-quarter sapper battalions, organized in three corps as a rapid advancement force. However, this was not achieved as planned and with limited resources allocated for this purpose, Russia would have been able to do so only by 1906 or 1907.[66] Had Japan waited, this projected large asymmetry in force level in the theater would have made its plans for a war of limited gains even more difficult to implement. The Japanese decision-makers were thus under intense time pressure to destroy the Russian Far Eastern Fleet not only before Russia added more ships to it but before it reinforced its land forces in the region.

The capability factor seems crucial to understanding why Japan did not go to war on two previous occasions. In 1895, when the Triple Intervention took place, the Japanese decision-makers decided not to go to war as their naval intelligence advised: "Japan might lose command of the Tsushima Straits, thus suffering the separation of her armies on the continent from their home islands, and might suffer the bombardment of her coasts, while her own squadrons were far away in the neighborhood of the Pescadores."[67] At that time the Japanese Army numbered only 67,000 and the Navy did not possess a single battleship.[68] During March–April 1901, a "war scare" arose when the Russian Foreign Minister Lamsdorff refused to accept a diplomatic note by the Japanese Minister in St. Petersburg. In that note, Japan had protested the provisions of the proposed Sino-Russian Treaty. This incident was followed by an atmosphere of crisis in Japan when several influential groups clamored for war. The army and navy strongly urged for war while the navy placed its forces on near fighting order. The Russian preponderance in capability was cited as one of the main reasons for no military response to this apparent humiliation. To Yamagata, Japan needed at least one more year to possess sufficient capability and to undertake adequate preparations for confronting Russia militarily.[69]

54

As noted previously, by 1903–4, Japan had procured sufficient offensive capability for waging a limited war with Russia. Its choice for war in 1904 was thus influenced greatly by its short-term offensive advantage in the theater of operations. Decision-makers in Tokyo viewed that their newly acquired land and naval capabilities would allow Japan to engage in a limited war. However, if they waited, they feared, the Russians would bring in an overwhelmingly preponderant force to the Far East, severely constraining any possibility for a successful war outcome.

Alliance configurations in 1904

Along with changes in capability, Japan's alliance relationships also underwent a transition during the early part of the century. In many respects, Japan did receive favorable alliance support in 1904. Historians generally agree that the Anglo-Japanese Treaty of January 1902 strengthened Tokyo's resolve to go to war against its more powerful adversary.[70] This alliance commitment made it certain that although Britain would remain militarily neutral in the war between Russia and Japan, it would intervene in case third parties joined on the side of Russia.[71] The Treaty also had recognized Japan's special interests in China and Korea. For all practical purposes, this allowed Japan a free hand in its war with Russia and foreclosed the possibility of French or German intervention on the side of Russia. The alliance relationship thus facilitated the localization of the war to the benefit of the weaker initiator; the prior anticipation of such a condition heavily influencing its military calculations.

By 1902, alliance relationships in the Far East had changed vastly in favor of Japan. The British defensive commitment to Japan practically eliminated the incentives for France and Germany to intervene on behalf of Russia.[72] Not only did Britain put its full diplomatic and political weight behind Japan, but the relationship also allowed Tokyo to borrow money for war efforts from the UK and the US. Additionally, the alliance helped Japan to buy brand new warships from Britain, while Britain prevented Russia from buying new ships from Italy. Britain also barred Russia's Baltic Fleet from using its ports all through the war, thus prolonging its arrival time in the Far Eastern waters by several months.[73] Prior to launching their offensive, the Japanese leadership tested the reliability of the alliance with Britain. The signals that Britain sent were positive and reassuring.[74]

In addition to the defensive commitment by Britain, Japan had received diplomatic and moral support from the US. Before launching its surprise attack, Tokyo had obtained a pledge from the US, promising neutrality in case of a war between Japan and Russia. Despite this public posture, there is strong evidence that President Theodore Roosevelt extended moral and diplomatic support to Japan consistent with a growing wave of public sympathy in the US for that country's steadfast opposition to Russian expansionism. For instance, just four weeks before the surprise attack, the administration announced a policy of benevolent neutrality, a position favorable to Japan. Immediately after the outbreak of war, the US Government sent diplomatic notes to all major European powers with interests in China to keep the kingdom's neutrality and territorial integrity intact, a move which showed interests in China's political future, but not that of Korea. Precluding Korea from the American strategic concern was in Japan's interests as Japan was claiming Korea as part of its sphere of interest. The Roosevelt Administration was opposed to a possible European intervention on behalf of Russia, because it wanted the Russians to loosen their control over Manchuria and avoid a partition of China.[75]

By the turn of the century, Germany also had balked out of its previous commitments to Russia. The German Ambassador to Britain informed the British Government that if a war broke out between Russia and Japan, Germany would remain benevolently neutral. The Germans gave assurances to Japan that they had not concluded any secret agreements with Russia. Their neutral position, the Germans assured, would also prevent France's involvement in the war.[76] The Russian effort to form a counter-coalition to the Anglo-Japanese alliance was not treated favorably by Germany. The Germans declared that their interests in the region were purely commercial and that they desired only to keep the sea-lanes open for free trade. Germany feared that if it allied with Russia, the US would be forced to join the Anglo-Japanese alliance.[77] The Kaiser's Government wanted the Japanese and the Russians to fight and weaken themselves in a prolonged war of attrition in the Far East so that Russia would divert its attention from Europe, resulting in the isolation of France on the Continent.[78] Although France had made a declaration to the effect that it intended to extend the Franco-Russian alliance to the Far East, in reality, Paris made every effort to convince the British that the declaration was a meaningless exercise made for propaganda purposes.[79]

Unfavorable alliance configuration was a major factor as to why Japan did not fight before 1904. The Franco-Russian alliance was active, which meant that Japan would have to simultaneously confront two European powers with strong interests in East Asia.[80] During the Triple Intervention in 1895, Japan found itself alienated completely as the three powers – Russia, Germany, and France – formed a formidable obstacle to Japan's ambitions in the aftermath of the Sino-Japanese war. At that time, Britain did not oppose the intervention, advising Japan to concede to the demands of the three powers.[81] Japan also received very little sympathy from potential allies such as the US. In 1895, a war with the combined forces of Russia, France, and Germany, especially at sea, would have been extremely risky for Japan to undertake. The Japanese naval experts had warned their leaders that Tokyo might not be in a position to confront the three powers together and that its naval control of the Tsushima Straits might be lost leading to the cutting off of its troops in China from Japan and a possible direct attack on the Japanese coastal areas.[82]

Thus for the Japanese decision-makers, the timing of a war with Russia was not opportune in 1895. A meeting of the national leadership concurred with Foreign Minister Munemitsu Matsu's recommendations that Japan had no alternative than to concede to the three-power demand for evacuating the Liaotung Peninsula. Matsu had hoped that Japan could withstand the pressures from the three powers by securing diplomatic support from Britain, the US and Italy.[83] While accepting this proposal, they wanted to search for the support of potential allies, implying that if they had a strong ally to provide defensive support, Japan would have resisted and, if necessary, gone to war against the three powers.[84] It also suggests that alliance commitment was a necessary condition for Japan to attack Russia.

Again in March 1901, Japan had announced its determination to go to war with Russia, if it was sure that France would not intervene on the side of Russia.[85] Many of the oligarchic leaders wanted war even if it meant defeat. The incident on March 25, 1901, when the Russian Foreign Minister Lamsdorff refused to accept a diplomatic protest by the Japanese Ambassador, led to a major crisis in their relations, ensued by a "war scare."[86] One of the major factors that seemed to have prevented war at that time too was an adverse alliance relationship. Admiral Yamagata, the father of the modern Japanese Army, had written to Prime Minister Ito in 1901 that sooner or later Japan would have to fight with the Russians. However, he warned that the Franco-Russian alliance made it difficult for Japan to challenge the Russian military single-handedly. Therefore, he urged the leadership to establish an alliance with Britain and Germany so that Japan could fight Russia in the future.[87] Ito himself was opposed to war fearing a

57

repetition of the 1895 experience. He was prepared to take the military initiative "only if assured that the international alignment was favorable."[88]

Thus shifts in alliance relationships did occur before Japan decided to commit to the war path. A major condition for the weaker state to go to war in this instance was favorable alliance support from a great power. The changes in the British and American positions, especially the defensive support from the former, meant that Japan could launch a limited war confined to Korea and Manchuria, unobstructed by other great powers such as France and Germany. Thus in 1904, the weaker challenger viewed a window of opportunity provided by the existing global alignment structure, favoring its taking military offensive against Russia.

Domestic changes

In addition to the external shifts caused by capability distributions and alliance configurations, what changes occurred by 1904 within the Japanese power hierarchy that might have contributed to the decision to go to war? Did shifts in the domestic balance of power influence in any way Japan's choice for war? By 1904, major changes in Japan's domestic power structure did indeed occur. It seems the ruling hierarchy, consisting among others of Prime Minister Taro Katsura; Foreign Affairs Minister Jutaro Komura; Home Minister Gentaro Kodama; War Minister Masatake Terauchi; Navy Minister Gonnohyoe Yamamoto; and Chief of the Army General Staff and elder statesman, Yamagata Aritomo, found war an advantageous option for internal as well as external reasons.

During a four-year period prior to the war the Genro, which had possessed immense control over the Japanese decision-making structure and had been a consistent opponent of the country going to war against a militarily superior Russia, began to lose its influence in decision-making. The Katsura Cabinet that came to power in June 1901 was controlled by second generation political leaders who were bent on making use of the Genro's prestige for their own advantage, while undermining its position within the decision-making hierarchy.[89] The Japanese reluctance to take military action until 1904 can be partially traced to the opposition of the Ito Hirobumi Cabinet which ruled the country intermittently until 1901. It instead sought to find ways to achieve a negotiated settlement. Ito, himself a Genro and his Foreign Minister, Nishi wanted to avoid any "adventurist policies" that would have caused an armed conflict with Russia. Therefore, when the

Russians annexed Port Arthur, they did not encounter the same opposition from Japan as one would have expected. "Safety first" was the watchword of the ruling elite which disliked the Russian activities in the region but could not find an ally that would stand with them on the sole issue of Russian behavior in Manchuria.[90] Subsequently Ito, the most powerful member of the Genro, opposed the conclusion of the Anglo-Japanese Treaty because he thought the alliance would provoke Russia to wage a war with Japan. Toward the goal of reaching an agreement with Russia, Ito himself undertook an unsuccessful trip to St. Petersburg in November 1901.[91]

Until the early 1900s, the Genro had within it powerful advocates of negotiations: Ito Hirobumi and Irou Karou. Proponents of an early war, including Foreign Minister Komura, agreed to continue negotiations right through 1903 as the elder statesmen insisted on avoiding an attack during the negotiations.[92] Within the domestic power structure, leaders such as Saionji Kinmochi of the Seiyukai Party, attempted to divorce foreign policy from party pressures and thereby reduce the influence of groups that clamored for a military solution to the dispute with Russia.[93] By 1903, when negotiations with Russia were not progressing favorably, several pro-war organizations had sprung up. Organizations such as Tairodoshikai (Anti-Russian Association) wanted immediate military action against the Russians. The impact of these organizations was profound on political parties, especially on the Seiyukai, whose leadership had earlier favored a negotiated settlement.[94] In September 1901, the Kokumin Domeikai (Anti-Russian National League), under the leadership of Prince Konoe Atsumaro, espoused continental expansion through railway building in Korea and Manchuria and clamored for resistance against the Russian occupation of these territories. Although this association was disbanded in April 1902 following the Russo-Chinese agreement to withdraw troops from China, it created a large constituency of diverse political viewpoints and strengthened the positions of militarists in various cabinets.[95]

Militaristic policies and colonial expansion had also been espoused by the "Black Dragon Society" which demanded abrogation of unequal treaties that were thrust upon Japan by the imperial powers.[96] The militarists were supported by the "Kogetsukai," an important pressure group of officials from the army, navy, and foreign ministry, which wanted to fight Russia even if Japan would lose the war. The group, comprising mostly middle ranking officials, argued that if Japan did not wage war at that juncture, the Russian military would advance to Korea and it would be extremely difficult to confront them in the future. They were supported by leaders such as War Minister Tera-uchi, Home Minister Kodama, and Foreign Minister Komura.[97] Other groups, such as "The Anti-Russian Comrades Society," were formed by the middle of 1903 and had received support from a broad spectrum of the Japanese elite, including Prince Kanoe and opposition leaders, Itagaki and Okuma.

Although militarism was already growing at the time of the outbreak of the Sino-Japanese War of 1895, it took almost a decade to crystallize and exert its full impact on Japan's foreign policy decision-making structure. For almost two decades prior to that war, the proponents of peace and diplomacy seemed to have won the debate and Japan was embarking on a course of internal development and quiet diplomacy. The constitutional crisis of 1894 and the desire on the part of the government to find a way out of it had been attributed as the reasons for the diversionary war with China. This period was also the time when ultra-nationalistic forces began to establish their roots in Japanese politics; the war with China was their first political victory.[98] The China War thus emboldened the military faction's strength in the Japanese power hierarchy. As discussed earlier, Prime Minister Ito attempted to renounce the militaristic policy, but did not succeed in his pursuit and had to resign in 1901.

Since 1896, the military faction of the oligarchy had attained such a preponderant position that they could easily topple any government that did not sympathize with their programs. The Itagaki–Okuma and the Yamagata Cabinets were overthrown one by one with the active connivance of the military faction. By 1900, pacifist parties and groups had been forced to assume a secondary role in Japanese politics, while the military factions became extraordinarily powerful.[99] The agreement in March 1898 between China and Russia to lease Port Arthur for twenty-five years marked the next active phase of the growth of expansionist groups in Japanese domestic politics. In November 1898, the East Asia Common Culture Society was established in an effort to revive Japan's position in East Asia, especially in China. The Boxer Rebellion of 1900 and the Russian troop movements into Manchuria resulted in the refocusing of these groups' attention toward Russia. By 1901, the Russians had clearly demonstrated their unwillingness to evacuate from Manchuria as promised, resulting in increasingly strengthened militaristic group activism in Japan. The Anglo-Japanese Treaty further reinforced their confidence in Japan taking the military offensive.[100]

The Katsura Government of 1901 typified the military's prowess in the Japanese power structure. The Anglo-Japanese alliance, the selling of open door policy in China to the US, and the massive rearmament in preparation for a war with Russia were undertaken under the supervision of this cabinet which was dominated by politicians who explicitly favored a military solution to the dispute with Russia.[101] The opposition to the war path was quite strong even in the early part of the twentieth century when the military factions under the leadership of Katsura had to face strong challenges from the Seiyukai Party, headed by Ito, on the national budget that called for more allocation for the naval building program. As he could not get the majority's support, Katsura dissolved the Diet. In the ensuing elections, the Seiyukai and the Real Constitutionalist Parties won an overwhelming majority. The Katsura Cabinet's lack of popular support was evident in those election results. Despite the opposition's victory, by 1903 Katsura managed to get Ito sidelined to the Privy Council, which greatly affected the Genro leader's ability to oppose the war. The Russian unwillingness to pull out troops from Manchuria as per the previous agreement with China also hardened the position of the proponents of war in the Katsura Cabinet and other pressure groups outside the regime.[102]

From this account one may conjecture that had Ito been in full control over the decision-making process in 1904, war would have been further postponed if not averted. Although Ito exerted some influence even in those later years as manifested in Katsura's willingness to continue negotiations, by the end of 1903, he was marginalized in the Japanese political setup by the militaristic groups. Katsura's reshuffling of the cabinet in June 1903 further strengthened the pro-war factions' position. By the end of 1903 the military factions had won the debate and the decision was taken to strike, and even soft-liners such as Ito were co-opted to the former's position that war was inevitable.[103] The final proposals that Japan submitted to the Russian Government contained very stringent conditions, showing that the hard-liners were sure of Russian rejection and thereby providing a good pretext for a military offensive.[104]

Internal factors did play a limited role in preventing war in 1895 when Japan considered a military confrontation with Russia. The leadership structure, comprising Prime Minister Ito Hirobumi and Foreign Minister Matsu opposed war as a meaningful policy at that time. Ito was especially opposed to the idea of a confrontation with Russia which he argued would invite both France and Germany to fight against Japan. Moreover, the domestic political situation was uncertain and the national finances were in disarray. Therefore, it was decided to postpone the war which many in the country regarded as inevitable.[105]

Explaining the Japanese decision to strike

This chapter has presented the four major factors that had arrived by 1904 and how they acted as causal variables in explaining Japan's decision to go to war against Russia, an opponent with more aggregate power capability. It was argued that the Japanese decision to attack the Russian forces in Manchuria was the result of the leadership's expectations of a successful limited aims/fait accompli strategy, achievable by surprise attack. The short-term offensive capability and the favorable alliance configurations also had a tremendous influence on the timing of Japan's offensive. Within the domestic political structure, the emergence of the Katsura Government and the prominence of individuals associated with the militarist movements had exerted some influence on military policy and Japan's willingness to bear the costs of war with a superior power in 1904.

Russia exacerbated Japan's sense of insecurity by expanding its political and military control of Manchuria and Korea. Its unwillingness to concede to Japan's major demands strengthened the Japanese decision-makers' resolve to fight, even if it meant defeat in the war. The Tsar and his advisers expected that their overall military and economic preponderance would deter Japan from going to war. They made confident statements without backing them up with adequate and timely military deployment. Their plans for additional stationing of troops in the Far East increased the Japanese fear and by early 1904 Japan was willing to exploit a short-term window of opportunity. Russia pursued neither a strategy of reassurance nor one of effective immediate deterrence, but relied on a general deterrent threat based on its overall superior military and economic capabilities.

In this case, all four factors of asymmetric war initiation were present in one form or other prior to Japan launching the war. The initiator's decision-makers expected a limited and short war and their calculations were based on a limited aims/fait accompli strategy relying heavily on surprise. The defensive support of a powerful great power ally and a short-term offensive advantage were also present. Also, the shifts in the domestic power structure brought about the rise of a group of decision-makers who valued war more favorably than continued negotiations. The timing of the war seems to have been tremendously influenced by these four factors. Although all four factors were present, in relative importance the limited aims/fait accompli strategy, defensive alliance support, and short-term offensive capability seem to be more critical in the Japanese calculations than the dynamics arising out of changes in the internal power structure. This conclusion is derived from Japan's rationale in 1895 and 1901 for not going to war. The lack of a powerful ally as well as sufficient offensive capability to confront Russia single-handedly were the main reasons for Japan abstaining from war during those periods, although the regime was controlled by less militaristic groups. By 1904, these two deficiencies were largely rectified. Although domestic changes favored an offensive in 1904, it is still possible to argue that Japan would not have gone to war without the British defensive support and the acquisition of sufficient short-term offensive capability, the two major conditions that allowed it to exploit a fast-closing window of opportunity.

The Russo-Japanese War brings forth the limitations of general deterrence. As Morgan characterizes, general deterrence is a situation in which opponents maintain armed forces sufficient to prevent attack by adversaries.[106] The Russians held overall military preponderance and expected that Japan with its limited military and economic capability would be deterred from initiating a war. Japan, the smaller power, circumvented its relative inferiority by choosing a strategy based on limited aims/fait accompli that relied heavily on surprise. The case illustrates that short, fait-accompli wars are antithetical to the success of general deterrence. Japan's expectation that the conflict would not end in attrition style warfare also influenced its choice for war.

4 THE JAPANESE ATTACK ON PEARL HARBOR, 1941

The Japanese attack on Pearl Harbor has been described as an "act of suicide," a "supreme folly," and a "strategically idiotic move."[1] This description has been largely based on a commonly held assumption that a relatively small state that wages war against an opponent who possesses superior power capability is indeed making an irrational choice. This chapter attempts to unravel the decision-making process of Japan's power hierarchy to see why the leaders opted to strike in December 1941 even when they knew that they were waging war against a country that possessed eight times more economic and industrial capacity and had the potential military power to destroy the Japanese state itself.[2] Going by the accounts of the Japanese decision-makers, it is clear that the leadership was aware of the potential as well as the existing strength of the adversaries whom they were confronting and the risks involved in a war with the US which meant fighting the Allied forces too.[3]

The disparity in overall capability between the two antagonists in 1941 was spectacular. The population of the US was nearly twice that of Japan and it held a seven times higher national income. In steel and coal, the US produced five times and seven times respectively as much as Japan. The average annual industrial production of the US during this period was seven to ten times higher than that of Japan.[4] The only sphere in which Japan could improve was in armaments and, through heavy investments, it was able to reach nearly 60 percent of the overall naval strength of the UK and the US individually. Against the combined British–US naval capability, Japan was still lagging behind with a total strength less than 40 percent. Although Britain was concentrating all its major efforts in the European theater, it was certain that the Royal Navy would intervene in support of the US in the Pacific once Germany and Italy were defeated.[5]

The origins of the US–Japanese conflict have been attributed largely to the incompatibility in economic and political strategies and objectives pursued by these two powers. Japan, the "Rising Sun of Asia," intended to achieve economic and political autarky through the conquest of vast areas of China and eventually of South East Asia. The Japanese intent was to create a sphere of self-sufficiency, encompassing these resource-rich regions. Japan's desire to achieve economic autonomy was partly derived from a predicament arising from its high external dependence for resources that it considered essential for building an imperial state with industrial and economic self-sufficiency. For instance, in 1938, the US supplied 75 percent of Japan's scrap iron imports, 93 per cent of copper, over 60 percent of machine tools, and 90 percent of oil. Besides the politico-economic incongruity resulting from this asymmetric dependence of Japan, at the grand strategic level the incompatibility sprang from the fact that the United States with its commitment to free trade and liberal international order formed the most formidable obstacle to Japan's achievement of politico-economic autarky through territorial expansion.[6]

Although this description of Japan's intent to achieve economic autarky provides a broad explanation for the conflict, it is still not clear why Tokyo decided to strike in December 1941 against its more powerful adversaries. Even though the naval plan for a carrier-based attack on Pearl Harbor was ready by January 1941 and the relations between the two countries had deteriorated rapidly during the early part of the 1940s, why did war not breakout prior to December 1941? In this chapter, I attempt to answer these questions by exploring the key causal factors and conditions that arose by December 1941 that might have allowed Japan to go on an offensive against an adversary that was superior in most indicators of power capability. First, the strategies that the opponents pursued on the eve of the war will be explored followed by a discussion on the changes in short-term offensive capability, alliance configurations, and domestic power structure within the initiating state.

The US strategy vis-à-vis Japan

The US and its ally, Britain, as defenders of the status quo in the Pacific, attempted to deter Japan from advancing southward through a variety of ways. The Allied deterrent strategy envisaged a blockade employing naval fleets operating from bases in the Philippines, Singapore, and the Pacific. The strategy was not to engage in war with Japan in the near future or to threaten an imminent military intervention, but to persuade Tokyo to give up its military expansion through economic sanctions and forward deployments. In that sense, it contained elements of both general as well as immediate deterrent threats. In the event of war, the US and its allies had planned to engage in an attrition style warfare, a slow blockade, and thereby compel Japan to give up its expansionist policies.[7]

However, during the early 1940s, the Roosevelt Administration's preferred policy posture was in the middle ground between no appeasement and no offensive military initiative. In June 1940, the administration's expectation was that with the UK able to keep up its resistance to Germany and the US maintaining its Pacific Fleet in Hawaii, Japan would be deterred from a major military move in the Pacific. In South East Asia, the administration further attempted a deterrence policy through a "calculated display of American power and Anglo–American–Dutch unity," and in China, by supporting Chiang Kai-shek's resistance against the Japanese occupation.[8] In a sense, this was a relatively inexpensive containment strategy, relying on economic pressure, military buildup and support to anti-Japanese forces in China.[9] However, by early 1941, the strategy increasingly became active coercive diplomacy, demanding Japan to withdraw from all its new territorial possessions. Japan's near total dependence on the US for major industrial materials convinced the administration that it would capitulate and withdraw from the adventurist policies in Asia, if the US remained resolute in its opposition to those policies. As the status quo power, the US hoped that its potential military and economic capability would bear upon the Japanese and convince them not to undertake any military action against it and its allies. Each step that the US undertook was predicated on the assumption that its gross capabilities were so superior that Japan would not dare to attack and would retract from its aggressive policies in China and South East Asia.

To a great extent, the American strategy toward Japan on the eve of war was one that demanded the challenger to give up all its military and territorial advances until then in return for an implicit pledge of not taking any military and economic retaliation by the defending status quo power. On one level, the US wanted to deter Japan without a major military effort, but on the other, it was not willing to provide any substantial concessions that would have satisfied the military leaders in Japan. The Hull Note, containing the final proposals that the US submitted to Japan on November 26, 1941, had asked the Japanese Government to withdraw from China and Indo-China, not to provide military, political, and economic support to any regime other than that of Chiang Kai-shek, and to nullify the Tripartite Pact with Germany and Italy. In addition, it had proposed that Japan conclude a non-aggression pact with the seven powers including the US, the UK, China, and the Soviet Union.[10] Japan was in effect asked to give up all the territories that it had acquired since the Manchurian Incident, which amounted to a complete withdrawal from the Asian continent.[11]

As evident in this proposal, the challenger was given no alternative other than to back down completely. All its investments and policies until then were to be forgotten for a promised state of no war which meant maintenance of a favorable status quo ante for the US and its allies. Thus, on the eve of the war, neither active deterrence nor credible reassurance characterized the US strategy towards Japan.[12] The US deterrent strategy suffered from at least three other drawbacks. First, the US decision-makers, while concentrating their major effort in Europe and the Atlantic, paid little attention to signals emanating from Japan on the impending attack.[13] Second, the limited deterrent efforts by the status quo state were viewed by the target state, i.e. Japan, as militarily provocative.[14] Third, the US grand strategy in the event of war with Japan was to engage in a gradual attrition style war that would compel it to sue for peace. However, the Japanese leadership was expecting to achieve its military and political objectives in a short war before the US could muster enough forces to wage an attrition style warfare. The threat of a long, attrition war was not credible to the challenging state.

Japan's strategic calculations

While the US and its ally, Britain, were relying on a general deterrent strategy combined with a coercive diplomatic posture, Japanese leaders made active preparations for war on the assumption that their superior strategy and tactics would offset Japan's inferiority in overall capability vis-à-vis its chief opponents. The military leaders were aware that in their effort to capture the resource-rich Dutch and British colonial possessions in South East Asia they would encounter serious opposition from the US, which might include a military intervention by its Pacific Fleet stationed at Pearl Harbor. By destroying that fleet and the naval facilities in the Philippines in a surprise attack, the Japanese leadership calculated that the US would be unable to take any offensive action for at least a year. Since the communications lines would be cut off, the US would be reluctant to fight with Japan in the short run. During this period a strong defensive perimeter in the Pacific could be established.[15] With the resources available from the newly conquered regions of South East Asia, Japan could wage a defensive war for some period of time. "As a result the Japanese leaders felt justified in their hopes that the US would be forced to compromise and allow Japan to retain a substantial portion of her gains, thus leaving the nation in a dominant position in Asia."[16]

The naval strategy, propounded by Admiral Yasuko Yamamoto, was based on the expectation that a surprise attack on the fleet at Pearl Harbor and its destruction would allow the Japanese Navy to deploy most of its forces in the southern areas without being diverted to confront the powerful American Navy. Further, the Admiral feared that the US might attack his naval forces in the Western Pacific eventually, thus forcing Japan to divert its naval strength before accomplishing the task of conquering the southern areas.[17] In Yamamoto's conception, taking the military initiative without delay was essential for an inferior navy such as that of Japan as otherwise the superior US Navy would determine the time and place of attack, forcing Japan onto the defensive. Waiting was also considered unfavorable to the extent that the Japanese Navy would be forced to engage in a diffused fighting mode to the detriment of Japan.[18] Thus the Japanese strategy was based on a premise that Japan could make major gains against the US if it was the first to attack. As Feis puts it, in 1941 "time had become the meter of strategy," and the Japanese decision-makers were "crazed by the tick of the clock."[19]

Japan's military planners were partially aware of the American naval strategy in the Pacific – "Orange" and "Rainbow Fix" – in the event of a war with Japan. This strategy had called for a slow US advance against Japan through the Central Pacific and an eventual defeat of the Japanese naval forces near their home waters.[20] The planners were thus convinced that the prevailing US strategy would not result in its early decisive victory and if a major blow could be inflicted upon the Pearl Harbor Fleet Japan could still attain its strategic objectives. An early tactical victory might alter the strategic balance in the Pacific in Japan's favor. For the military planners, it was therefore imperative to destroy the US Pacific Fleet at the very outset so that the navy would receive the necessary freedom to protect the army's advances in the southern areas. By moving fast, a breathing space could be gained, in addition to the acquisition of strategic resources sufficient for waging a protracted war, if necessary. The shock of the initial Japanese victory and the prospects of waging a two-ocean war single-handedly, especially if Germany won its campaign against Britain, might convince the US to reach a negotiated settlement, allowing Japan to keep its newly acquired territories.[21]

In the first phase of this strategic plan, the Japanese forces were expected to conquer Malaya and the Philippines within fifty days and all of the southern areas within ninety days following the Pearl Harbor strike. The anticipation was that a surprise attack and quick occupation of the southern territories would provide Japan with important tactical advantages, such as preventing the Allied powers from sending reinforcements as the forward bases would be under Tokyo's control, and thereby present them with an irrevocable fait accompli.[22] During the second and third phases, Japan would assume a defensive position, exploit the resources of the newly acquired territories, reinforce the defensive perimeter extending from the Kuriles, the Marshall and Bismarck Islands to Java, Sumatra, and Burma, and engage in a war that would destroy the US will to fight.[23]

Japan clearly wanted to wage a war of limited objectives with the US, as it had no intention to conquer the mainland US or to defeat the enemy decisively. The Japanese expectation was to achieve its aims in South East Asia in a short war and then come to a negotiated settlement with Washington.[24] Its decision-makers were convinced that a rapid advance into South East Asia would offset America's military and industrial capacity and that the prospects of a protracted defensive war would deter the Americans from resisting Japan's military moves.[25] This outcome was likely, given the possibility of Germany winning in Europe and the American people not making the sacrifice as high as war for the cause of China.[26] The Japanese leaders were cognizant that their forces were sufficiently equipped and had reserves that "she was prepared as she ever would be for a short war, even against opponents possessing enormous resources and great industrial potential."[27]

The Japanese strategic calculations were thus based on short-range considerations. This was manifested in Japan's failure to formulate concrete and clearly defined strategic or tactical plans regarding the offensive and defensive operations against US targets after the Pearl Harbor attack. Its decision-makers seemed to have given little thought to the long-range consequences of their actions in terms of the adversary's likely response and the ability of their forces to fight a long and bloody war if the US chose to do so. In the words of a Japanese historian, Japan's military leadership could anticipate neither the scale of the war nor its intensity (which eventually involved the whole strength of the nation, was fought with weapons of all kinds, and spread over a vast area). Essentially, what they conceived was a traditional war on the model of the Russo-Japanese War of 1904–5.[28] Admiral Yamamoto had recognized the impracticality of waging a protracted war with the US, lasting more than a year and a half, although the navy failed to convince the army leadership of the possibility of not winning "a long-drawn conflict."[29]

The short-range calculation was evident in the attack itself. The Japanese struck only the Pacific Fleet, especially its battleships and the airfields, disregarding the more vital ship repair, maintenance, and oil storage facilities on the Hawaiian Islands. The destruction of these facilities would have further delayed the American retaliatory response.[30] The Japanese naval planners also did not seriously consider occupying the Hawaiian Islands as they were not completely confident of the success of the surprise attack when the plans were formulated. If they had done so, Japan would have deprived the US Navy of a major functioning base in the Pacific, thereby making its operations in this vast ocean extremely cumbersome, at least in the short run. The attack on Pearl Harbor was conceived as a supporting operation, purported to prevent the US Navy from interfering with the Japanese operations in the South.[31] The decision-makers gave orders to destroy the more tangible and immediate threat with the hope that the war would be short during which Japan's initial advantage would sustain, thus prompting an early US withdrawal from the conflict.

The strategic calculations of the initiator played a significant role in its final decision to go to war against a militarily and economically superior adversary. The Japanese leaders clearly expected a limited war with the US; a fait accompli war in which the stronger power would not be able to cancel out the initial tactical and strategic gains that Japan would accrue through a surprise attack. The decision-makers were under time pressure given that an attack in 1941–42 promised the best chances for the success of this strategy. The stronger power was expecting a longer, attrition style war which it believed would deter Japan from going to war since the materially superior power would invariably be the winner of such a conflict. But in Tokyo's calculations, the war would be concluded before the US could direct its full strength and military potential against Japan.

Changing capabilities

Two pertinent questions that require answers in the Japanese decision-making context are: (1) what offensive capabilities did Japan possess in December 1941 that allowed a war with the US? and (2) what role did changes in the military balance between Japan and its principal opponents – the US and the UK – play in Tokyo's calculations in 1941? At the time of the war, the Japanese Navy possessed a total of eleven battleships, ten aircraft carriers, with 3,000 aircraft, in addition to some efficient land-based bombers and torpedo-carrying squadrons. It also held six fleet and four light cruisers with 6-inch or smaller guns, one hundred destroyers, and sixty-three submarines.[32] The short-term advantage in aircraft carriers was a determining factor in Japan's selection of Pearl Harbor as a target. The naval strategists recommended taking the initiative when Japan held the advantage by striking first and destroying the opponent's aircraft carriers.[33]

Although officially Japan had adhered to the Washington and London naval arms-limitation treaties, during the 1930s it built weapons beyond the treaty limits. Japan's limited economic and industrial capacity – smaller than those of its chief antagonists, Britain and the US – did not prohibit its decision-makers from building more aircraft and ships than those two powers during a short period of time. By 1931, Japan had built three carriers – the 38,200-ton *Kaga*, the 36,500-ton *Akagi* and the 7,470-ton *Hosho* – and had started the construction of the 10,600-ton *Ryujo*. The *Kaga* and *Akagi* were larger than the US's *Lexington* and *Saratoga*. Japan also possessed seventeen naval aircraft squadrons and 284 naval aircraft, a formidable force in the Pacific during that period.[34] By the early 1930s, the navy had identified the US and the UK as Japan's major challengers in the naval arms race and wanted to attain a qualitative edge in the number of capital ships, aircraft carriers, destroyers, and cruisers. The navy adopted six naval rearmament replenishment plans during the period before World War II in an effort to build the maximum capacity allowed by the Washington Treaty and to catch up with the US. During the first two plans, Japan built two more aircraft carriers of 10,050 tons each, the *Soryu* and the *Hiryu*.[35]

Making use of various loopholes in the Washington Treaty, Japan announced plans to build more cruisers, destroyers, and submarines. In the cruiser field, Japan expressed its determination to build 10,000-ton cruisers with 8–inch guns.[36] The Navy's aim was to achieve a limited qualitative edge in the Pacific over Japan's main opponents, the US and the UK. The special tactical systems that it developed were expected to allow Japan to wage "decisive fleet action in the course of interception operations, stressing employment of the 'balanced fleet principle,' with battleships as the backbone."[37] Submarines formed another key part of Japan's "invincible armada." The I-class fleet submarine was capable of cruising up to California without refueling, while the smaller Ro-class boats could cruise to the Hawaiian Islands and back on a single fuel load.[38] In the Japanese strategic calculations, torpedoes and aircraft also held a major role. The Type 91 aerial torpedo enabled the launch aircraft – Type 97 (Kate) – to fly at high speed, "at an altitude of several hundred feet."[39] Japan was the only country that possessed the capability to torpedo battleships from the air in a shallow anchorage like Pearl Harbor with a depth of twelve meters.[40]

High-quality aircraft played a crucial role in Japan's strategic calculations in 1941. Of them, the Type 97 B5N1 attack plane with a range of 1,000 miles and the Type 97 (Kate) which carried the Type 91 torpedo were two significant models that came into service in 1937. In 1939, the dive bomber, the Type 99 (Val), went into operation. It had a range of 1,250 miles and a 241 mph top speed at an altitude of 9,000ft. The Nakajima A6M-Zero-sen was one of the most valuable aircraft in Japan's possession. In many respects, it was the world's first strategic fighter. With a range over 1,200 miles, its possession was considered a necessary precondition for the Pearl Harbor attack. According to some naval historians, had the Zero not been capable of covering the distance from Taiwan to the Philippines to attack General MacArthur's Luzon-based American Air Force, Yamamoto might have been forced to use his fleet carriers for that task, thus abandoning his project to strike Pearl Harbor. This aircraft fitted perfectly into the Japanese conception of "rapidity of fire and minimum of risk."[41]

Japan also built three super-battleships of 72,000 tons each: *Yamato*, *Musashi*, and *Shinano*. The plans for these ships were underway even when Tokyo was observing the letter of the naval disarmament treaties. Japan's decisions to scuttle the Second Naval Disarmament Conference in London in January 1936 and to withdraw from the 1922 Washington Treaty when it expired in 1936 were influenced by the Fleet Faction, under the leadership of Kato Kanji, vice chief of the Navy General Staff, and Captain Suetsugu Nobumasa.[42] This faction wanted to build a powerful fleet comprising bigger and better naval systems before the other powers caught up. By 1936, members of the fleet faction had gained dominance over their opponents, the pro-Washington Treaty faction, which lost much of its clout within the navy. The Navy Minister, Admiral Osumi Mineo, a strong supporter of the fleet faction, made tough proposals that were to be tabled at the London Preparatory Conference. Opposition from other countries to the Japanese proposals for declaring an upper limit on the number of warships, increasing the defensive units such as submarines, and reducing combatant units, prompted Tokyo to withdraw from the conference, a major victory for the fleet faction.[43] Following its withdrawal, Japan accelerated the construction of battleships and other offensive weapon systems. The Japanese decision-makers realized that time was not on their side and that if they waited too long the US and the UK would build more battleships of superior caliber. All that Japan could hope for was to build quickly some qualitatively superior naval systems that would give it a decisive bargaining advantage in diplomatic dealings with Western powers and short-term offensive military capability in the event of war.[44]

The growth of the Japanese Army during this period was also spectacular. Between 1936 and 1941, Japan's Army doubled its size from twenty divisions to fifty and fifty air squadrons to 150.[45] The General Staff's 1936 National Defense Plan had envisaged a five-year arms buildup program and a six-year re-equipment program.[46] By December 1941, Japan had raised fifty-one active service divisions, ten depot divisions or training units, and about thirty independent brigades and garrison troops. Japan had thus trained over a million regular forces and two million reserves.[47] In addition, the army possessed powerful mobile artillery as well as 2,000 aircraft which also included the Zero fighter, faster and more maneuverable than any European-made aircraft of the times.[48]

The interesting question for this study is what bearing did the capability factor have on the timing of attack? The Japanese Navy and Army feared that Japan's advantage would be only short-lived and that the United States would become overwhelmingly preponderant in the Pacific in a year or two. They calculated that by March 1942 the US reinforcements in the Philippines would reach a higher level and that the Allies would greatly augment the defenses of Malaya and the Philippines, making the southward advance virtually impossible.[49] In their assessment, Japan's destiny as an imperial power was at stake if it was losing the naval advantage to other countries. The alternative to war would be Japan's eventual submission to other naval powers.[50] The perceived short-term advantage over the US in certain categories of weapons played a key role in the Japanese timing of attack. Navy Chief Osami Nagano told an Imperial Conference on November 5, 1941: "The ratio of our fleet to that of the US is 7.5 to 10; but 40 percent of the American fleet is in the Atlantic Ocean, and 60 percent in the Pacific ... The US would need considerable time if she should withdraw ships from the Atlantic Ocean and come to attack us."[51]

Foreign Minister Shigenori Togo shared the confidence that the army and the navy officers had in their newly acquired capabilities. In his words: "The Army having devoted the major part of its appropriations since the beginning of the China affair to mechanization, felt that its fighting power had been vastly enhanced, the Navy confident of its fleet (which since the abrogation of the Naval Limitation Treaty, had come to include types of vessels particular to Japan) believed itself invincible."[52] However, the rapid modernization of the US Navy meant that Japan would soon lose its short-lived window of opportunity in the Pacific. By the early 1940s, the US had launched a program to build a powerful two-ocean navy. In 1941, it was constructing 17 battleships, 12 aircraft carriers, 48 cruisers, 160 destroyers, 78 submarines, and 11 minesweepers. The Roosevelt Administration had also planned to manufacture 50,000 aircraft, and several cargo ships were ordered to be converted into escort carriers.[53] The time pressure arising from the changing military balance between the two adversaries was evident in Navy Chief of Staff Nagano's statement to the 50th Liaison Conference: "In various respects the Empire is losing materials: that is, we are getting weaker. By contrast, the enemy is getting stronger. By the passage of time we will get increasingly weaker, and we won't be able to survive . . ."[54] Thus in 1941, the Japanese decision-makers were confronted with a "now or never" situation. Japan's short-term offensive capability in the Pacific theater was about to be overtaken by its Anglo-American adversaries. A short war promised a better chance for Japan to attain its military and economic objectives and the existing capability made the waging of such a war possible.

Changing alliance relationships

Apart from changes in military balance between Japan and its major opponents, what alterations occurred in the global alliance structure by 1941 that might have had an influence on Japan's strategic calculations prior to the attack? What role did the protracted negotiations that led to the Tripartite Pact and the competing and changing interests of Germany and Japan play in Tokyo's decisions leading to the Pearl Harbor attack? The contention here is that changes in the global alliance structure during the late 1930s and early 1940s did affect Japan's calculations. Among these changes, Tokyo's new alliance with Germany was a crucial factor in the timing of war initiation. A look at the vicissitudes in negotiations on the alliance could give clues on how Japan's decisions with respect to war or no war evolved over time. In June 1938, Japan approached Germany to form an alliance against the Soviet Union. The leadership's, especially the army's, calculation was that Germany would pressure the Chinese nationalists to concede to its demands and deter Russia from intervening on behalf of the Chinese resistance and even abandon its support for Chiang Kai-shek. They also believed that the Pact would provide a defensive insurance in case Japan engaged in war with Russia.[55] Germany wanted to include the Western powers also as potential enemies within the purview of the alliance. Japan's refusal to this demand put a halt to the endeavor for the time being. Disagreement over the gamut of the proposed alliance with Japan partially encouraged Germany's signing of the non-aggression pact with the USSR in August 1939. Japan followed suit by concluding a neutrality pact with Moscow.

However, the German victories over Holland, Belgium, and France in the summer of 1940 changed Japan's perceptions with regard to the utility of an alliance with Germany. In the Japanese calculations, Germany's victory against the European powers provided Tokyo with a unique opportunity to gain control over their colonial possessions in Asia. The military leaders feared that Germany would claim jurisdiction over those colonies and that the US and the UK might occupy the Dutch East Indies in order to prevent a Japanese or German takeover.[56] The difficulties on the British front prompted Hitler to reconsider the alliance question seriously. An alliance relationship with Japan was viewed by the Nazi leader as a means to accelerate Britain's defeat by alienating the US from its side. The Japanese leaders perceived an alliance with Germany as a way to obtain greater freedom in concluding the China war in its favor and strengthening its strategic and military position in South East Asia. These calculations finally led to the conclusion of the Tripartite Pact on September 27, 1940.[57]

The Pact provided Japan with several advantages. Germany recognized Japan's economic and military hegemony over South East Asia, promised technical assistance in improving Tokyo's war industry, and agreed to settle the former German colonies in the Pacific in the former's favor. For Japan, the most significant aspect of the Pact was the German promise of unilateral military help in a prospective war with the US and military aid in the event Britain and Japan engaged in combat.[58] During negotiations for the Pact, the German Foreign Minister Joachim von Ribbentrop convinced his Japanese counterpart, Matsuoka Yosuke that the alliance would neutralize the US military position in the Pacific. The Japanese leaders hoped that through the Pact they could render the US inactive in the Pacific, conclude the China war as the US support to Chiang Kai-shek would cease, and move into South East Asia unhampered. The Germans, on the other hand, believed that the alliance would not only isolate the US in the Atlantic and in the Pacific, but would prevent it from getting involved in the European conflict as well.[59]

Article 3 of the Pact called upon the three signatories – Germany, Japan, and Italy - to assist "one another with all political, economic, and military means if one of the three contracting powers is attacked by a power at present not involved in the European war or in the Chinese–Japanese conflict."[60] Yet great uncertainty persisted in the alliance relationships among the three powers. Japan was not consulted on Hitler's invasion plan of the Soviet Union. The Nazi attack on Russia had in fact created severe challenges to the Japanese military plans and therefore serious bitterness in Tokyo. Meanwhile, by 1941, Japan's relations with the US had deteriorated rapidly over the China question and Japan's moves into South East Asia. The new Japanese regime under Tojo was preparing for war in earnest, but the question of German alliance support still remained murky, chiefly because of Tokyo's unwillingness to join Hitler's war against Russia.

However, the German response to the Japanese queries whether the former would declare war against the US in case Japan decided to attack came in the affirmative. Although Germany was bound to support Japan only in the event of the latter being attacked, on November 21, 1941 Ribbentrop assured that Germany would declare war against the US if Japan decided to go on the offensive. On November 25 the three signatories of the Tripartite Pact also signed a memorandum extending the Anti-Comintern Pact by another five years.[61] At a meeting on 28 November with Hiroshi Oshima, the Japanese Ambassador to Berlin, Ribbentrop pointed out that if Japan decided to go to war against Britain and America, it would not only be to the mutual advantage of the two countries but would be of greater benefit to Japan. The Japanese Ambassador reported to Tokyo that the "attitude of Germany towards the US had considerably stiffened and that she would not refuse to fight her if necessary."[62] The German assurance of support thus preceded the Japanese decision to strike Pearl Harbor and can be considered as a determining factor in the timing of the attack.

The alliance support was more political than tactical or strategic in nature, although militarily it prevented the US from deploying all its forces in the Pacific. In reality, the Axis partners fought separate wars on different parts of the globe. The political nature of the alliance relationship was evident in Germany and Japan's failure to devise a joint strategic coordination plan even after the Pearl Harbor attack. The talks they held before signing the Pact were political in nature with little attention being paid to military planning. Each country essentially formulated its own naval strategy without giving much consideration to the other.[63] However, by November 1941, the Japanese military planners had given serious consideration to the possibility of Germany and Italy defeating Britain in Europe and in the Middle East while Japan was doing the same in Asia. These two allies were also expected to "deprive America of her will to continue the war."[64]

Although the Japanese–German alliance has been described as

"hollow", the contention here is that the alliance had a powerful impact on the Japanese decision to go to war with the US. The alliance support seems to have exerted both direct and indirect impacts upon the decision. The Japanese expectation that Germany would defeat Russia and Britain and the belief that the US would not fight a long war single-handedly were paramount in their decision to strike Pearl Harbor. Even if Germany did not succeed immediately, the European war would be prolonged and intense, forcing the US and the UK to devote most of their forces there. This would allow Japan to take independent action in the Pacific. The indirect effect of alliance configurations was thus the freedom with which Japan could out-maneuver the superior aggregate capability of the adversary while it committed its main forces in the European theater.

Significant changes also occurred in Japan's relations with the USSR during this period. A major concern of the Japanese decision-makers was how to prevent a war with Russia while advancing into the south. The Soviet–Japanese Neutrality Pact of April 13, 1941 served the purpose of allaying those fears to a great extent as the Pact stipulated the maintenance of respect for each other's territory, and neutrality in case either party was being attacked by one or more third powers.[65] The Pact provided Japan with some assurance that the Soviet Union would not get involved in a military confrontation with the former if it were engaged in war with the UK or the US during the course of Japan's southward expansion.[66] It provided Japan with some freedom of action in China and in the southern regions as it prevented the Russian forces along the Manchurian border from engaging in a hot war with the occupying Japanese forces. Although the Russians were actively helping Chiang Kai-shek's struggle against Japan and were constantly engaging in border skirmishes with the Japanese forces, war was avoided to the relief of Japan's military leaders who were bent on a southward thrust.

The Neutrality Pact endured Germany's invasion of the Soviet Union, helping to maintain Japan's position vis-à-vis Russia. Some advocates of continental expansion in the Japanese power hierarchy, especially Foreign Minister Matsuoka wanted to take advantage of the situation by attacking the USSR.[67] However, Matsuoka's replacement, Toyoda Teijiro, promised the Soviet Envoy Konstantin Smetanin at their meeting on August 5, 1941 that Japan would abide by the Treaty unless the Soviet Union granted military bases to other powers in the Far East and signed pacts with countries involved in East Asia that were antagonistic to Japan. A week later, the Soviets reaffirmed their commitment to the Neutrality Pact. On November 22, 1941, Foreign

Minister Togo held consultations with Ambassador Smetanin and sought reassurances that Moscow would abide by the Neutrality Pact and would not provide bases to third parties. The Ambassador reaffirmed that the Soviet Union would neither form an alliance with other countries against Japan nor provide military bases. The Japanese Foreign Minister repeatedly asked for the same assurances on November 28 and December 6, 1941 and on both occasions the Soviets reaffirmed their commitment to the Pact.[68]

The significance of alliance relationships in the Japanese calculations was evident from proceedings of the 63rd Liaison Conference held on October 28, 1941 at which the possibility of postponing the offensive until March 1942 was discussed. Foreign Minister Togo argued that the threat from the Soviet Union would be much less if the war was postponed. In response, Army Chief of Staff Sugiyama argued that the Soviets could join hands with the US and thereby "the alliance that is encircling Japan would get stronger. Also Japan's relations with the Soviets would become more uneasy. Oil and other materials would diminish, while the other side's military preparedness would be improved."[69]

Changes in the contours of global alliance structure, especially the shifts in German position and its victories in Europe, encouraged the Japanese decision-makers to go an offensive against the US, lest, they feared, they should "miss the boat." The German military and diplomatic position toward the end of 1941 and the expectations in Tokyo regarding Berlin's support could thus be viewed as determining factors in the timing of war by the weaker initiator in this case.

Domestic changes prior to December 1941

Besides the external changes caused by alliance configurations and the capability distribution affecting Japan and its adversaries, what internal changes took place that might have had a bearing on the decision to attack? Major power shifts did in fact occur within the Japanese decision-making structure prior to the war. Factions that professed militaristic policies gained control while relatively moderate groups lost ground in a power struggle lasting well over a decade. The 1920s had witnessed the emergence of liberal and civilian governments in Japan which were opposed to imperial expansion in Asia. This moderation was evident in the Japanese acceptance of the Washington Naval Limitation Treaty of 1922 and the London Treaty of 1930, the Four Power Treaty that conferred the status quo in the Pacific, and the Nine Power Treaty that guaranteed the territorial and political integrity of

78

China.[70] These treaties were looked down upon by some factions in the Japanese power hierarchy, especially in the army, that saw the arrival of an opportunity to reassert their claims following the economic turmoil caused by the Great Depression. The strengthening of the military's control in China was fostered by young army officers who sought to redeem Japan of its economic and political problems through territorial expansion.

The years between 1924 and 1932 had been referred to as the period of normal constitutional government (*Kensei Jodo*) dominated by party cabinets. The early 1930s witnessed the military factions slowly gaining control over the power structure. A failed coup attempt in March 1931 that was actively supported by elements within the General Staff, the Manchurian Incident of September 1931, and the assassination of liberal Prime Minister, Inukai Tsuyoshi in May 1932, were the precursors to the army factions gaining control over the government and its foreign policy making process.[71] From 1932 to 1936, the last civilian government struggled to retain control against the onslaught of the militaristic factions that were assuming dominance. Prince Saionji, the last major Genro, and a liberal politician, also supported the civilian groups in their failed efforts to keep the rightist forces away from positions that would have allowed closer contacts with the Imperial Palace.[72]

By 1935, the Prime Minister was totally ineffective in controlling the forces in the field. By then, the key military decisions pertaining to field operations were being made by bureau and section chiefs of the Kwantung Army in Manchuria, rather than the civilian leadership in Tokyo. One of the most glaring examples was when the cabinet's directive to limit the area of the September 18, 1931 Manchurian Incident was disregarded by the field units.[73] The Army High Command threw its full support to the field officers, by way of first accepting cabinet orders to restrict the military advance and then allowing them to be ignored under the pretext of operational requirements. The army constantly justified expansion of areas under occupation by this technique, presenting the Japanese civilian leaders and diplomats "with a series of faits accomplies."[74] The two most prominent factions within the army were the "Imperial Way Group," (Kodo-ha) comprising mostly young field service officers and two key generals, Sadao Araki and Jinsaburo Mazaki. Their opponents, the "Control Group" (Tosei-ha) consisted of senior officers and was led by generals such as Nagata Tetsuzan, Jiro Minami, Iwane Matsui, Seishiro Itagaki, Hideki Tojo, Yoshitsugu Tatekawa, and Jotaro Watanabe. The Control Group believed in the expansion of Japan through the occupation of China, while the Imperial Way Group – being staunchly anti-Communist – propounded war against the Soviet Union. The February 1936 Incident and the subsequent suppression of the mutineers involved in it resulted in the demise of the Imperial Way Group and the coming into prominence of the Control faction. The ascendancy of the Control faction was manifested in the government's adoption of a seven-point program which stepped up the arms buildup and the aggressive moves in China.[75]

The February 1936 Incident, or The Young Officers' Revolt, thus exerted a pronounced impact on the rise of militarism in Japan in the mid-1930s. The event occurred on February 26, 1936 when 1,400 soldiers, under the command of some junior officers, seized the center of Tokyo and succeeded in assassinating a number of key officials. Although the rebellion was subsequently suppressed, its effect on Japan's domestic politics was profound as in its aftermath the army, especially the Control faction, strengthened its role in the governance of the state. Following the Incident, the Koki Hirota Cabinet accepted the military's demand to appoint only officers on active duty as eligible for cabinet positions of War and Navy Ministers. This change in the governing structure had a far reaching impact on Japan's domestic politics and external policies as, henceforth, all state policies had to be to the satisfaction of the military. Otherwise, the War Minister would resign and the army would refuse to nominate a successor, thus forcing the cabinet itself to give up power.[76] The Incident also ended the prospects of a liberal civilian government assuming power. The Hirota Cabinet included Hisaichi Terauchi as War Minister, a strong proponent of military expansion. Hirota was successfully persuaded by Terauchi to increase the arms buildup. It was the Hirota cabinet that launched the new naval buildup and concluded the Anti-Comintern Pact with Germany in November 1936.[77]

The increasing influence of the military in foreign policy making was evident in Japan's decision to withdraw from the League of Nations and from the Washington Naval Treaty when the latter expired on December 31, 1936. With the arrival of the new cabinet under the premiership of Prince Fuminaro Kanoye in 1936, the internal stumbling blocks to the full-scale conquest of China were all cleared. However, moderate political leaders continued to exert some influence intermittently prior to 1941. The Yonai Mitsumasa Cabinet that was in power from January to July 1940 opposed the alliance negotiations with Germany but was eventually prevailed upon by the army. Yonai had temporarily acted as a check on factions within the military that wanted closer ties with Germany and Italy and desired to create a totalitarian party system in Japan. Yonai rejected those demands fearing Japan's involvement in the war in Europe. In fact, his Foreign Minister, Arita Hachiro, made efforts to improve relations with the US and the UK. The army did not tolerate this for very long and compelled War Minister General Hata to leave the government and then refused to nominate a successor. The Yonai Cabinet was thus forced to resign.[78]

Its successor, the second Kanoye Cabinet, assumed power in July 1940, marking the end of most of the civilian control in governance. Kanoye made his major decisions after heeding the army's advice. Kanoye's appointment of General Hideki Tojo as War Minister, Yosuke Matsuoka as Foreign Minister, and Naoki Hoshino as President of the Planning Board further strengthened the military's grip on the ruling apparatus.[79] This was the cabinet that decided to conclude an alliance with Germany and which drafted the document, "Outline of Basic National Policy," which supported the Army's China policy and its southward expansion. It also had approved negotiations with the USSR on the Neutrality Pact, while maintaining a tough posture toward the US.[80] The fluid domestic situation prior to the war generated conditions that gave rise to total control of the system by the army leaders who were bent on taking the military initiative. Although Kanoye presided over a cabinet that made the decision to conclude the Tripartite Pact with Germany and Italy, he seemed to have been opposed to a war with the US. Kanoye's intention in signing the Pact was apparently to bring the Soviet Union to the alliance eventually and thereby restrain the US from intervening in the European war. This, he thought, would also result in settlement of the war in China. However, the sudden German attack on the Soviet Union in June 1941 thwarted Kanoye's plans. Fearing Japan's involvement in the European war, Kanoye began to step up his efforts to negotiate with the US.[81]

Kanoye was not only less risk-acceptant than other military and political leaders, but was more realistic in his assessment of the possibility of Japan fighting a prolonged war. In an attempt to make some headway in the negotiations, he tried in vain to meet with President Roosevelt in August 1941 and thereby convince the army of the futility of going to war. Tojo and other key members of the Army General Staff opposed the idea of signing a short-term agreement with Washington by arguing that any delay in the war with the US would be disastrous. Although the Liaison Conference finally approved Kanoye's summit proposal, it was not acceptable to Washington.[82] Kanoye's intention was to give limited concessions to Chiang Kai-shek in the form of abolishing the Nanking regime, agreeing to an eventual withdrawal of troops from China, and providing limited autonomy to Manchuria. His attempt to convince Tojo to commit to withdrawing from China did not succeed. Tojo contended that giving some concessions would lead to more concessions and that if Japan withdrew, the morale of the armed forces would suffer. On the basis of this disagreement, Tojo and the army withdrew their support from the cabinet, forcing Kanoye to resign.[83] With Tojo's arrival as the Prime Minister, the military's control of the foreign policy making structure was complete. Opponents of war were denied access to the Emperor while all advice to him was carefully screened by Tojo and his military allies.[84] The rise of Tojo to power thus gave the General Staff and the Control Group supreme authority over the country's foreign policy making. Quick reappraisals of national strategy followed suit. The new regime stressed operational necessity and exhibited a desire to move fast on the military front under severe time pressure, thereby giving diplomacy little chance to succeed.[85]

Why no war before 1941?

An important question that needs to be addressed for the purposes of this study is why neither the army nor the navy took serious decisions for war with the US and other Western powers until January 1941 despite the fact that an attack on Pearl Harbor had been in Japan's military training programs since 1931. To some historians, the basic plan had been evolving since the early 1930s. The theoretical possibility of such an attack had been discussed by graduates of the Japanese Naval Academy since that time. In their final examinations, a hypothetical question was repeatedly asked: "How would you carry out a surprise attack on Pearl Harbor?"[86] Prior to 1931, the National Defense Plan in 1923 had identified the US, the Soviet Union, and China as Japan's potential enemies. In addition, the tactical plan that was adopted during that time had called for the occupation of Guam as well as the Philippines by the army in cooperation with the navy in the event of a war with the US. In 1924, the Army General Staff had set up a committee to study preparations for war against the US.[87] The Japanese Army had incorporated the earlier strategic and tactical plans for a war with the US since 1925. Over time, the army's annual operational plans had contained detailed strategic programs for implementation in the event of a conflict with the US. The 1925 plan had called for the invasion and occupation of Luzon, Lingayen, Lamon Bays, and Manila and eventually the Philippines before the US Navy could send a major naval fleet to defend the territories. These plans were modified in 1936 when the UK was added to the list of potential enemies which by then included the US, the USSR, and China.[88] These plans remained essentially on paper, at the theoretical level, as part of the larger operational strategy of the army. No serious effort was made to implement them until after 1939.[89]

What prompted the army and the navy to change their defensive posture toward the Western powers to an offensive one? Morton argues that the earlier stance was not because of any great confidence in diplomatic negotiations but was based on a realistic assessment of Japan's economic weaknesses and lack of strategic resources.[90] The conceptual planning for a carrier-based attack on Pearl Harbor was prepared by Yamamoto in 1940 and was ready by early 1941. The plan called for a task force made up of aircraft carriers, cruisers, and destroyers, to "deliver an annihilating aerial strike against the US fleet in Pearl Harbor." Yamamoto wrote to his friend, Admiral Sankichi Takahashi on December 19, 1941: "The plan of launching a surprise attack against Pearl Harbor at the outset of war to give a fatal blow to the enemy fleet was decided in December of last year, when the fleet strategy was revised."[91]

It is also known that the Japanese decision-makers grappled with the question of fighting a war with all three powers – the US, the UK, and the Soviet Union. At the 30th Liaison Conference held on June 12, 1941, the policy paper, "Acceleration of the Policy Concerning the South" was presented with a clause that if Britain, the US, and The Netherlands tried to obstruct Japan, and if it was necessary for its survival, it "would not refuse to risk a war with Britain and the United States." The Liaison Conference on June 16, 1941 approved the document, after deleting this clause.[92] The Imperial Conference on July 2, 1941 acknowledged the possibility of war with the US as a result of Japan's moving into South East Asia. At the 40th Liaison Conference on July 21, 1941, the Navy Chief of Staff Nagano argued that there was a chance of victory if a war was fought at that time. To him, "by the latter half of next year, it will already be difficult for us to cope with the US, after that the situation will become increasingly worse."[93] At the Imperial Conference of September 6, 1941, to the Emperor's query as to how a war with the US in the South Pacific would conclude, the Army Chief of Staff replied that the operation would take three months.[94] What factor or cluster of factors prevented war in previous periods, especially from January till December 1941, and why was war initiated in December 1941? The arrival of what factor or constellation of factors facilitated war initiation at this critical juncture?

83

Explaining the Japanese decision in 1941

Although all four factors of asymmetric war initiation seem to have arrived prior to December 1941, in relative importance the changes in alliance configuration appear more critical than others. Even the ardent supporters of war were fairly conscious of the formidable forces that Japan was expected to fight. The Pearl Harbor strike plan was under serious consideration by the Japanese High Command for about a year. But Japan had to wait for favorable alliance configurations to emerge before it could launch an offensive. The German advancement in Europe and the congenial political conditions arising from the Tripartite Pact prompted the Japanese leadership to go for a surprise attack against the US, fearing that Japan would otherwise miss the brief window of opportunity. The timing was also greatly affected by the leadership's expectations in a successful limited aims/fait accompli strategy and the calculations regarding US reluctance to wage a costly war with Japan. They expected an outcome similar to the Russo-Japanese War, in which the stronger opponent would concede Japan's territorial gains through a negotiated settlement. The short-term offensive capability was viewed as a necessary condition in the choice for war. The advantage in terms of "force in being" was deemed as critically important in determining the final outcome, as striking first entailed the possibility of success. The arrival of Tojo and the military factions' gaining of full control of the decision-making structure further increased the pressure on Japan to go for an offensive against its more powerful adversaries.

The US strategy also had an impact on Japan's calculations. The US economic sanctions were intended to coerce the Japanese to modify their aggressive policies, but they had the reverse effect. On the military front, the Japanese leaders realized that the immediate defensive and deterrent capability of the US in the Pacific was limited and that Japan enjoyed a window of opportunity. The issue that prompted Japan's aggressive policies toward South East Asia was its desperate need for oil, while the systemic changes caused by German successes provided the Japanese leadership with an opportunity they had been waiting for all along. The willingness of the decision-making group to make use of that opportunity resulted in military advances that were previously ruled out.

This case study points to the weaknesses in implementing general and, to a limited extent, immediate deterrent policies. The preponderance of the US in aggregate capability did not act as a deterrent against Japan undertaking offensive action. Japan's calculations were that in

84

the short-run it could wage a fait accompli war and achieve its objectives before the adversary mobilized its formidable power resources. The global alliance structure would assure its victory in such a war. Deterrence was unlikely to have obtained in such a situation, unless it was backed by an overwhelmingly preponderant military force and credible retaliatory threat in the theater of operations. Additionally, reassurance was not seriously attempted as backing down was the chief option offered to the challenger by the defender. The stronger power all along pursued coercive diplomacy on the expectation that its overwhelming aggregate power capability would compel Japan to back down, partly because of the difficulties in pursuing another strategy for internal political reasons.

5 THE CHINESE INTERVENTION IN KOREA, 1950

On October 14, 1950 several divisions of the Chinese People's Liberation Army (PLA) crossed the Yalu River to confront the advancing US/UN forces in Korea under General Douglas MacArthur.[1] China's decision to intervene militarily in the second stage of the Korean War against the far better equipped and well-trained US/UN forces is a major case of asymmetric war initiation in this century. The US, together with its coalition partners, possessed overwhelming advantages in the air and at sea, as well as a qualitative edge in artillery, tanks, and other key sources of modern conventional and nuclear military power capability.[2] In some respects, this intervention is slightly different from other cases in this study as it was a pre-emptive attempt by the weaker side against a perceived threat to its security from the US, its main adversary at that time. Moreover, the Chinese offensive occurred after the initiator sent several warning signals with regard to its intention to intervene in protection of its interests and to deter an invasion of North Korea by the UN forces under General Douglas MacArthur.

Yet the question remains as to why the Chinese decision-makers, even after assessing their country's weaknesses vis-à-vis the US and other participating countries in the UN force, decided to commit their poorly equipped forces on the war path. Deliberations among them prior to the intervention reveal a clear awareness of China's disadvantages in fighting an adversary, far superior in all key aspects of military and economic power.[3] Moreover, in a telegram to Stalin in October 1950, Mao Tse-tung warned about the possibility of an American declaration of war on China and the bombing of Chinese cities and industrial bases by the US Air Force and attacks on coastal areas by the Navy.[4] This case of asymmetric war initiation has relevance to general deterrence theory since the US possessed nuclear capability and had signalled its determination to use it against military threats emanating from Communist countries.[5] While deciding to intervene, the Chinese leaders had in fact recognized the possibility of a US nuclear attack.[6]

In this chapter, I seek to explain why China decided to intervene in Korea in the Fall of 1950 by exploring whether the key hypothesized determinants of asymmetric war initiation pertaining to the initiator apply in this case, i.e., expectations of a successful limited aims strategy and limited war, defensive support of a great power ally, possession of short-term offensive capability, and changes within the domestic power structure of China as well as the compulsions arising from the insecurity of the newly established regime due to the perceived internal as well as external threats. First, what strategic assumptions did the defender and the challenger hold in 1950 that might have had a bearing on the timing of intervention?

The US strategy in Korea

The US/UN strategy went through three major phases during the course of the Korean War. During the first stage, the strategic objective was to contain the North Korean offensive. However, after the Inchon landing in September 1950, the US and its allies went on a "strategic, operational, and tactical offensive with the objective of rolling back Communism and liberating North Korea." When China intervened in November 1950, the Allied forces re-assumed a defensive posture and tactical withdrawal from North Korea.[7] The broader strategic calculations of the US were based on elements of deterrence by denial, deterrence by punishment, and reassurance. A calculated display of force, including that of nuclear weapons, and an implicit threat of their use if China intervened, formed the core of the deterrent effort. New studies based on declassified archival materials suggest that, on a few occasions, the Truman Administration considered the nuclear threat in an effort to deter China. One such instance was the decision to dispatch nuclear configured B-29s to the Pacific at the end of July 1950. Again, following the Chinese intervention, Truman made a statement on November 30, 1950 that he would take all steps necessary to deal with the situation and that the use of nuclear weapons had "always been under active consideration."[8]

At various stages of the crisis, the US decision-makers, especially the military leadership, believed that the Chinese, lacking the necessary requirements for a successful offensive or defensive operation against the world's most modern army, would be deterred and that if deterrence failed it would be the result of China's foolishness and miscalculation. Additionally, the US attempted to reassure Peking that it did not possess any predatory motives against the Chinese mainland and that the advancing forces were not intending to cross the Yalu.[9] The US political and military leadership assumed that Washington's military action in Korea did not threaten China's interests in any serious way and that the Chinese leaders were preoccupied with their country's internal reconstruction. MacArthur's successful Inchon landing, the failure of Moscow to make any military moves, congressional pressures on the administration to achieve Korea's unification, and the distrust of Chinese warnings and their transmitting channels, all compounded the existing assumptions on the low probability of Chinese intervention.[10] The administration generally worked under the premise that the declared goodwill gestures of the US would reassure the Peking leadership that the US would confine its military operations to Korea and would cease them once the peninsula was reunified under South Korea.[11]

The US strategic and tactical expectations were based on a premise that a poorly equipped China with serious domestic problems would not intervene in the war. If the Chinese were going to intervene they would have done so before October 1950 when the US/UN forces were thin enough to be susceptible to inflict a severe blow by their military action.[12] In the administration's thinking, during this period the USSR would be more prone to intervene in support of North Korea than would China and, in the American logic, if the Chinese had felt a severe military threat, they would have intervened when the North Koreans were still in control of Seoul or Pyongyang.[13] In both strategic and tactical senses, China passed up the most opportune time to stop the advancing US/UN troops. This view was shared by various segments of the US Government. In July 1950, the Joint Intelligence Committee (JIC) report observed that PLA's past combat experience, involving hit-and-run guerrilla tactics, was not appropriate to Korea. "They had never met a well-trained force with a high morale, equipped with modern weapons and possessing the will and skill to use those weapons. In addition, China had 'practically no capability' of reinforcing or supporting the North Korean Navy and not much in the way of an air force either."[14]

General MacArthur's response to President Truman's query at their Wake Island Conference on October 15, 1950 on what chances there were for the Soviets or the Chinese to intervene was, "very little." According to MacArthur it would have been decisive had they intervened during the first or second month. "We no longer stand hat in hand. The Chinese have 300,000 men in Manchuria. Of these, probably not more than 100,000 to 125,000 are distributed along the Yalu River. Only 50,000 to 60,000 could be gotten across the Yalu River. They have no Air Force." Since the US had air bases in Korea, "if the Chinese tried to get down to Pyongyang there would be the greatest slaughter."[15] Regarding the Soviets, they had made no ground troops available for North Korea. Although they had a fairly strong air force in Siberia, if the Russians attempted to provide air support to Chinese infantrymen, it would result in them bombing "the Chinese as often as they would bomb us." MacArthur discounted the possibility of Chinese ground troops advancing with Russian air support on the basis that neither possessed the necessary experience in joint air–ground operations.[16] The Secretary of State, Dean Acheson also believed that China had nothing to gain by supporting the North Koreans as their invasion was launched solely under the auspices of the Soviet Union. Acheson was convinced that the military advances of MacArthur and a delay in diplomatic parleys with China would provide the US with an opportunity to conduct negotiations from a position of strength, forcing the Chinese to concede the reality of American troops closer to their border. In Acheson's words: "It would be sheer madness for the Chinese Communist Government to enter the Korean War on the side opposing the free nations of the world."[17]

The belief on the part of the American military and political leadership that China was incapable of engaging the US was evident in General MacArthur's expectation that in a classic campaign, with the Eighth Army driving to the border and the X Corps moving northwest, the Chinese forces would be crushed between the two.[18] The division of his forces and little coordination between the two reflected MacArthur's expectation that his army could squeeze an ill-prepared and ill-equipped Chinese guerrilla force and reach the Yalu River more or less unchallenged. On November 24, MacArthur announced his famous "Home by Christmas Offensive," clearly suggesting that the General failed to grasp the situation caused by a determined adversary thrust within Korea against his troops. MacArthur was convinced: "Only a resolute action would forestall extensive Chinese intervention."[19] The General's overconfidence was rooted in the expectation that the Chinese Army, without air power, tanks, armored vehicles, motorized transport, and sufficient number of rifles "could even attempt to challenge the strongest country in the world." The previous Chinese successes against a better equipped Japanese Army were not considered by the American military leadership in Korea as being of any significance.[20] MacArthur firmly believed that American "air-power would stop the Chinese reinforcements from crossing from Manchuria and would destroy Chinese troops already in Korea."[21]

The Truman Administration allowed MacArthur to cross the 38th Parallel on September 27, 1950 on the basis of NSC-81 which author-ized him to destroy the North Korean Army and advance until he encountered Soviet or Chinese forces. MacArthur was permitted to exploit the advantages accruing from the surprise landing at Inchon and the failure of Russia or China to defend their retreating North Korean allies.[22] It was assumed that the Soviets would not run the risk of direct confrontation with the US and that they would "back down in the face of American firmness," which was already clear in their behavior during the Berlin Blockade.[23] In the administration's view, the US gestures of goodwill and non-aggression toward Peking would constitute sufficient assurance against an intervention by China, and therefore their "threats of intervention were considered as bluff."[24] As a continuation of this strategy of reassurance, on November 7, 1950, the UN Interim Committee on Korea declared that the UN troops would fully support the Manchurian frontier.[25] On November 10, a Six Power Resolution introduced in the Security Council reaffirmed the Chinese frontier with Korea as "inviolate" and the determination to fully "protect legitimate Chinese and Korean interests in the frontier zone."[26] On November 15, Acheson expressed readiness to talk with the Chinese on their "legitimate" interests on "both sides of the North Korean–Manchurian border." He warned that if China entered the war, it could cause a "a world-wide tragedy of the most colossal nature."[27] The drawback of this strategy of reassurance was that for China it had little credibility as past US assurances were flouted by MacArthur and his army divisions.

The US strategy in Korea, until the Chinese intervention, was based on an offensive doctrine that was practiced in World War I and World War II, i.e. the total destruction of enemy forces; in this case, the North Korean Army.[28] Although the strategy underwent minor modifi-cations, it seems the objective was to reunify Korea and destroy the North Korean Army as a fighting force. MacArthur, being educated in the traditional military school of thought, believed that the "best defense was offense" and that a bold course of destroying the enemy completely was preferable to an indeterminate defensive strategy.[29] However, the unexpected Chinese intervention changed the strategic objective. Since then, the major goal was to consciously limit the war to the Korean Peninsula. Korea was the first major limited war experi-ence for the American troops in this century. For the US, warfare in the twentieth century was global and total, requiring the complete mobilization of the country's resources to defeat the enemy thoroughly. As Bernard Brodie contends: "The prevailing axiom among the American military at the time the Korean war began, existing since World War I and reinforced by World War II, was: 'Modern war is total war.'"[30]

The major constraint of fighting a limited war was however, the conscious effort on the part of the administration not to bomb Manchuria, although occasional incursions occurred. Such a self-proclaimed restraint prevented the stronger power from using its air power effectively. The restraint was adopted, because in the US view, the political costs of escalation outweighed the immediate benefits of full mobilization and infliction of unacceptable costs on the weaker adversary. It is not clear whether the Chinese leadership was aware of a likelihood of the US delimiting the war to Korea before it decided to intervene. However, there was speculation that the Soviets had informed China of the possibility of the US waging a limited war confined to Korea. The restraint that was imposed on the US forces was partly a function of the world-wide containment strategy and partly the fear of fighting a global war with the Soviet Union, especially in Europe. An additional consideration was the possibility of the disintegration of NATO if the war spread beyond the Korean border.[31]

China's strategic assumptions

While deciding to initiate military action in Korea against the advancing US/UN forces, the Chinese leadership seemed to have adopted a mixture of strategic concepts from the Maoist guerrilla warfare and the precepts of traditional limited war, fought for limited objectives. The first phase of the intervention was a limited one, mainly purported to give the US a warning of the Chinese intent to prevent reunification of the Korean peninsula under the South Korean/US auspices. The key strategic objective was to achieve a military and political fait accompli in Korea through which the status quo ante, i.e. re-establishment of the two Koreas, would be secured. This, they hoped, would be accomplished by the establishment of a major bridgehead on the Peninsula between October and mid-December, 1950.[32] During this period the Chinese forces were expected to establish a defense perimeter along the Kusong, Taechon, Kujang-dong, Tokchon, Yongwon, and Oro-ri line in North Korea.[33]

Although Marshal Peng Dehuai, Commander of the Chinese People's Volunteers (CPV) that intervened in Korea, did not exactly follow this original plan to establish the defense line for the sake of maintaining surprise, the limited strategic objectives were clear in the initial movement of his troops. Consistent with the limited war plans, despite early successes in forcing the US troops to retreat, the Chinese leadership decided to halt their successful push at the 38th Parallel after just three weeks of military campaign.[34]

The larger politico-military objective of China when it decided to intervene was evidently to prevent a total defeat of North Korea and the reunification of the Peninsula rather than the complete surrender of South Korea or the complete withdrawal of US forces from Korea. Additionally, in the leadership's calculations, the war could be localized in Korea through surprise intervention, and thereby a major future conflict with the US could be prevented. The Chinese press justified the intervention later on as a necessary measure "to keep the wolf from the door." The leadership had estimated that a quick and decisive offensive might succeed if it took place before the US brought more than four additional divisions to Korea. By launching a forceful thrust, the Chinese leaders estimated that they could dislocate the advancing US/UN troops and unsettle American public opinion, thereby forcing Washington to negotiate.[35]

Mao Tse-tung and his decision-making group believed that it would be better to engage the American troops in Korea where the risks of the action would be manageable. Such an intervention would provide forward defense to Manchuria and thereby keep the war limited to Korea and preclude a possible US attack against Chinese territory.[36] Mao believed that if China did not send any troops and allowed US forces to reach the Yalu River, "the international and domestic reactionary bluster would surely become louder ... The whole Northeast Border Defense Army would be tied down there, and the electric power in South Manchuria would be subject to the control [of the enemy]."[37] It was assessed that even if the US did not engage in an immediate attack on China, the deployment of its troops along the Sino-Korean border "would have still constituted a grave threat to northeast China, the most advanced industrial area of the country." China would have carried a tremendous burden by keeping large forces on the border in order to provide a passive defense. Premier Zhou En-lai expressed the Chinese leadership's thinking in these words: "How many troops are needed to guard the Yalu River of one thousand kilometers? Moreover, they have to wait there year by year without knowing when the enemy comes."[38] As evident from this statement, the leadership was under intense time pressure as the more advances the US/UN made in Korea, the lower were the chances that China's limited strategic objectives would be successful.

In the Chinese view, the CPV intervention became necessary given the threat posed by the US forces crossing the 38th Parallel, following General MacArthur's successful landing at Inchon. This also coincided with talks of rearming Japan.[39] These actions prompted the Chinese leaders to believe that their territory, especially Manchuria, was in great danger and that the US would be in a position to attack China if the North Korean buffer was removed.[40] Premier Zhou En-lai argued at a top Communist Party meeting on October 24, 1950 that as soon as the US crossed the 38th Parallel it would start attacking Chinese territory.[41] Preserving North Korea at any cost was evident in a statement made at the top-level meetings that decided to intervene: "When the lips are gone, the teeth feel cold."[42] The Chinese leadership was also concerned that if the US succeeded in its initial objectives, there was nothing that could prevent it from making more demands or advancing further.

The record of the US in the region, especially its support to the Nationalists during the Civil War and their shielding in Formosa afterwards, gave additional reasons to the Chinese leadership to fear that "a determined opponent from a position of strength in a unified, independent, and non-Communist Korea could exploit many opportunities inside China."[43] Although the invasion of China was not a declared aim of the US at this time, from the Chinese point of view, every previous advance that MacArthur had made led to a change in the US strategic goals. Initially, the US had declared no interest in crossing the 38th Parallel, and once it did that, the modified objective was to halt military operations 150 miles north of the Parallel. However, in the changed military situation, following the routing of the North Koreans, the South Korean troops were to continue until the Peninsula was reunified.[44] This scenario gave a warning to China that MacArthur's objective might change again once his forces reached the Yalu and that he might turn his troops against Manchuria itself, contrary to assurances from Washington. It would have been impossible for Truman and Acheson to repudiate the General when he was on a winning streak. They thus had very little reason to trust the American promise of restraint given the past behavior of its leaders in Korea.[45]

Marshal Peng Dehuai echoed these concerns in these words: "The US occupation of Korea, separated from China only by a river, would threaten Northeast China ... The US could find a pretext at any time to launch a war of aggression against China. The tiger wanted to eat human beings; when it would do so would depend upon its appetite. No concession could stop it."[46] The American policy of protecting Chiang Kai-shek and arming his troops and providing military aid to France in its colonial war in Indo-china, in addition to the possibility of a re-armed Japan in alliance with the US confronting China were factors that raised concerns among the Chinese decision-makers of the possibility of larger future threats if the US advance was not nipped in the bud.[47] To the Chinese leadership, a major conflict with the US was inevitable, whether in Korea, Vietnam or Taiwan. Korea provided the most favorable terrain for the PLA forces to wage a Maoist style warfare and the surest way to receive Soviet support.[48]

When the Chinese leadership launched the first major assaults against the US/UN troops, they expected a limited, short war and achievement of quick battlefield successes that could be translated into political and strategic gains.[49] Although Mao and his decision-making group were aware of the risks of a two-front war resulting from American support to the Kumingtang, they were also confident that the US would be preoccupied in Korea and would not be able to launch such a war from Formosa.[50] The quick war expectation was evident in Marshal Peng Dehuai's report to Mao in March 1951 that after nearly five months of fighting, the war could not be won quickly as anticipated. Mao replied: "Win a quick victory if you can; if you can't, win a slow one."[51] The leadership was also concerned about the possibility of stalemate on the battlefield. In his telegram to Stalin on October 2, 1950 Mao said that if the American troops, especially the Eighth Army, were defeated in Korea and even if the US had declared war on China, the "ongoing confrontation would not be on a large-scale, nor would it last very long." The most unfavorable situation would be the failure of Chinese forces to destroy large numbers of American troops in Korea and thereby a stalemated war of attrition." In Mao's calculations, the first scenario was the most likely one, i.e., a quick attack and destruction of US forces in Korea and an early settlement.[52]

During deliberations prior to the Chinese entry, Marshal Peng debated with the supporters of intervention in the Chinese High Command on the nature of the prospective military action and agreed to lead the PLA forces on the condition that China would respond in a limited way at least during the initial stages, mainly to provide a warning to the Americans.[53] "Our first response to an American invasion of North Korea should be limited. The PLA has not the equipment, the supplies, or the time to launch large scale operations

94

deep into Korea. If by some mischance the Americans and their allies ever invade the DPRK, we should halt them north of Pyongyang at the narrow neck of the Korean Peninsula," Peng was quoted as saying at a September 10, 1950 staff exercise session.[54] The objective of preventing a massive direct military retaliation by the US and an all-out war was evident in the renaming of PLA troops going to Korea as Communist Party Volunteers (CPV). Mao specifically instructed Peng Dehuai to rename the troops as volunteers so as to make the conflict a localized one and not to give the US a pretext to attack China.[55]

According to the initial plan that Mao and Peng adopted, the American troops would merely be stopped north of Pyongyang. This initial action was expected to compel the US decision-makers to alter their plans to advance toward the Yalu. The Chinese leaders hoped that in the aftermath of this limited, luring operation, the US would negotiate with them on restoring the two Koreas and maintaining China's territorial sanctity.[56] The Chinese desire to limit the war was further evident in its partial force withdrawal from Korea in early November.[57] The massive intervention in late November was in response to General MacArthur's final offensive to end the war by Christmas. Subsequently, on December 13, 1950 Mao ordered Peng to cross the 38th Parallel in order to make use of the favorable political situation, despite the General's hesitation to do so before Spring. The leadership considered President Truman's promise to British Prime Minister Attlee not to use atomic weapons in Korea as a favorable opportunity worth exploiting.[58] Even after the failure of the first limited attempts to send warning signals to the US, China still wanted to limit the war, as evident in the Chinese unwillingness to use its limited air capability in attacking US lines of communications, airfields, and ports in South Korea and Japan. The MiG-15 forces did not provide any aerial interdiction and close air support to the ground troops, but concentrated their efforts on defense against US/UN fighter bombers in northwestern Korea.[59] Although Mao decided to drag on the war despite signals from the US/UN for negotiations, the objective of continued fighting was to gain more bargaining power vis-à-vis the superior adversary rather than a decisive victory.[60]

Surprise was a key element in the Chinese strategic planning. In his telegram to Peng Dehuai on 23 October, 1950, Mao said the military outcome of the intervention would depend on whether the campaign "will make use of a surprise attack which will be completely unanticipated by the enemy."[61] Total surprise and tactical mobility, especially during the first two weeks of intervention, were made possible by the fact that the Chinese troops advanced mostly under the cover of darkness, leaving behind little trail of their movement. They could achieve this because they possessed mostly hand-carried supplies.[62] The Chinese strategic thinking relied heavily on a war scenario in which resolve and superior tactics of the revolutionary volunteers would play a key role in resisting the more advanced technological and military capabilities of the adversary. The leadership was willing to sacrifice several thousand soldiers in order to "stop the enemy by the age-old method of putting so many men in his way that he could not proceed."[63] The determination to resist the US through human-wave tactics was also based on a calculation that in land warfare the Chinese Army would prevail. For instance, China's Acting Chief of Staff, General Nieh Yen-jung, during conversations with the Indian Ambassador to Peking, K.M. Panikkar, stated: "Americans can bomb us, they can destroy our industries, but they cannot defeat us on land."[64]

The Chinese leadership constantly downplayed the effectiveness of a US nuclear attack against its vast and dispersed population. Mao told Peng in early October that the Soviet Union had broken the American nuclear monopoly and that "nuclear blackmail will not work," especially "when coping with a huge population and extensive land." The determining factor in the outcome of the war would be human power and not modern armory.[65] A directive released as part of the "Resist America" campaign said that nuclear weapons are not a deci-sive factor in a war as they cannot be employed as battlefield weapons. "[They] can only be used against a big and concentrated object like a big armament industry center or huge concentration of troops. There-fore, the more extensive the opponent's territory is and the more scattered the opponent's population is, the less effective will the atom bomb be."[66] The leadership believed that the outcome of the war would be determined by human factors and that the US would be concerned about the adverse world opinion its nuclear attack would bring forth. If the US used only one or two atomic bombs, it would not make much impact on Chinese policy as it would not entail a decisive defeat for Peking, while a massive use of nuclear weapons would inevitably result in getting the Soviet Union involved, leading to a global war.[67]

From defense to offense

The primacy of defense in the Maoist doctrine of warfare was only partially applied in Korea. Mao had expected that the war would be protracted at the strategic level, but short and quick at the tactical level.[68] In the Maoist conception, a mobile warfare would be followed by guerrilla warfare in which active defense and strategic counter-offensive form key organizing concepts. Although Mao's military doctrine during the Civil War was described as defense dominant, it was in fact one of active defense or "defense through decisive engagements." This operational doctrine was generally implemented whenever the Red Army faced superior force, and had to break the opponents through their "encirclement and suppression." The doctrine also called for strategic retreats whenever confronted with a stronger enemy so as to conserve strength and time for counter-offensives. The counter-offensives were to be facilitated by conditions such as support of the local population, favorable terrain, ability to concentrate unit-level forces, discovery of the enemy's weak spots, and forced demoralization of the adversary.[69] Such strategic and tactical approaches helped the PLA to defeat the eight million strong US-backed forces of Chiang Kai-shek and to gain valuable experience in fighting a better equipped adversary.[70]

Despite the primacy given to defense in early Maoist strategic thinking, in Korea, the dominance of the professional army's strategy and doctrine was evident in the offensive–defensive doctrine adopted by the PLA: an approach in which Chinese forces would engage in limited offensive operations; followed by a defensive posture during which attempts would be made to lure the superior forces to engage in semi-protracted warfare.[71] In actual operations, luring the enemy deep into strongholds of well-entrenched CPV units was successfully practiced by Peng's forces. This tactical concept was adopted as the Chinese forces could not engage a better equipped enemy in frontal, positional warfare. The tactics entailed keeping the main body of the Chinese forces unnoticed in favorable locations while allowing small units to engage with the enemy forces. While these small units retreated, the opponent would be forced to follow them and establish positions. The main Chinese forces would then attack from the rear in full force and engage them at close quarters with grenades and bayonets, thereby making the adversary's superior firepower ineffective.[72] The possession of light infantry and huge manpower allowed the CPV to practice the classic tactics of combining frontal attacks and, subsequently, enveloping moves on the flanks, as well as cutting off retreat routes.[73] In addition, the tactics relied on complicated tunnels through which troops could move around without being noticed.[74]

The Chinese intervention in Korea illustrates that the strategic approach of a weaker initiator has a determining effect on its choice for war against a more powerful adversary. The Chinese leadership

97

thought that they could wage a short, fait accompli war with superior strategy and tactics, as well as surprise; concepts derived largely from the Maoist style of warfare. The strategy had a high element of limited aims, although it contained principles of attrition warfare as well. The initiator expected a war confined to the theater of operations, i.e. Korea, even though the possibility of US nuclear attack on the mainland was considered, but was ruled out.

Weapons capability in Chinese calculations

What offensive capability did China possess in 1950 that possibly gave incentives to go to war against the superior US/UN forces? It seems that the PLA held little or no modern weaponry when the Chinese leadership decided to confront the huge forces arrayed against it. The Chinese Army, despite containing five large field armies, was essentially an infantry force which lacked heavy artillery, armored vehicles, and ammunition. Their commanders lacked knowledge of modern technological warfare and operational tactics, such as joint operations and combined arms, involving armor, infantry, artillery, and close air support.[75] Modernization was also not on the cards. In fact, in May 1950, the leadership had decided to demobilize and redeploy thousands of PLA units in order to use them in the economic reconstruction of the country. The army's strength was expected to be slashed from 5.4 million to 4 million under the charge of Zhou En-lai. The demobilization process began on June 20, 1950, just five days before the outbreak of the Korean War.[76] In 1950, the Chinese Army remained largely a guerrilla force that was trained to conduct long marches on small amounts of food and with light weaponry, such as submachine guns, rifles, grenades, and light mortars. These weapons were mostly of Japanese, Soviet, and American make. The American weapons were: M-1 rifles, Browning Automatic Rifles (BARs), Thompson submachine guns, light and heavy machine guns, 60mm and 81mm mortars, and 105mm howitzers, captured from the two million odd surrendering Nationalist forces.[77] None of the weapons that the Soviets promised arrived before the intervention. In fact, the Soviet supply of substantial amounts of weapons started only in Fall 1951, about a year after the intervention started. Additionally, the 500–odd aircraft that the Chinese Air Force possessed by the end of 1950 were mostly propeller driven.[78] The lack of capability had been attributed to the PLA's development of "infantry small-arms syndrome," and the "defense syndrome."[79]

In the Chinese calculations, high morale and a belief in the just cause of fighting made the opponent's superior military capability less threatening. A high-level officers' meeting of the Northeast Military District at Shenyang on August 13 analyzed China's advantages and the US disadvantages and concluded that the US had to divide its forces between Europe and Korea. The US forces in Korea suffered from low morale, while the Chinese Army possessed high morale. In addition, it was calculated that transportation of huge numbers of forces and equipment from the US would be time consuming, while China possessed the advantage of proximity to Korea. However, this was proven to be of limited value since China lacked air superiority. Yet the decision-makers were well aware of China's deficiency in transportation vehicles, personnel and anti-tank weapons.[80] At an early October 1950 meeting Mao told Peng that Stalin had promised him air support and China's ground forces were capable of engaging the US single-handedly. To Mao, the US disadvantages included an extended front line, with the naval forces spread across several oceans and the ground troops extended from Western Europe to the Far East. The US troops would take a long time to refurbish in Korea, while the morale of its troops stationed in Japan was low. Moreover, the US Allies would not send many troops.[81]

This brief description of Chinese capabilities clearly suggests that the possession of offensive weapons did not play a major role in the Chinese thinking prior to the intervention. Although there were promises of Soviet weapon support, the Chinese calculations were mostly based on military strategy and tactics and morale that would compensate for their disadvantage in capability vis-à-vis the US and the UN forces.

Soviet support in China's calculations

The full account regarding the position of the USSR in the Korean War and its role in the Chinese decision to intervene in support of North Korea is yet to unfold. The limited evidence available on this question points toward an active influence that Russia might have exerted in China's decision to intervene. Although China was clearly not a proxy of the Soviet Union during this period, the tacit support from the USSR might have still been a critical factor facilitating Peking's decision to intervene. The Chinese vacillation during the period from August till October 1950, the several Sino-Soviet meetings prior to the intervention, and the Chinese statements that the limited Soviet nuclear capability would deter the US from using nuclear weapons, are elements giving credence to the contention that the leadership expected defensive support from the USSR in the event the war turned against it decisively or the US escalated the conflict by attacking mainland China itself.

The relations between the two Communist giants were not very strong when the Chinese Party won the revolution in 1949. Stalin was suspicious of Mao's tactics in the Civil War, and was afraid that the latter might become another Tito by opposing Soviet influence in China. Mao later revealed that Stalin was hesitant to sign the Friendship Treaty and had made serious attempts to make China a pawn. He stated:

> After the victory of the revolution he next suspected China of being a Yugoslavia, and that I would become a second Tito. Later, when I went to Moscow to sign the Sino-Soviet Treaty of Alliance and Mutual Assistance, we had to go through another struggle. He was not willing to sign a treaty. After two months of negotiations he at last signed. When did Stalin begin to have confidence in us? It was at the time of the Resist America, Aid Korea campaign, from the winter of 1950.[82]

A key aspect of the Russian support to China was that it was defensive and political in character. The Chinese leadership considered the alliance's strategic and political value especially in confronting internal as well as external threats while maintaining the "lean on one side" policy. The alliance relationship was also considered as a means to buy time to accomplish economic reconstruction and to consolidate internal security. An NCNA editorial, published in February 1950, noted that although Article I of the Sino-Soviet treaty specifically mentioned an attack by Japan, the part dealing with "states allied with it," clearly implied that it covered a threat from the US as well.[83] The Chinese leadership, when it decided to intervene in Korea, seemed to have received assurances from the Soviet Union that if the US escalated the war to Manchuria Moscow would intervene on behalf of China. According to one account, during late September, Stalin had warned Mao that the US troops were fast approaching the Yalu River and that they would pose a direct threat to Manchuria. With the hope of China sending troops to Korea, Stalin offered Soviet air cover for Chinese soldiers if they intervened.[84] After receiving support from his internal decision-making group, Mao sent Zhou En-lai to Russia for Stalin's approval for his decision to intervene. Stalin met with Zhou at his vacation retreat at Sochi and extended the Soviet Union's full support for the intervention.[85]

According to an account by two Chinese scholars, a special Politburo meeting of the Chinese Communist Party on October 2 had approved

Mao's plan for intervention "provided that the Soviet Union could provide the CPV with Air Force support and war materials." This decision received Stalin's approval who in turn agreed to provide China with air support and military equipment. However, soon afterwards the Soviet leader changed his mind, fearing that Soviet involvement in Korea would lead to a larger US–Soviet military confrontation. Mao asked Zhou to convey to Stalin his determination to pursue the offensive even without direct Soviet air support. In response to this Stalin made promises to expedite the training of Chinese pilots, although he ruled out the Soviet forces' direct participation in the fighting. However, once China confirmed its decision to intervene, the Soviet leader agreed to provide major aid.[86] Mao had telegrammed Stalin on October 2 informing him that in the early phase of the operations, the Chinese troops would deploy defensive tactics and remain north of the 38th Parallel, fighting only the US troops that were entering the northern regions. "Meanwhile, our troops will be awaiting the arrival of Soviet weapons and being equipped with those weapons. Only then will our troops, in cooperation with the Korean comrades, launch a counter-offensive to destroy the invading American forces."[87]

Ambassador Panikkar, who had extensive contacts with the Chinese leaders, stated that the Chinese were assured that if Manchuria were attacked, the Soviets would intervene on their behalf.[88] Marshal Peng Dehuai had also confirmed that what made him agree to Mao's decision to intervene was the belief that because China had a "national government and Soviet assistance, our situation was much better than it had been during the War of Resistance to Japanese aggression. We should despatch troops to Korea to safeguard our national construction."[89] China's leaders also seemed to have expected a limited Soviet nuclear retaliatory threat as a factor in deterring a possible US nuclear attack. At a CCP Military Commission meeting in early August 1950 (attended by Nie Rongzhen, the Commander of North China Field Army, Peng Dehuai, and Generals He Long and Zhu De), He Long queried whether there was any possibility of America's using nuclear weapons against China in the event of a Chinese intervention in Korea. Nie's response was that although the possibility existed, since the US no longer enjoyed an atomic monopoly, and since the Soviets had conducted their first test a year ago "they may be less eager to use it nowadays."[90]

Yet the Soviet support to China seemed to be confined to limited political backing and military supplies as evidenced in Stalin's unwillingness to provide any major military assistance during the initial phases of the war. Outwardly, the Soviet approach seemed cautious so that the war would not assume global proportions or end up in a US–Soviet nuclear exchange. The Russian reluctance in confronting the US in Korea was evident in its earlier withdrawal of Soviet technicians from North Korea after the US/UN troops crossed the 38th Parallel.[91] Despite this cautious posture, the Soviets did in fact step up their propaganda campaign in October, urging China to intervene without delay to protect North Korea, its fraternal neighbor.[92] The caution with which the USSR supplied weapons to China during the first year of intervention also showed that the Soviet leaders wanted the war to be limited. When the tide began to turn against China, the Soviets commenced their massive arms supply, invoking the February 1950 Treaty of Friendship, Alliance and Mutual Assistance, which contained provisions for bilateral assistance in the event of an attack on either party by Japan or other states allied with it.[93]

There is some evidence of early coordinated efforts of the two states' military forces. For instance, in August 1950, the Soviet Army Chief, Marshal Shtemenko; the Commander in Chief of Soviet Far East Military Area, Marshal Malinovsky; the Soviet Air Force Commander in the Far East, Klazovsky; and the Soviet Anti-Aircraft Forces Commander met with Chinese commanders, including Peng Dehaui, and discussed the conditions under which the Soviet Union would extend full-scale support to China, as well as arms and advisers. Additionally, they agreed to set up a Joint General Staff in Shenyang by the middle of September, with "Soviet Lt. General Kuzman Derevyanko as Chief and the commander of the PLA's 40th Corps, General Han Hsien-ch'u as Deputy Chief." Yet these were mostly defensive preparations in the event that the US/UN forces engaged in a direct attack on either Chinese or Soviet territory. The Chinese decision to intervene was taken at a later stage.[94]

This case points towards a fairly strong impact exerted by the great power ally on the war choices of a weaker challenger. The great power at times showed ambivalence in its commitment towards the weaker ally, yet the latter expected defensive support from the former if not direct involvement in war. The Chinese leadership anticipated Soviet defensive cover against a massive punitive strike on its territory, especially on Manchuria, by the US and its allies. They viewed the Soviet nuclear capability as a deterrent against the US from launching a nuclear attack on China. We may also conclude that the Chinese leadership expected a limited war confined to Korea largely due to the Cold War and the Soviet global position vis-à-vis the US.

Domestic compulsions and the decision to intervene

Apart from external conditions arising from alliance commitment and the interaction resulting from conflicting strategic objectives of the opponents, what internal factors might have contributed to the Chinese leadership's decision to intervene in Korea in the Fall of 1950? Can the internal dimension of the decision to enter the war be explained within the context of the new regime's attempts to secure its legitimacy and control over wide regions of China following the successful conclusion of the Civil War in 1949?

Indeed in 1950, the Chinese regime was confronting severe internal challenges. The threats to the new regime came not only from external sources, such as the one mounted by the US and the Nationalists from Taiwan, but from several regional warlords who commanded regular forces and bandits while resisting the central authority in Peking. An estimated 400,000 bandits operated through secret agents, while resorting to economic sabotage, assassinations, and guerrilla activities. The Chinese leadership believed that the US and Chiang Kai-shek were supporting and financing these groups through associations like, the Sino-American Cooperation Organization, and the Sino-American Information Bureau.[95] These threats and the immediate learning experience resulting from the struggle against Kumingtang led to what is termed as a "civil war syndrome" in Chinese military thinking and strategic approach.[96] The legitimacy of the new regime was also in question given the precarious nature of its position internally. According to one Chinese historian, if China gave in to the US, the Communist Party would have lost the support of the people.[97]

The chief external threat to China after the revolution seemed to have come from the US because of its occupation of Japan and its support for the Kumingtang. A historian notes that between 1948 and 1950, the US was "viewed as the primary enemy of the revolution not only internationally but also domestically." Mao characterized China as "semi-colonial" and "semi-feudal" and argued: "The imperialist countries not only threatened the nation from without but also were themselves domestic political actors using their control of domestic political forces, their cultural influence, and their tremendous economic power to stymie the revolution from within." Therefore, in order to achieve China's full liberation, "all the sinews of imperialist power would have to be removed."[98] The leadership thus feared that if it acquiesced to an American military victory in Korea, it would encourage the US as well as Chiang Kai-shek to engage in military operations against China while the internal opposition would strengthen its hold among the masses. This was evident in Mao's message on October 12, 1950 to Zhou En-lai who was in Moscow: "If we adopt a policy of non-intervention and let our enemy to press the bank of Yalu river, the reactionary arrogance inside and outside the country will be inspired."[99]

In this case, major changes in the domestic power structure did occur with the advent of the revolutionary regime into power in 1949. Within the ruling elite, there was some opposition to the intervention, although Mao remained the key decision-maker with respect to the choice for war. More than internal power shifts, it was the perceived sense of threat to the regime that acted as a determining factor in the leadership's calculations prior to the intervention. There is an inter-linking of internal and external variables here as forces of internal threat to regime survival were also supported by external powers, mainly the US. Therefore, removing the external threat became imperative for the regime's internal legitimacy and control.

Why intervention was delayed

It is not clear from most Chinese accounts why China did not inter-vene in August and instead waited until October even though the leadership seriously considered military involvement in Korea. For instance, Marshal Nie Rongzhen in his memoirs stated that on August 5 the Party Military Commission had instructed General Deng Hua to prepare for war within one month.[100] Prior to that, Mao had ordered the redeployment of the 13th Army Corps from the Central-South Military region to the Yalu River area where this army combined with the local army and was renamed the Northeastern Frontier Defense Army, which eventually became the Chinese Peoples' Volunteers (CPV) that entered Korea. After the redeployment that began in mid-July, over 180,000 of China's best-trained forces were available to intervene in the proximity of Korea. In spite of the fact that the Northeast Frontier Force was formally designated to safeguard the security of the frontier and to assist North Korea in its fight against the US as and when necessary, they were simply asked to await further orders.[101] On July 10, China had also organized the "Committee of Chinese People against US invasion of Taiwan and Korea," and on August 5 the Central Military Commission had ordered the frontier force to be ready for operations by early September.[102]

Although these steps could be considered as defensive measures against a possible attack by the US on Chinese territory along the Yalu

River area, for preventive reasons China should have joined hands with the North Korean forces early on to stop any US/UN counter offensives. It could be argued that the leadership was waiting to see what forward action General MacArthur would take and how far he would go in reunifying Korea, before entering the conflict. Only when MacArthur decided to cross the 38th Parallel did the Chinese leaders feel the need to intervene. Although this could be true, it seems to be an insufficient explanation for the delay given that while it waited, China was in fact allowing the US forces to entrench deeply into Korea, making their removal even more difficult.

The reluctance of the Chinese leadership stemmed partly from opposition to the plan expressed by some key party and military men. PLA leaders who opposed the intervention feared that it would result in China being "bogged down in a protracted war." To some, the US threat was not as imminent as feared. Despite attacks on North Korea and border incursions into China, no large scale-invasion had yet occurred.[103] Nie Rongzhen makes repeated comments in his auto-biography on the long and intense debate within the Party and the army hierarchy on the pros and cons of intervention. According to him, Lin Biao, among others, opposed the plan to send troops to Korea, forcing Mao to appoint Peng as commander of the Chinese forces that eventually intervened.[104] Ch'en Yun, the most important economic policy maker in the regime and Jao Shu-shih, a key official from the East China region, also opposed the intervention, fearing that a protracted war with the US would adversely affect China's economic recovery.[105] This opposition came to the surface at a Politburo meeting of the Communist Party on October 1 that was convened to make the final decision to intervene. Lin Biao and Gao Gang, Chairman of the Northeastern region, opposed the intervention by contending that China did not have sufficient economic and military capability to wage war against the powerful US forces. To them, China also had "less consolidated rear defenses."[106] Mao finally made the decision after overruling the opposition's argument about the likelihood of waging a protracted war and China's vulnerability vis-à-vis a superior enemy.

Explaining the Chinese intervention

In summarizing the proximate causes of China's decision to intervene in Korea against a militarily superior adversary, three factors seem significant. The calculations derived from a limited aims/fait accompli strategy with some characteristics of attrition, seem to be an important determining factor. This strategy, relying on surprise, offered the

possibility of removing the US presence from North Korea and preventing reunification of the peninsula. Moreover, the leadership
anticipated a limited war and limited retaliatory response from the US.
The Soviet defensive support was expected to prevent an all-out
nuclear and conventional attack by the US/UN forces on China. It may
be concluded that the expectation that China held a superior strategy
and a conviction that the war could be localized to Korea provided
major incentives to its decision-makers to order an offensive in
October 1950. The third condition, the possession of short-term offensive advantage, seems to be of little pertinence to this case, as China
held very little modern weaponry at that time. The timing of the
offensive bears to a certain extent on regime insecurity, as the newly
established Communist government feared a US presence in Korea
emboldening internal opposition forces. However, the debate among
top leaders regarding the protracted nature of the war and the
uncertainty about the Soviet position seem equally critical to
explaining China's vacillation from August till October 1950 regarding
the timing of intervention. Opposition by many key PLA commanders,
including Lin Biao seems to have prompted Mao to ponder over the
feasibility of operations for quite some time. In the end, the fear of
increased challenges to the newly established regime became a critical
factor in the decision.

The stronger power's strategy neither deterred China nor provided
adequate reassurance to Peking that there was no intention to
threaten Chinese territory. The US deterrence efforts failed partly
because the threat of retaliation was at times ambiguous and partly
because China viewed the US actions as extremely provocative. The
previous shifts in US goals were considered by the Chinese as a sign
that once the North Korean buffer was removed, the US might
advance into its territory, making it difficult to wage a successful
limited war. The US reassurance efforts were not credible because the
statements of benign intent were not followed up by concrete actions.
The Chinese also failed to convince the Americans of their ability to
intervene as the US could not believe that a weaker opponent would
engage in a highly risky operation against superior military forces.
This case challenges general deterrence theory to some extent, and it
proves that a highly motivated adversary state need not feel deterred
by the massive forces, including nuclear weapons, arrayed against it.

6 THE PAKISTANI OFFENSIVE
IN KASHMIR, 1965

The second Kashmir War between India and Pakistan began on August 5, 1965 with the infiltration of specially trained guerrillas into Indian held Kashmir from Pakistani controlled Azad Kashmir.[1] The initial Pakistani operation, code-named "Gibraltar," was actively planned and implemented by officials from Pakistan's Foreign Ministry and Army and was intended to capture the Kashmir Valley from India through urban insurrection. If that mission failed, the operation was expected to raise the prospects for serious negotiations by bringing the Kashmir issue to renewed international focus.[2] The important question for this study is why did the Pakistani leaders decide to commit to a military solution to the Kashmir dispute in September 1965 even when they knew that India held a nearly 3:1 numerical advantage in the Kashmir theater and a 5:1 superiority in overall military and industrial capability?[3]

The balance of capabilities in 1965 was as follows. The Indian armed forces comprised 870,000 men in sixteen divisions as compared to Pakistan's 230,000 under eight divisions. Of the sixteen divisions, India had deployed two infantry divisions in Kashmir and eight along its border with Pakistan and the rest on the Chinese border. Pakistan had a total of seven divisions confronting India in West Pakistan and one division in East Pakistan. India possessed two armored divisions, one each of Centurion and Sherman tanks; while Pakistan had one armored division with American built M-47/48 Patton tanks, and a few other regiments with M-4 Sherman medium tanks and M-24 Chaffee light tanks. In air capability, India held over 700 aircraft, mostly the French Mystere IVs, British Canberras and Hunters, and Indian-made Gnats. Pakistan had a total of 280 aircraft that included 168 Sabres, and 12 F-104A Starfighters. The naval strength was also in India's favor although the war did not involve any major naval operations.[4] In quality many of Pakistan's aircraft and tanks were of superior caliber, but the absence of proper training for their crews somewhat nullified this advantage. With its four times larger territory and population,

107

India had the added advantage of defense-in-depth and a domestic arms industry to support a long war. In addition to the favorable overall balance of capability, the Indian leadership had made limited deterrent threats regarding its intention to retaliate at strategic points beyond Kashmir if Pakistan launched an attack in Kashmir. For instance, in April 1965, the Prime Minister, Lal Bahadur Shastri had warned that Pakistan's intrusion into Kashmir would result in India taking retaliatory action along the international border; the time and place would be of its choosing.[5]

The Kashmir dispute had its origins in the partition of the sub-continent in 1947 when the princely ruler of the largely Muslim populated Jammu and Kashmir decided to accede to the Indian Union.[6] The accession was justified as a necessary measure to prevent the incursion of tribal warriors or Mujahids into the state from Pakistan who were determined to occupy the territory forcibly. Following the accession, the Indian Army responded militarily against the advancing tribal forces while the Pakistani regular army units came to the rescue of the latter. The war ended with an armistice in 1948; the result of which was a heavily armed border, patrolled by UN peace-keeping forces. Subsequent governments had reiterated Pakistan's claim over the entire Kashmir on the grounds of the territory's contiguity, large Muslim population, and strategic significance. The Indian claim had been greatly derived from the legality of the instrument of accession by the princely ruler and the strategic value of the territory, especially magnified by the 1962 Sino-Indian War. It was also based on the Indian notion of secularism which contends that the country should not be further bifurcated on religious grounds. Pakistan argued that without Kashmir's accession to it, the partition of the sub-continent would be incomplete.[7]

These claims and counter-claims had led to mutual acrimony and tensions between the two South Asian nations, often bringing them to the verge of war. Several border skirmishes occurred between 1948 and 1965. In this chapter, I probe the question of why a large-scale war did not occur previously and why it did erupt in August–September 1965. Specifically, why did the Pakistani leadership not initiate hostilities in 1962, when India and China were fighting on the Himalayan border, despite military recommendations to do so? The effort here is to find an answer to this question as well as an explanation for the decision to initiate war in 1965 by looking at the strategic calculations of the belligerents – especially the initiator – and the role of changes in short-term capability, alliance configurations, and domestic decision-making structure within the initiating state.

India's strategy: a failure to deter?

The Indian strategy towards Pakistan in 1965 was a combination of defense and deterrence by punishment. This was based on the expectation that India's larger forces would prevail in a long war, and therefore that Pakistan could be deterred from engaging in war. It was also rooted in a belief that New Delhi held sufficient deterrent capability and kept the option to launch an attack on Pakistan's international border in the Punjab, should war in Kashmir turn to its disadvantage. Thus a threat to escalate war to the more vulnerable parts of the opponent's territory was the key component of Indian deterrent strategy against Pakistan prior to 1965. This strategy had been evolving since the early 1950s. In 1952, Prime Minister Nehru had warned that if Pakistan "by mistake invades Kashmir, we will not only meet them in Kashmir, but it will be a full scale war between India and Pakistan."[8] As previously mentioned, Prime Minister Shastri also had made a deterrent threat in April 1965, revealing the Indian intention to escalate the conflict in response to Pakistan's limited military actions in Kashmir. Despite these warnings, there was still some question regarding the credibility of the deterrent threat. An effective Indian deterrent could have been hampered by the following factors. First, although verbal commitments were made, they lacked credibility to the challenger, as India's past responses to limited wars were not to escalate them beyond the immediate theater of operations. Second, India's major strength lay in its depth, population, and military potential, which were not sufficient to deter a short and limited attack by Pakistan. Third, the Indian commanders themselves agree that they were wavering in their effort to deter Pakistan as they were unsure of their own capabilities in the short run.[9]

The Indian military's expectations regarding a long war can be inferred from its reluctance to use its air force with its full might at the initial stages of the war. The Indian Army commanders thought that the war would be prolonged and therefore they attempted to conserve their forces for major counter-offensives.[10] Critics of the Indian strategy contend that in the battlefield, such reluctance strengthened Pakistan's expectation that the Indians were not keen on fighting a major war. The main plank of the strategy was to wean the Pakistani forces away from Kashmir towards Punjab and there were no long-range plans for capturing or occupying other areas of Pakistan.[11] Although the Army Chief, General J.N. Chaudhuri and the Defense Minister, Y.B. Chavan were in favor of continuation of hostilities, the Prime Minister decided to terminate the counter-offensive, largely due to international pressures from the UN, the US and the UK.[12] The strategy thus had more elements of defense than deterrence. In a defensive war, the Indians were somewhat vulnerable to a short, intense attack given that the army was going through reorganization. It has been argued that although the commanders were expecting a long war, it is unclear whether they were fully ready for one in 1965.[13]

In the political sphere, the strategy was to integrate Jammu and Kashmir into India constitutionally and legally so as to remove the dispute from international attention for ever. In February 1954, the state's National Assembly ratified the accession to India. In October 1956 a new state constitution was adopted, thereby effectively making the state a legal part of India, although Article 370 of the federal constitution which accorded a special status to the state was preserved. On January 26, 1957, India declared the accession of the state as irrevocable, and on January 20, 1960 the Indian Supreme Court assumed jurisdiction over the state's legal authority.[14] By 1965, a number of incidents within Kashmir increased the unrest in the state. The theft of a holy relic from the Hazrat Bal Mosque near Srinagar in December 1963 was a precipitating event leading to large-scale disturbances. The arrest of Kashmir's most prominent leader, Sheikh Abdullah in May 1965 for his alleged anti-Indian activities abroad led to a spate of violence. In December 1964, Article 356 of the Indian Constitution was extended to the state, which allowed the President to declare central rule over Jammu and Kashmir by toppling the state's elected government.[15] It is argued that all these political measures aggravated the Pakistani leadership's time pressure as they feared that the Kashmir issue would be frozen or forgotten for ever unless they went to war.[16] The Indian Government's backing away from an earlier made promise to conduct a plebiscite in the state on its status further increased the Pakistani pressure to act militarily. New Delhi's policies in Kashmir failed to generate enough support among the Kashmiris for continued association with India. The recurring turmoil in Kashmir created windows of opportunity for Pakistan to exploit with the expectation that the Kashmiri people would support a military operation.[17]

Pakistan's strategic calculations

While the Indians were preparing for a defensive war with a limited deterrent threat of escalation in order to prevent an attack from their smaller neighbor, the Pakistani leadership was planning a short,

110

limited war to be waged in the Kashmir area. The initial strategy had some elements of Mao's guerrilla warfare, but was largely one of limited aims/fait accompli, which was intended to infiltrate Jammu and Kashmir with guerrilla forces and thereby foment an uprising among the local population. According to this plan, about 7,000 to 8,000 specially trained Mujahid raiders, code-named "Gibraltar Force," were pushed into Kashmir with the short-term objective of "dislocating and disorganizing the Indian Army."[18] These raiders were expected to sabotage Indian military installations such as airfields, communication centers, bridges, headquarters, ammunition facilities, and military camps, and eventually distribute arms to the Kashmiri people in an effort to initiate a guerrilla movement in the Kashmir Valley. They would also establish special training camps for Kashmiri volunteers in order to intensify the liberation struggle. The Indian troops would attempt to suppress the rebellion, which in turn would create an international outcry, forcing India to modify its position. The expectation was that when the guerrilla movement gained momentum, the Indians would find their continued occupation of Kashmir too expensive in men and material. The international reaction would bring further pressure on the Indians to go to the negotiating table for a settlement.[19] Pakistan's Foreign Minister, Zulfikar Ali Bhutto, believed that even "if the war could be fought to a standstill, it was equivalent to a victory. While the action smouldered, the loser could only be India."[20]

Mohammed Asghar Khan, a former Pakistani Air Force chief, suggests that the acceptance of this plan by the military leadership was based on three important premises: (1) There was widespread support within Jammu and Kashmir for its success; (2) in response to this action, India would not resort to a large-scale military offensive against Pakistani-controlled Azad Kashmir; and (3) the Indians would not cross the international frontier in either East or West Pakistan.[21] These strategic assumptions were reinforced by a belief that several conditions for the success of the operations were met, as there was a "worthy cause, difficult terrain, a determined war-like people (Pakistanis), a sympathetic local population (Kashmiris), the availability of weapons and equipment, and strong leadership."[22] The strategy contained offensive plans involving regular forces if the Indians detected and retaliated against the guerrilla operation. In order to counter a possible Indian retaliatory response, the Pakistani Army had planned another operation; an offensive through the Chaamb Valley in an effort to capture Akhnur – a strategic point of Indian defenses in Kashmir – through concentrated artillery fire.[23] The basis for this

111

operation was also an expectation that the Indian response would still be confined to Kashmir.

President Ayub Khan was convinced by his Foreign Minister, Bhutto, that the Indians would neither extend the conflict to other parts of the border, nor cross the international frontier, especially in the more vulnerable Punjab.[24] The rationale for this belief was that the lines separating the two portions of Kashmir and the international border dividing Pakistan and India in the Punjab were different in their legal character and that the latter was inviolable even if the former was violated. Kashmir being a disputed territory, a military initiative there would not be tantamount to an attack on India. In this perspective, an intrusion of guerrillas into the Kashmir Valley from Azad Kashmir would remain distinct from any action that India might undertake in retaliation along the mutually accepted international border.[25] The leadership did not take seriously Prime Minister Shastri's warning that India would be compelled to cross the international border if Kashmir was attacked.[26] When the war escalated, the Indian forces, according to a pre-declared strategy, crossed the international border in Punjab with the objective of severing the main Grand Trunk Road behind the border city of Lahore, which came as a surprise to Pakistani commanders.[27]

The war was a classic example of the initiator pursuing a limited aims strategy. In launching the operation, Pakistan's major aim was to achieve territorial and political objectives in a short and swift, fait accompli operation.[28] The Pakistani military strategy was based on the expectation of successfully waging a short war: a "fast moving and hard-hitting operation to stun and paralyze the much larger Indian armed forces" before they could respond. The military leadership feared that if the war slid into a prolonged conflict, it would be to the benefit of India. Therefore, an important basis of the operation was to deny India the advantage of time.[29] Limited war calculations were also a function of the US control over the supply of spare parts for the advanced weaponry that it had supplied and that those supplies would last for only three weeks of fighting, unless Washington decided to accelerate the shipments.[30] The military leadership calculated that a "big push" with the available weapons and spare parts would provide Pakistan control over some portions of Jammu and Kashmir which would strengthen its negotiating position. The United Nations as well as the great powers might intervene in support of the Pakistani position following a fait accompli operation.[31]

The Indian military behavior during past conflicts provided an important rationale for the assumption that the defender's response would be limited and defensive in character this time too. The lessons that Pakistan learned from the Rann of Kutch skirmishes of April 1965 reinforced the leadership's expectation that the Indians would not engage in a prolonged war, nor would they escalate the conflict to the internationally accepted border.[32] In that battle, which lasted from April 9 to April 29, Pakistani forces managed to outmaneuver Indian troops at several points and achieve limited tactical gains. Pakistan also had some successes in employing its newly acquired American weapons against the numerically superior opponent. This battle – involving artillery, armor, and infantry – was considered as a test of India's will and determination to resist quick attacks. The Indian tactical retreat was followed by an agreement to leave the dispute to international arbitration which surprised the Pakistani leaders as India had always opposed arbitration in Kashmir. From the outcome of this conflict, the military regime learned the lesson that with a strong show of force, limited to certain areas, the Indians would allow international arbitration in Kashmir too. Such arbitration would most likely be favorable to Pakistan, or would at least alter in some way the territorial status quo which had remained advantageous to India since 1947.[33]

The military success in Kutch, in the words of former Pakistani Air Force chief, Asghar Khan, bolstered President Ayub Khan's rising faith in the Pakistani Army's inherent strength. It increased the army leadership's morale and helped to create a belief that the Pakistani forces were superior to their Indian counterparts.[34] These operations also provided a good testing ground for Pakistan's weapon systems, newly acquired from the US, such as Patton tanks and F-104 Starfighter aircraft. There were no reprisals from Washington, although the armaments were supplied under explicit conditions that they be used only to resist possible aggression by Communist forces from the northwest.[35] The Pakistani leadership also had the experience of fighting a limited war in 1947–48 in the first major flare-up between the two countries. The Indian forces did not escalate the war into Punjab even when they had to wage a difficult campaign to keep up their supply lines to Kashmir.[36] Thus the most important lesson that was learned from the Indian response in the Kutch battles and in the 1947–48 Kashmir War was that India would not escalate the conflict beyond the immediate area of confrontation to other parts of the border. Additionally, the failure of India in the war with China in 1962 confirmed the Pakistani leadership's lack of esteem for India which many started to view as a "paper tiger."[37] Some members of the military leadership also believed that Pakistan could choose the battlefield as well as the timing of various offensive operations.[38] In addition, there was a general expectation that the Pakistani soldiers were better fighters than their Indian counterparts and they would therefore be able to achieve definite results in a controlled, intense battle.[39]

Changing military doctrine: dominance of offense

In 1965, the confidence in Pakistan's military prowess was reflected in the army's new tactical and doctrinal approaches. In tactics, by 1965 the Pakistani military leadership had emphasized new methods that would raise the combat efficiency of the troops, and techniques that would "relegate numbers to a secondary position." The most prominent characteristic of the new tactical concept was the use of a limited number of troops for ground-holding purposes so that maximum effort could be devoted to offensive and counter-offensive operations. In order to achieve optimal use of limited resources, emphasis was given to mobility and fire power.[40] With the arrival of new and high-quality weapons in the early 1960s, Pakistan's military doctrine underwent changes. The new doctrine was based on the idea of "bold and vigorous offensive-defense". Prior to the acquisition of these weapons, the Pakistani doctrine was primarily "defensive-offense," in which the emphasis was placed on deploying one-third of the forces for offensive or counter-offensive purposes, while keeping the remaining two-thirds for holding the ground in defensive positions. The new "offensive-defense" doctrine dovetailed the deployment of one third of the forces on the ground for defensive purposes while keeping two-thirds for offensive action.[41]

The offensive operations were to be greatly strengthened by the employment of high-quality artillery in concentrated fire by "a large number of mixed calibers."[42] The doctrine of "offensive-defense" envisaged taking the initiative in an acute crisis and engaging in a short, sharp war that would achieve limited military and political results. Such a doctrine also presupposed "the availability of high performance armor and aircraft and superior generalship"; two key factors that could somewhat offset India's overall numerical superiority.[43] Although doctrinal, strategic, and tactical changes had been slowly incorporated since late 1950s, their full impact was felt only when the Pakistani Army tested these concepts in the Rann of Kutch operations of April 1965. The offense-dominant doctrine was also based on a conviction that Pakistan enjoyed certain tactical advantages over India in the Kashmir sector. Given the rugged nature of the terrain and short communication lines – both favorable to Pakistan - a quick and limited operation from the West would yield substantial results if Pakistan attacked first. The Indian military traditionally had been uncomfortable in confronting the Pakistani forces in Kashmir due to these reasons. The Pakistani leadership was well aware of the Indian uneasiness which seemed to have had its effect in reinforcing their conviction that a quick victory was possible in a short war.[44]

Politically too, the Pakistani posture began to change with the death of the Indian leader Jawaharlal Nehru in 1964. The new "leaning on India" policy emphasized aggressive patrolling on the border and strong international pressure to gain control over Kashmir with the support of Pakistan's great power ally, China.[45] The new Indian leader, Lal Bahadur Shastri was considered weak and therefore an easy target for military pressure. The expectation was that the Shastri Government would not risk a wider war beyond Kashmir.[46] Taking the military initiative was also considered an important part of the strategy to gain international attention for Pakistan's cause and to solidify Pakistan's ties with other Islamic countries and China in support of its struggle with India.[47]

Offensive capability in 1965

The strategic and doctrinal changes did not occur without parallel improvements in Pakistan's military position. During the first half of the 1960s, Pakistan's offensive capability had substantially increased due to arms aid from the US. What influence did the arms acquisitions have on Rawalpindi's calculations and its decision to launch an offensive in Kashmir? It may be argued that the possession of new weapons played a significant role in the leadership's timing of the offensive. Pakistani analysts generally agree that the arrival of new weapons gave the army a major incentive to take military action in 1965.[48] In the leadership's assessment, Pakistan had a short-term qualitative edge for a limited offensive operation. The Pakistani military had recognized the 3:1 to 3:2 quantitative superiority that India held in Kashmir. At the same time, it was confident of a limited qualitative advantage in its possession of 200 M-47/48 Patton tanks, twelve high performance F-104A Starfighter and F-86 Sabre aircraft, and twelve T-33 jet trainers, although India had more aircraft in its arsenal. Moreover, several of the Sabres were equipped with state of the art Sidewinder air-to-air missiles.[49]

President Ayub Khan and his key advisors knew that the Indian window of vulnerability was fast closing with its five-year defense modernization program gathering momentum and its acquisition of large quantities of weapon systems from the USSR, the US, and the

UK. Whatever short-run advantage in certain categories of offensive weapons Pakistan held would be offset if it waited too long. Moreover, the Indians were yet to fully integrate their newly acquired Soviet MiG-21 aircraft into service. The Pakistani decision-makers thought they had a short-run qualitative edge in armor, artillery, and aircraft, which would have disappeared in a year or two. The incentive to use the limited advantage for coercive bargaining when it would have made a difference was greater during this period. If they lost the window of opportunity, they feared the Kashmir issue would be frozen for ever.[50] Foreign Minister Bhutto confirmed these calculations by stating that Pakistan had to act in 1965 because the "ordnance factories which India had established had not gone into full production and once they did, India would have been too strong to be beaten." In his words:

> There was a time when militarily, in terms of the big push, in terms of armour, we were superior to India because of the military assistance we were getting and that was the position up to 1965. Now, the Kashmir dispute was not being resolved peacefully and we had this military advantage, we were getting blamed for it. So it would, as a patriotic prudence, be better to say, all right, let us finish this problem and come to terms, and come to a settlement.[51]

Both Bhutto and the President, in several statements prior to the war, had expressed their unhappiness with the Indian buildup. Although the chief rationale for the Indian arms acquisition was to compensate for its failure in the 1962 war with China, to Ayub Khan, the increased capability would eventually be used against Pakistan. In his contention, once India settled its dispute with China, it might well turn its newly acquired capability against Pakistan when an opportune moment arrived.[52] India need not engage in a direct military assault on his country; all that was needed to humiliate Pakistan was "simply to possess a greatly superior military force and threaten, bully, and tease the vulnerable halves of Pakistan in order to neutralize and isolate the country and turn it into a satellite of India."[53] The Ayub regime felt that once the Indian modernization program was completed, the military balance on the sub-continent would alter "drastically" and "irrevocably" in India's favor and that it would strengthen the Indian intransigence and resolve not to settle the outstanding territorial disputes with Pakistan.[54]

Bhutto echoed Ayub Khan's views in several of his statements before the war. In his view, the rearmament program would allow India: "To be able to dictate to a neighboring country from a position of strength ... Time is running out. With the passage of time, as the military and economic strength of India increases, the possibilities of its agreeing to a peaceful and reasonable settlement of our outstanding disputes with it are correspondingly reduced."[55]

Following its defeat in the 1962 war with China, India had launched a five-year modernization program, starting from April 1964. The plan proposed the raising of an 825,000-strong army under twenty-one divisions, with substantial modernization of equipment, the creation of a forty-five-squadron air force, and the establishment of a major indigenous arms-building capability. The total expenditure for this program was about Rs. 5000 crores (over one billion US dollars). The program had also envisioned the construction and improvement of communication facilities in the border areas.[56] By 1963–64, the Indian defense expenditure had risen from the 1960–61 level of 2.1 per cent of the GNP to 4.5 percent. In real terms, this was from Rs. 312 crores ($65 million) to Rs. 816 crores ($170 million). This was a major increase considering that during the period between 1951–52 and 1961–62, the Indian defense budget never surpassed 2 percent of the GNP.[57] Although much of this spending was for raising ten mountain divisions to be deployed on the China border, for Pakistani leaders the increase represented a long-term threat. They believed that the capability could increase the Indian intransigence on Kashmir and strengthen its offensive capability, allowing New Delhi to take independent action in the territory.

Some Pakistani officials argued that the Indian buildup would give it an 8:1 numerical superiority, as opposed to the previous 5:1 overall superiority. According to observers, once the buildup was complete, India might have had 6:1 superiority, although a good portion of the forces would still have been pinned down on its border with China.[58] Therefore, in some respects the Pakistani plans were based on a partially preventive motivation; i.e., prevent the adversary from emerging as a well-armed military power and thereby perpetuate the status quo.[59] Offense dominance was thus a critical factor in explaining Pakistan's choice for war in 1965. This case illustrates that a challenger who is weaker in overall power capability could exploit its short-term offensive advantage in a war fought for limited objectives. The Pakistani leaders were under time pressure to make use of their short-run and limited offensive advantage and their choice for war was largely a function of this perception.

Changing alliance configurations

In addition to changes in the military balance between the antagonists, what alterations occurred in Pakistan's alliance relationship before September 1965 that might have had an impact on its war calculations?

The most prominent shift in this respect was the strengthening of relations between China and Pakistan. By 1963, the Sino-Pakistani relations had altered dramatically from normal neighborly ties to a tacit alliance. High-level official visits were followed by agreements to open air traffic between the two nations, despite strong opposition from the US. These agreements were matched by official statements that clearly indicated the conclusion of a strategic alignment of these two Asian neighbors. The alliance relationship became more apparent in June 1963 when Premier Zhou En-lai openly declared that China would defend Pakistan throughout the world.[60]

Although in the early 1960s China had put out feelers for strengthening friendship with Pakistan, the Pakistani leaders were reluctant to commit themselves because of the fear that the US would oppose such a relationship.[61] But by 1963, this fear had largely evaporated, with the development of new strains in US–Pakistan relations. The increasing rapprochement between Pakistan and China was manifested in the border agreement they signed in March 1964 which removed all the existing territorial disputes between the two countries.[62] During negotiations for this agreement, the Chinese leaders began to openly endorse the Pakistani position that the Kashmir problem should be resolved in accordance with the wishes of the people of the territory.[63] In February 1964, Premier Zhou En-lai and Foreign Minister Chen Yi visited Pakistan and made statements that clearly deviated from the earlier Chinese position of neutrality on the Kashmir dispute to one more favorable to Pakistan, i.e., supporting the demand for a plebiscite in the state.[64] Even before Premier Zhou En-lai's visit, on July 17, 1963, Foreign Minister Bhutto made a statement before the Pakistan National Assembly that an attack on Pakistan by India "would no longer confine the stakes to the independence and territorial integrity of Pakistan." It would also "involve the security and territorial integrity of the largest state in Asia."[65] Bhutto's declaration suggested that he had received assurances that should Pakistan be attacked by or become involved in a war with India, it would receive China's diplomatic and material support. An opportunity to test the Chinese support came during the Rann of Kutch skirmishes in April 1965 when China declared total support to the Pakistani position, while stepping up its criticism of India. This strengthened Bhutto and his supporters' conviction that the Chinese leadership would indeed stand by Pakistan in its next war with India.[66] Anticipation of Chinese defensive support was thus a crucial factor in the Pakistani calculations while launching the offensive as the relations between the two countries "were at its best."[67]

By 1965, the positions of the super powers vis-à-vis the sub-continent also underwent changes. Although the Soviets had supported India on Kashmir at the UN, by early 1965, they seemed to have shifted to a neutral stance toward the dispute. President Ayub Khan had visited Moscow in April 1965, a trip largely resulting from the improving Soviet–Pakistan relations. During the Rann of Kutch operations, the USSR took a less partisan position; thereby signalling neutrality in the event of a major war breaking out between India and Pakistan.[68] Bhutto's personal contacts in Moscow convinced him that if the US did not provide assistance to Pakistan, the Soviet Union would remain neutral in a prospective war.[69] The Pakistani leadership thus believed that the USSR would not get involved in a military conflict on the sub-continent in India's favor.[70] During the UN Security Council debates on Kashmir on February 3 and May 18, 1964, the Soviets changed their position on the dispute from unqualified support in favor of India (as was evident in their veto of the resolution on Kashmir in 1962) to a neutral position. This was evident in the Soviet statement that the dispute between India and Pakistan should be settled by the parties concerned and "exclusively by peaceful means."[71] The Soviets were clearly unhappy with the Indian acceptance of economic and military aid from the US and the UK and the subtle tilt in Indian foreign policy towards the West following the 1962 war with China.

This was also the period when the US was taking a low-key interest in the region, mainly because of its deeper involvement in Indo-china and strained relations with Pakistan. The Pakistani leaders were aware that the US attention was focused primarily on South East Asia due to its military involvement in Vietnam.[72] The US had remained neutral during the Kutch battles and thereby provided a signal to Pakistani leaders that a similar position could be expected in another limited war confined to Kashmir. The Pakistani leadership thus anticipated no major adverse reaction from the US if it launched an offensive on Kashmir.[73] On the other hand, the military leaders believed that the US would take the Pakistani case on Kashmir seriously if it proved successful in a military venture and might not even raise serious opposition if the offensive remained limited.[74]

Thus, in effect, the Pakistani leaders perceived the state of great power alliance configurations in 1965 as favorable to them. While Pakistan received strong backing from China, India lost its support from the USSR. The Pakistani leadership seemed to have concluded that the opportune time had arrived in terms of great power alliance support for its position and that war would not bring any major adverse reactions from the key international actors. The Pakistani case suggests that the alliance factor could be a key determinant in explaining asymmetric war initiations. A state weaker in overall power resources could still go to war with a stronger opponent if it anticipated defensive support from a great power ally. The shifts in alliance relationships, especially the position of great powers vis-à-vis the defender, could also be in the calculations of the weaker initiator as perceived lack of adverse reaction from the powerful actors in the international system could be conceived as a favorable condition for war initiation.

Shifts in decision-making structure

What effect did the changes in Pakistan's decision-making structure prior to 1965 exert on its foreign policy posture and the final decision to send troops into Kashmir? What was the army's role in Pakistan's decision-making structure in the early 1960s? The Pakistani Army from its inception in 1947 until the mid-1950s generally kept out of civilian politics. Because of serious instability in the civilian government system from 1954 till 1958, the army began to take a more aggressive posture in national politics. Although the army takeover of power by its chief, General Ayub Khan, was under the instruction of the civilian President Iskander Mirza, the ground for such an event was already laid by 1958.[75] Despite the militarization of Pakistan's internal politics, the key formulators of the 1965 war plans were civilians who held the support of important military officials. The death of Foreign Minister Mohammad Ali Bogra on January 23, 1963 and the elevation of Zulfikar Ali Bhutto to the post resulted in some dramatic changes in Pakistan's foreign-policy outlook. Bhutto proposed closer ties with China while moving away from Pakistan's somewhat intimate relationship with the US. The new Foreign Minister constantly urged Ayub Khan to take a hard-line position on Kashmir, partly to bolster the President's image at home and partly to fulfil his own political ambitions.[76] As a young, dynamic minister and Pakistan's leading spokesman on Kashmir at the UN, Bhutto had already acquired the confidence of Ayub Khan who regarded Bhutto as a "political troubleshooter," and "awarded him the Hilal-e-Pakistan, the country's highest civil award."[77]

In Bhutto's conception, any qualitative alterations in the status quo in Kashmir could be achieved only by "sustaining the tempo and degree of tension." Bhutto expressed his philosophy at a later date; "confrontation, confrontation," he claimed, was "the key to the India–Pakistan dispute."[78] In pursuit of an aggressive foreign-policy posture, Bhutto actively cultivated friendship with China.[79] While supporting the Chinese position on key world issues, Bhutto also stepped up his criticism of Western countries. In December 1964, when India applied Articles 356 and 357 of its Constitution to Kashmir, Bhutto reinforced his view that India did not want to give up control of the territory. He argued that diplomacy was not the answer to break the Indian intransigence on Kashmir. Unless India was pressured militarily, the Kashmir problem could never be resolved.[80]

Although Ayub Khan approved the military action, it was not he who prepared the plan to send guerrillas into Kashmir. He was a reluctant player and a risk-averse decision-maker. Ayub Khan was selected as the Commander-in-Chief in 1950 by the then Prime Minister Liaquat Ali Khan as a counterweight to the "older" officers who desired to renew the war with India in Kashmir. Ayub was expected to neutralize the alleged conspiracy that the generals were hatching.[81] Ayub Khan was also instrumental in disbanding the paramilitary forces attached to the Muslim League Party which were preparing for infiltration into Kashmir in support of the insurgent movement.[82] Kochanek argues that with the adoption of the Basic Democracy Constitution in 1962, the decision-making system in Pakistan was transformed into a "centralized military-bureaucratic system," under which the President delegated considerable freedom of action to his trusted ministers and bureaucrats while retaining his authority to decide disputes among them. Over time, Ayub's dependency on these selected people for decisions increased dramatically, although the cabinet as a whole was not given much power. Instead an informal inner cabinet decided most of the key policy questions. Ayub also attempted to keep the military generals in the background by offering patronage and special privileges.[83] However, a few generals in the military hierarchy still played crucial roles in policy decisions with regard to Kashmir.

It is in this context that a small group – comprising civilian and military officials – could influence Ayub Khan in taking the decision to launch military action against India in 1965. The key decision-making group consisted of Bhutto, Foreign Secretary Aziz Ahmed, Defense Secretary Nazir Ahmed, and General Akhtar Malik, the Commanding Officer for the Kashmir area. Bhutto's biographer cites an interview in which Bhutto revealed that none of the other ministers of Ayub Khan's cabinet was aware of the plan.[84] Knowledgeable Pakistani sources believe that the plan was first formulated by Bhutto and Akhtar Malik and then brought to the President for approval. They also kept the army chief, Mohammad Musa, out of the initial planning process.[85] However, Musa tacitly endorsed the plan, even though his General

Staff at the army headquarters and the Commander of the Special Services Group, Colonel Mehdi, attempted to impress upon him that the operation was a "non-starter."[86] In the assessment of the skeptics, sending commandos into Kashmir was doomed to fail because of Pakistan's disadvantages in terms of short preparation time, logistics, and follow-up support.[87]

While recommending military action, Bhutto wrote to Ayub: "If we wanted to pursue a policy of confrontation with India, time was running out. We had to act now or it will be too late."[88] Bhutto also convinced Ayub Khan that India would not react decisively to the guerrilla operation and that Pakistan's incursion into Azad Kashmir would not provoke New Delhi to extend the area of hostilities along the Indo-Pakistani border.[89] In his estimation, India was not in a position "to risk a general war of unlimited duration for the annihilation of Pakistan."[90] India's poor performance in the 1962 War with China, its tactical reverses during the Rann of Kutch operations, and the unrest in Kashmir were cited as factors that pointed to an opportune moment for Pakistan to launch an offensive.[91]

Thus shifts in internal power structure did indeed occur prior to the 1965 military operation. The significant change was in the elevation of Bhutto as a principal foreign and military policy maker, someone who had staunchly argued for a solution to the Kashmir dispute through the use of arms. Another internal factor, the condition of regime legitimacy, seems to have played a limited role in the Pakistani leadership's decision for war in 1965. President Ayub Khan's popularity among the rural population was reasonably high, largely due to his economic successes. This was evident in the presidential elections in January 1965 when Ayub Khan defeated his opponent, the Combined Opposition Party's Fatima Jinnah, with over 62 percent of the popular votes. In the ensuing National Assembly elections in March 1965, the President's Muslim League Party won 120 seats while the Combined Opposition Party won only 11.[92] Although he received strong support among the rural people, Ayub was determined to bolster his credibility among the masses and the intelligentsia by achieving dramatic changes in the Kashmir imbroglio. Ayub Khan was also committed to changing the perception in the army that he failed to take advantage of the 1962 opportunity to gain Kashmir militarily. Additionally, he wanted to alter the belief among a large section of the Pakistani public that their President was following the "dictates of his US advisers."[93]

Why no war in 1962?

The significance of the four factors of asymmetric war initiation in the Pakistani case may be determined by looking at the previous period when war was considered by the decision-makers. Available evidence suggests that during the Sino-Indian War in 1962, the Pakistani Army recommended military action in Kashmir by taking advantage of India's weaknesses that could arise from having to fight a two-front war.[94] Lack of support from Pakistan's closest ally, the US, seemed to be the major factor that prevented an offensive at that time. Ayub Khan was strongly urged by President Kennedy and the British Prime Minister, Macmillan not to take any action that would have further jeopardized the Indian defenses against the forward thrust of Chinese forces. These leaders urged the Pakistani President to observe a "freeze" on the Kashmir issue until the Sino-Indian conflict was resolved. Ayub himself and his then Foreign Minister Bogra admitted that the reason why Pakistan did not utilize the Indian vulnerability in 1962 was the American pressure against such a move.[95] The Pakistani leadership attempted to convince Kennedy to pressure India to settle the Kashmir dispute while the war was in progress. In a letter to Ayub Khan on October 28, 1962, Kennedy wrote that such an action would be a "totally wrong response to the threat facing India," and instead pressed Pakistan to offer a no-war pledge.[96] Kennedy stated that he was familiar with the history of the Kashmir dispute and that he did not make his suggestion lightly. India, he believed, would recognize the threat coming from the north as more dangerous than regional quarrels on the sub-continent. In these circumstances, a generous Pakistani move would "bring about a sensible resolution of Pakistan–India differences."[97]

With respect to capability, Pakistan was still receiving arms deliveries from the US.[98] Ayub Khan was also aware that the Indian Army, despite its preoccupations on the China border, still retained a large number of troops on its border with Pakistan and held a superiority of 3:2 over Pakistan in Kashmir.[99] In 1962, the existing capability was probably sufficient for Pakistan to engage in a limited war, confined to Kashmir, but the possibility of a larger conflict involving the Western powers was conceivable. Both the US and Britain were supporting India in its war against China. Within the domestic spectrum, there was no civilian or military leader of Bhutto's stature to persuade President Khan to agree to the army commanders' recommendation for military action. It may therefore be argued that Bhutto's arrival in 1963 as the new Foreign Minister resulted in some important changes

123

in the domestic balance of power and decision-making structure itself which were mirrored in the regime's strategic calculations.

Explaining the Pakistani decision in 1965

The major conclusion from the discussion on the Pakistani decision to launch the offensive in Kashmir is that by 1965 all the four conditions were present to some degree. The military and political calculations of the Pakistani leadership were based on a limited aims/fait accompli strategy. Pakistan had acquired sufficient short-term offensive capability for a short war, confined to Kashmir, and waiting would have been to its disadvantage. The alliance structure also shifted in its favor, largely as a result of China's alignment with Pakistan and the expected US neutrality in the conflict. The Pakistani leadership did not anticipate any major opposition from the US, as in 1962. In the domestic spectrum, the arrival of Bhutto into the decision-making structure made the most significant change in 1965, favoring war initiation by the weaker side. The deterrent threats that India made were not credible given India's past behavior in conflicts involving Pakistan and China. Its political steps in Kashmir increased the civil unrest there, providing Pakistan with another favorable condition for military operation.

To rate the relative importance of factors that favored war in 1965, the alliance relationship, the calculations based on a limited aims strategy, and the short-term advantages in quality weapons seem most critical. This is largely inferred from the fact that the Pakistani unwillingness to go to war in 1962 was the lack of an alliance support. The strategic calculations of Pakistan had changed dramatically by 1965, with the successes in the Rann of Kutch operations and the shaping up of the offense-dominant military doctrine by the army. In 1962, there was no guarantee that the war would remain limited or that Pakistan would achieve its strategic goals in a fait accompli operation. The acquisition of short-term offensive weapons seems to be the third crucial factor that played a key role in the calculations. The leadership feared that Pakistan's short-term advantage in armor and aircraft would soon be overtaken when India completed its defense modernization program. The changes in the decision-making structure could be considered the fourth factor. The rise in influence of Bhutto in the governing structure made a difference in choosing the war option in 1965, especially with his ability to convince Ayub Khan that the President's credibility and popularity would improve if Pakistan went on the offensive in Kashmir.

This case strongly supports the hypotheses on war initiation in asymmetric conflicts as presented in chapter 2. The weaker initiator expected a limited war fought by pursuing a limited aims/fait accompli strategy. To the initiator, a war confined to a small theater of operations, i.e. Kashmir, was expected to raise considerably the prospects for gaining control of the disputed territory. The expected great power alliance support and the inaction of the super powers were perceived as providing a favorable systemic condition. Changes in the short-term offensive capability and shifts in internal power structure were also crucial factors in this case of asymmetric war initiation on the Indian sub-continent.

7 THE EGYPTIAN OFFENSIVE IN THE SINAI, 1973

The Egyptian offensive in the Sinai in 1973 provides a test case of an asymmetric conflict in which the relatively weak side initiated the war.[1] The Egyptian leadership was well aware of the Israeli superiority in the air and on the ground – the two crucial determinants of military power in the Middle Eastern strategic context – when it undertook the attack.[2] In other indicators of military and economic capability, despite the disadvantage in terms of total population (Egypt's was ten times greater), Israel could still muster a larger pool of skilled human resources than Egypt.[3] As a result of the 1967 War, Israel assumed a better geo-strategic position than its Arab opponents, as it could deploy forces deep into Sinai. In terms of economic power, both states had a gross national product of approximately $7 billion, although the Israeli per capita income remained much higher than that of Egypt.

In more tangible indicators of military capability, Israel held advantages in air power, especially in deep penetration and reconnaissance capability, close air support, and tactical air-lift, as well as in armor and other ground weapons. The Israeli soldiers were better trained in the handling of sophisticated weaponry and were better marksmen than their Egyptian counterparts. The technological superiority of Israel in 1973 also enabled it to possess much greater firepower than Egypt. In 1972 these advantages were so vivid that one analyst observed: "Israel is in a more superior military position vis-à-vis Egypt than at any time in its short history."[4] By some accounts, Israel also possessed nuclear weapons capability in 1973 as an ultimate deterrent against a massive Arab attack.[5] Moreover, Israel had the full-fledged support of the US, which in reality was stronger than the corresponding backing that Egypt could have expected from the USSR. The Egyptians were well aware that the US would offer full diplomatic and military support in protection of the Jewish state if its existence was militarily threatened by the Arab countries.

In this chapter, I address the question of why President Sadat and his advisers committed their nation to the war path even when they knew Israel held a clear-cut military superiority and when the risks of a disastrous defeat at Israeli hands as in 1967 were present. An explanation based on political factors would contend that, by 1973, the preconditions for the war were in the making. During the post-1967 War years, the Middle East entered a period of missed opportunities, failed attempts at negotiation, and an unwillingness on the part of both the Arabs and the Israelis to give up their long-standing claims and political positions. While the Israeli strategy centered on preserving the favorable territorial status quo until full recognition came from the Arab states, Egypt and the other Arab countries refused to negotiate directly with Israel without it making a commitment to withdraw from the occupied territories. By the early 1970s, President Sadat and his close advisers had calculated that Israel was clearly content with the military and political situation that resulted from the 1967 War and was bent on creating a fait accompli vis-à-vis the occupied Egyptian territory. The Israeli construction of the Bar-Lev line along the Suez Canal was considered by the Egyptians as a sign of that country's determination to hold on to Sinai at any cost. Viewed from Cairo, that line represented the creation of an impregnable Israeli presence, intended to perpetuate the status quo along the Suez Canal. Egypt's major effort under President Nasser to alter the situation, the War of Attrition, failed in its key objective of destroying the Line even after heavy and continual artillery bombardment by its forces.[6]

It has been suggested that the failure of US Secretary of State, William Rogers' plan and Sadat's own peace initiative reinforced the Egyptian leader's belief that a military solution was the only realistic option left.[7] The Jarring mission's attempt to find a peaceful solution also failed, largely because its proposals were not acceptable to Israel. In those proposals, announced on February 8, 1971 by UN representative Ambassador Gunnar Jarring, both sides were asked to make simultaneous commitments in order to achieve a negotiated settlement. These proposals included the withdrawal of Israeli troops from the Sinai, subject to secure arrangements for freedom of navigation through the Suez Canal and the Strait of Tiran, and acceptance of Israel's right to exist in peace, within secure boundaries.[8] In the next round of diplomatic activity, secret parleys were held between President Sadat's National Security Adviser, Hafez Ismail and his US counterpart, Henry Kissinger in February and May 1973 which also did not produce any major changes in the diplomatic positions of the parties concerned.[9]

Yet, despite all these failures to find a negotiated settlement, it is still not clear why Egypt chose the war path in October 1973 as there was the possibility of a stronger Israeli military response than the one in 1967 which would have spelled disaster to Egypt's Army a second time in six years and imperilled the survival of Sadat's regime itself. For this study, the key questions are (1) what were the military and political calculations of the Egyptian leadership that made war in October 1973 a reality? and (2) what were the specific conditions that arose that contributed to the outbreak of war? As in other case studies, answers are sought to these questions by looking at four factors – the strategic calculations of the initiator, changes in alliance relationships, short-term offensive capability, and domestic power structures within the initiating state – and their presence or absence prior to the conflict in order to see whether they played separate or additive roles in the choice for war by the Egyptian decision-makers.

The Israeli strategy in 1973

A discussion of the defender's strategy is imperative as the strategic choices and options of the initiator depend greatly on its expectations regarding what the defender's strategy would be and what responses it might receive during and after the war. The Israeli strategy in 1973 was primarily one of deterrence by punishment, relying heavily on superior weapon systems for retaliatory threats. To its military planners, Israel's preponderance in the air and on the ground provided a credible deterrent against an attack from Egypt and other Arab states. The backbone of this deterrent capability was a superior air force, advanced intelligence and warning systems, quick and efficient mobilization, and an ability to counter-attack through the Golan Heights or by crossing the Suez Canal.[10]

As was evident in 1973, the Israeli strategy, based on retaliatory punishment did not prove sufficiently credible because the Egyptians were not anticipating winning a major war. To the Israelis, launching a war by the Arabs was not viewed as a "viable option, so long as victory was not assured."[11] They, like other stronger powers in asymmetric conflict situations, believed that an opponent would go to war only if it had the necessary military superiority to achieve its objectives. The Israeli leaders could not accept the possibility that Israel's superior air capability was not sufficient to deter an adversary that was highly dissatisfied with the status quo. Neutralizing the Israeli superiority in the theater for at least a short while was the key objective of the Egyptian strategy, a contingency that was not adequately considered by the Israeli leadership. The Egyptian planners correctly estimated that the SAM-2, SAM-3, and SAM-6 missiles and other anti-aircraft weapons would provide an effective umbrella over the Suez area, thus effectively scuttling the Israeli deterrent strategy based on superior air strength.[12] A major weakness of the Israeli grand strategy was its exclusive reliance on military means to resolve political disputes and an unwillingness to believe that the adversary was under intense pressure to do something drastic to alter the status quo. Subsequent Israeli governments could not conceive a long-term plan or a solution to the dispute with their Arab neighbors. The rejection of the Israeli proposals for direct negotiations by the Arabs was considered by the Golda Meir Government as a sign of intransigence on the part of the latter. In fact, it was received with relief by the Israeli leadership, as the continuation of the territorial and political status quo looked more attractive than any compromise settlement with the Arab states.[13]

Prime Minister Golda Meir and Defense Minister Moshe Dayan, strongly believed that the military and political status quo resulting from the 1967 War should continue for the foreseeable future. As Kissinger notes, to Meir the Israeli military position was impregnable and therefore there was no need for any major changes in its policy towards the Arab states. She also believed that the more time that Israel gained, the better would be its claim over the occupied territories.[14] Dayan was one of the key decision-makers who had convinced himself that the Arab states would not launch an attack because they could not achieve battlefield victory.[15] To the Israeli leaders, they offered the Arabs a reasonable political alternative when they invited the latter to conduct direct, face-to-face negotiations without preconditions.[16] Although the Israelis viewed this invitation as generous, for the Arabs it was tantamount to accepting "Israeli dictation from a position of strength."[17] Moreover, the Israeli leaders did not adequately recognize the windows of vulnerability in their strategic posture. After the War of Attrition, the Israeli planners felt vindicated by their strategic concept that emphasized a fortified defense system, manned by a limited number of regular forces, allowing the reserves time to mobilize in a contingency.[18] However, the Israeli Army, mostly a citizen force, needed time to mobilize against a concentrated surprise attack. Additionally, even when full mobilization could be achieved and the war turned in its favor, there was always the possibility of super power intervention for a cease-fire.[19]

Israel, like most other status quo powers, could not conceive the Arabs engaging in a limited war for limited gains. In the Israeli General Staff's estimates, the Egyptians would not be able to launch an offensive until the end of 1975.[20] In their assessment, until the Arabs attained sufficient air capability (such as medium-range fighter bombers), they

129

could not launch a successful attack on Israeli airfields, something viewed as a necessary condition for neutralizing the Israeli Air Force. As known to the Israeli leadership, the Egyptian strategic doctrine had also emphasized the possession of long-range bombers and missiles that could reach the population centers and airfields within Israel as a precondition for launching a major military offensive.[21] The Israelis also believed that Egypt would not go to war until it neutralized the Israeli edge in tanks and armored vehicles. However, the Egyptians countered the Israeli preponderance not by achieving superiority in tank-to-tank ratio, but by deploying anti-tank Saggar and Snapper missiles.[22]

Both Meir and Dayan, on various occasions, expressed confidence in the Israeli preponderance and the improbability of a credible military challenge from the Arabs. In Dayan's words: "The overall balance of forces is in our favor. Our military superiority is the dual outcome of Arab weakness and our strength. Their weakness stems from factors that will not change soon ... Low level of their soldiers' education, technology and integrity, disunion among the Arabs and the decisive weight of extreme nationalism."[23] This overconfidence in the Israeli capability to deter an attack and defend, if deterrence failed, did not take into account the impact of surprise in a weaker adversary's war strategy. Because of its superior capability, the Israeli leadership also expected that Israel would be the initiating state of any major war between them and the Arab states.[24] The Israeli belief that it possessed sufficient military capability to deter any attack from the Arab countries was shared by the US. For the US policy makers, Israel's superiority seemed unchallengeable and the Egyptians would surely lose should they risk an all-out attack. A limited war would also be thwarted by the Israelis, the result of which would be a further stalemate on the diplomatic front.[25]

Egypt's strategic assumptions in 1973

While Israel and the US were counting on Tel Aviv's preponderance in tangible military power as the primary means to deter an Arab attack, Egypt was planning a limited war for limited gains. The Egyptian leadership's strategic calculations were based on the notion that war could be used as a means to attract super power attention to the continuing, but stalemated dispute. They were convinced that the US would not take seriously the Egyptian demands for an Israeli withdrawal from Sinai without a bold show of force.[26] President Sadat and his advisers believed that although the Soviets could provide weaponry, only the Americans could exert pressure on Israel to come to the negotiating table. War was thus conceived as the best method to attract serious superpower attention to the dragging conflict, especially that of the US.[27]

The Egyptian leadership's strategic calculations in 1973 were based on limited war expectations, relying heavily on strategic and tactical surprise. Limited war characteristics were pronounced in the objectives, duration, size of the battlefield, and the number of troops deployed on the battlefront. On the Western front, the battlefield was confined to an area about twenty miles either side of the Suez Canal, while on the northern front to an even smaller area.[28] As for duration, the Egyptians thought they could fight a war lasting three to four weeks.[29] General Shazly, the Egyptian Chief of Staff in 1973, contends that the military planners adopted a limited aims strategy after they realized that it was impossible for Egypt to

> launch a large scale offensive to destroy the enemy concentrations in Sinai or to force the enemy withdrawal from Sinai and the Gaza Strip. All that our capabilities would permit was a limited attack. We could aim to cross the Canal, destroy the Bar Lev Line and then take up a defensive posture. Any further more aggressive moves would then need different equipment, different training, and a lot more preparation.[30]

Additionally, Egypt was convinced that the US would not allow its troops to enter Israel proper and thereby endanger the existence of the Jewish state.[31]

General Shazly cites three main considerations behind the adoption of a limited aims-fait accompli strategy. First, the Egyptians knew the weaknesses of their air force very well, and therefore, wanted to avoid direct air contact with the enemy. Second, the static SAM missiles could permit only a limited offensive operation as they would provide air cover only up to six to eight miles beyond the Canal. Finally, an entrenched defensive position by Egypt, eight miles east of the Canal, would force Israel to retaliate and this would eventually raise their casualty rate, a painful choice for the Israelis to make. In this way, Israel's will to fight could be reduced.[32] Adherence to the initially determined limited strategic goals was evident in the decision not to extend the area of operations, even after the attainment of preliminary tactical successes that were beyond what the Egyptian leadership had anticipated. Thus, although during the first five days of the war their forces had made crucial gains, the Egyptians decided not to advance further and capture the strategic Mitla and Giddi passes. Despite recommendations by Chief of Staff General Shazly to move quickly eastward and occupy those main passes, the leadership decided to assume a defensive posture after the initial victories. By October 10, the Egyptians had advanced nearly 80,000 troops and 700 tanks onto the east bank and had occupied an area just over ten miles deep along the Canal. But they assumed a static defensive position under the cover of anti-aircraft SAM missiles and long-range artillery. General Ismail believed that with the infantry and the anti-tank weapons at the front, and the armor behind them, the Egyptian forces would become "the rocks upon which the Israeli waves would be shattered."[33]

The 1967 Israeli successes against their forces had taught the Egyptian leadership a crucial lesson: surprise was an essential element in any military success in the Middle East and the initiator could gain significant tactical and strategic advantages if it undertook military action undetected by the adversary.[34] The Egyptians also knew very well that a forewarned Israeli Army would be highly difficult to confront. There was an expectation that by launching a surprise attack with the help of offensive weapons, certain strategic and tactical advantages could be achieved, which would be difficult to cancel out later on. Although they did not anticipate a decisive victory, the expectation was that whatever tactical gains Egypt would make in the limited war could be used for a politically favorable settlement in the future. The means to achieve these strategic objectives, according to President Sadat's spokesman, was the employment of "incremental" tactics, the purpose of which was to reach a "threshold in the theater" that would inflict enough pain on the adversary to make negotiations "inevitable."[35]

The Egyptian strategy in the War of Attrition (March 1969 to August 1970) was intended to inflict maximum casualties on the casualty-sensitive Israeli forces, and thereby raise the tempo of negotiations. The result of the implementation of this strategy was an increasingly combative Israel attacking more and more civilian targets inside Egypt. The war failed to produce any decisive results; the Egyptians could neither break the Bar-Lev Line, nor capture any portion of the territory they lost in the 1967 War. Once the Israeli Air Force began its offensive deep within Egypt proper, the Egyptians lost their offensive momentum and were forced to assume a defensive posture.[36] The learning experience from the War of Attrition had thus exerted a pronounced impact on Sadat and his advisers' strategic calculations in 1973. They realized that a prolonged attrition war would result in Israel retaliating massively without producing any political effects on the status quo. In order to counter the Israeli reaction to an attrition battle, Egypt would have to expend disproportionate military resources.[37] General Ismail opposed an attrition style military venture in 1973 on the ground that a small tactical operation would result in a big Israeli response which would have little political or military value. Therefore, Sadat and his military advisers agreed that Egypt's "blow to the enemy should be a large one, and we should be prepared for a major blow from the enemy in return."[38]

The 1973 Egyptian strategic calculations were based on the expectation that the duration and the level of conflict could be controlled and that even if the Israelis did not follow the Egyptian conception of war, a decisive defeat could be averted by the timely intervention of super powers. The Egyptians had signalled to the Europeans, the Americans, and to some extent the Israelis that they had neither the capability nor the intention to conduct "the last war."[39] Thus the Egyptian leaders calculated that the safety valves in the situation allowed them to end the war quickly if the tide turned against them, and therefore that an offensive confined to the Sinai carried with it only limited risks.[40]

The possible possession of nuclear weapons by Israel did not deter Egyptian decision-makers as they discounted their use in limited war situations. They were confident that Israel would not use those weapons of mass destruction against Egypt in order to protect the occupied Sinai. Unless the population centers in Tel Aviv were attacked and Israel proper was in great danger, the Egyptian leadership calculated there was little chance that Israel would unleash its nuclear weapons.[41] By confining the attack to the Sinai and not threatening Israel's pre-1967 border, the Egyptian leadership calculated that Israel could be prevented from introducing nuclear weapons during the war.[42] There was also an expectation that Israel had reached the limits of its ability to occupy and control the Egyptian territory and would confront serious tactical and strategic obstacles if and when it crossed the Suez Canal.[43]

The timing of the attack was also based on the consideration that the Israeli response would be limited since it would take them longer to mobilize, given that early October was the time of the Yom Kippur holidays and that the nation's attention would be greatly diverted by the run-up elections to the Knesset toward the end of the month.[44] Additionally, the Egyptian military planners knew that the main strength of the Israeli forces, the reserves, would take a few days to mobilize on a war footing. When these forces were mobilized, the Egyptian commando units, already positioned in strategic points in the Sinai, would prevent their advance. Major attacks were planned to be launched on the Israeli bases in Sinai, with the objective of destroying the command and control system and thereby taking the teeth

133

away from the Israeli counter-offensive.[45] The broader strategic plan included an attack along the whole length of the Suez Canal, forcing the Israelis to spread out their counter attacks. As the operation would be dispersed, the opponent would not be able to detect, at least for some time, the main concentrations of Egyptian forces and therefore would be forced to pause before launching the counter-attack.[46] The Chief of Staff, General Shazly had reassured President Sadat prior to the war that Israel would take at least two days to mobilize and that, at a minimum, tactical surprise was possible. However, in actual operations, Egypt could achieve both strategic and tactical surprise.[47]

The Egyptian military doctrine in 1973 was one of offensive–defensive, the main characteristic of which was to launch an offensive in first phase by crossing the Suez and defeating the Israeli forces in Western Sinai. As soon as the Egyptian forces reached the passes on the eastern side of the Canal, they would assume a defensive posture in order to create a fait accompli situation, by protecting the areas that they had occupied. The ensuing engagements with the Israeli forces were planned to be of a defensive nature.[48] The discussion thus far points to a conclusion that the strategic approach that Egypt adopted in 1973 greatly facilitated its engagement in a war with a militarily superior adversary. The limited aims/fait accompli strategy and the offensive–defensive doctrine precluded major strikes on Israel's pre-1967 border, thereby limiting the likely response from the defender and its super power ally. A quick land-grab strategy, it was expected, would invite super power intervention, which could in turn increase the chances of attaining a political settlement of the territorial conflict.

Weapons in Egyptian war plans

Besides the interaction resulting from incompatible strategies of the adversaries, what impact did weapons play in the Egyptian leadership's calculations in 1973? Did Egypt gain offensive and defensive capability prior to the war sufficient to affect Egypt's calculations on the timing and the type of operation that it could mount? Was the Egyptian leadership under time pressure to exploit its short-run capability which would have been lost had they waited too long? Evidence clearly puts the answers to the above questions in the affirmative. President Sadat, in his conversations with Mohamed Heikal on September 10, 1973, said that Egypt was having its last chance and that "if we did not seize it we should have finally missed the bus. For one thing, Egypt was not going to receive any more arms than it already had and was at the peak of its military capacity."[49] General Shazly contends that the Egyptian offensive planning had begun "as early as 1968; but it ran far ahead of our offensive capabilities. Over the next four years our capabilities steadily grew while our planning became more realistic. The gulf between them, enormous in 1968, shrank with each year's exercise until, in October 1973 when exercise became reality, planning and capability were one."[50]

A key aspect of the Egyptian strategic calculations was the reliance on defensive weapons for offensive purposes. The military planners hoped that the SAM-2, SAM-3, SAM-6, and SAM-7 missiles that they had acquired from the USSR would enable them to neutralize the Israeli air superiority and remove its threat of deep penetrating attacks.[51] These defensive missiles did indeed form a major part of the offensive capability that Egypt had acquired before the war. The SAM-2 missiles, with a range of twenty-five miles and the SAM-3, with a range of sixteen miles, were expected to provide sufficient air cover over the area of operation extending to the east bank. The SAM-6, with a range of twenty-two miles was more critical as, unlike the other SAMs, it was a mobile missile and more effective with its radar-lock capability. The SAM-7 mobile missile batteries could fire four to eight missiles at a time. These missiles were deployed with the objective of neutralizing the Israeli Air Force. Additionally, a number of anti-tank missiles were deployed in BRDM armored anti-tank missiles carriers.[52] Cairo had also received MiG-21 FMs and MiG-23s that could facilitate attack on selected Israeli targets. Another missile that played a key role in the Egyptian calculation was the Scud which it had received by April 1973. This missile, with a range of 180 miles, was considered a deterrent against Israel escalating the war to the Egyptian interior as it had the range to hit civilian targets within Israel. The importance of this missile in Egyptian war plans was evident in President Sadat's reported statement that his final decision to go to war was made in April 1973 when the first Scud missiles arrived in Egypt.[53]

Acquisition of short-run offensive and defensive capability thus contributed to the Egyptian leadership's decision to go on an offensive in October 1973. This capability allowed Egypt to engage in a short war, confined to the Sinai. In Cairo's calculations, the capability would help Egypt to achieve a territorial fait accompli, while imposing constraints on the defender to cancel out the possible gains that would accrue to it from the war. Egypt's previous failures to start an offensive as planned were partly due to limitations in offensive capability; by October 1973 that situation had changed as it received the offensive and defensive weapons necessary for launching a limited war.

Alliance commitment in Egypt's calculations

Other than changes in the acquisition of weapons for offensive capability, what was the impact of alliance relationships on Egypt's timing of attack? Was there a favorable alliance relationship with a great power in 1973 which allowed Egypt to carry out its limited war plans? Although Egypt's relations with the USSR had become strained following the expulsion of Soviet experts in July 1972, the ties between the two countries did not terminate at that point. To a great extent, the direct Soviet military presence until 1972 in Egypt worked as an impediment to Sadat and the military from making their own independent decisions regarding the military operation. The Soviets had their own global strategic objectives which did not necessarily coincide with the Egyptian desire to liberate the occupied territories by force.

With the exit of an active Soviet military presence from the Egyptian soil, Sadat and his military could devise their limited war strategy more effectively. Support from the Soviet Union, in the form of military supplies and political backing, was crucial to their strategic calculations. Had the Soviet military presence continued in Egypt beyond 1972, this strategy would probably have been vetoed by the Russian leadership. The expulsion allowed the Egyptians to make their own decisions regarding the war, while the Soviets increased their support to the military challenge by way of accelerated supply of promised weapons and by providing political backing. Heikal contends that after the expulsion, Moscow did in fact expedite the arms supply to a considerable extent. "It was as if the Russians were telling Sadat if he did not proceed to the battle he had been so long talking about he could not blame them for his failure."[54] The expulsion did help to alter Moscow's views of President Sadat. The Soviets seemed to have realized the strong determination that the Egyptian leader possessed in altering the status quo militarily. The change in Soviet tactics was all the more apparent after Egyptian Prime Minister Aziz Sidqi's visit to Moscow in October 1972. During that visit, the Soviets promised to expedite supply of the weapons that the Egyptians urgently needed to engage in a limited operation. Details of the arms package were agreed upon when the War Minister General Ahmad Ismail visited Moscow in February 1973. By March 1973, large-scale supply of Soviet arms to Egypt commenced. The most critical of these weapons for the Egyptian war calculations were the SAM-6s, SAM-7s, and the Saggar anti-Tank missiles.[55]

As early as April 1973, Sadat said the Russians were "providing us now with everything that is possible for them to supply. And I am now quite satisfied."[56] The supply level was such that Sadat told Heikal: "They are drowning me in new arms."[57] Heikal cites President Sadat as saying after the Soviet arms began to arrive: "It looks as if they want to push me into a battle."[58] To Sadat, with the arrival of new weapons, military action became a highly attractive option in order to unfreeze the status quo. It is clear from the Russian actions that they could no longer veto an Egyptian decision to wage a limited war. Supporting the Egyptian position appeared to be the best policy alternative in order to maintain their strategic position in the Middle East. The Egyptian expulsion seemed to have prompted the Soviets to treat the Arabs more seriously. They stopped their dismissal of Sadat's previous talks about the impending war as "bombast" and suspended their efforts to dissuade the Egyptian leader from taking the military course. The nature of the arms supply also changed as the intent at this point was not to gain immediate political influence but to demonstrate Russian goodwill to its most important ally in the Middle East.[59]

Moscow's concern regarding losing Egypt was that it had made its biggest global strategic investment outside of Eastern Europe in that country and that the Soviet military was especially interested in keeping Egypt as a strategic asset. The Soviet Army was concerned that Egypt's fiasco on the battlefield would be treated as tantamount to its own failure.[60] With the visit of Prime Minister Sidqi to Moscow in October 1972, Soviet–Egyptian relations were again on a normal course. The USSR promised Egypt one squadron each of MiG-23 and SU-20 aircraft which would be delivered before the end of 1973 and a brigade of Scud missiles with a range of 150 miles to be supplied by early 1973. General Shazly concluded that with the Egyptian premier's visit, "we have begun to reconstruct the crucial alliance."[61]

The strongest indication of Soviet support came a few days before the outbreak of war. In early October, President Sadat met with Soviet Ambassador to Cairo Vladimir Vinogradov and informed him that Egypt was going to move fast on the military front and wanted to convey this message to Brezhnev. On October 4 Brezhnev replied that the decision when to fight must be for Sadat alone to make and that the Soviet Union would give him the support of a friendly nation.[62] Sadat had also calculated that the Soviets had little choice other than to support Egypt in a war with Israel. Egypt was a major prize to leave given that a substitute springboard for Soviet presence in the Middle East was lacking. Sadat seemed to have felt the time pressure regarding this relationship in that the Soviets would soon become disinterested in a military solution to the stalemate. With the improving relations between the US and the USSR, it became apparent to the Egyptian decision-makers that time was not on their side.

The Egyptian leader was convinced that the Soviet Union, Egypt's most important ally in its conflict with Israel, was slowly getting into a détente relationship with the US. He told the Egyptian National Security Council that the "two super powers appeared to be reaching agreement on all subjects, including the Middle East, which made this the last chance for action."[63] Conferring with Heikal, President Sadat expressed the time pressure that he was experiencing as a result of the burgeoning super power détente. When Heikal said, "the détente will set conditions for the Middle East Problem instead of the Middle East problem setting conditions for détente," Sadat replied: "Maybe we will just be able to catch the last part of the tail of the détente."[64] During the Nixon–Brezhnev summit in May 1972, the super powers began to talk of joint efforts for a relaxation of military tensions in the Middle East. As Sadat commented: "It was a violent shock to us because we lagged at least 20 steps behind Israel and so military relaxation in this context could mean nothing but giving in to Israel."[65]

General Shazly acknowledges the crucial role that the Soviet support played in Egypt's strategic calculations in these words: "Without the help of the Soviet Union our battle would have been impossible ... No other country or group of countries simultaneously could and would have supplied Egypt with the arms in the profusion and sophistication needed to combat Israel ... The Soviet Union was, in my view, the best available ally for an Egypt bent upon liberating its lost territory."[66] Despite the support they extended to the Egyptian cause, it is not fully accurate to believe that the Russians were instrumental in Egypt's decision or its planning of the operations. The anticipated Russian support was indirect in nature, mostly in terms of military equipment, spare parts, and political and diplomatic support, and a last bastion of defensive support in case the war went beyond Egyptian strategic calculations.

Apart from the Soviet Union, Egypt also expected the US intervention to restrain Israel if the latter escalated the war beyond the theater of operations. In the Egyptian calculations, the US would not allow Israel to escalate the conflict beyond certain limits. President Sadat anticipated American mediation in order to get a cease-fire once his limited military objectives were achieved. This was evident in Sadat's approaches to Kissinger, through his National Security Advisor Hafez Ismail, to intervene when the tide of the war turned against Egypt.[67] Egypt was also assured of receiving political and economic support from other Arab states, especially Syria, which opened a second front, and Saudi Arabia, which employed oil as a weapon. In addition, Cairo expected diplomatic support from the non-aligned countries. Sadat expressed this assurance when he told Heikal: "From the international point of view, Egypt had all the backing which had ever been dreamed of – among the Arab nations, the non-aligned, at the UN and everywhere."[68]

On the eve of the war, the initiator was expecting diplomatic and military support from its super power ally, the Soviet Union. The anticipation was that the super powers, especially the USSR, would help prevent a massive retaliation by the defender and thus help limit the duration and intensity of the conflict. The anticipation of super power intervention in order to terminate the war before the defender could escalate it was thus a major factor in Egypt's decision for war in October 1973.

Domestic politics and war initiation: Egypt in 1973

Were changes in the external environment, resulting from new alliance configurations at the super power and at the regional level, parallelled by domestic changes within Egypt that might have had a bearing on the calculations of the Egyptian leadership? In this section, I explore the major changes on the internal front that might have influenced the decision to go to war in 1973. Two key questions in this context are: (1) did shifts in the decision-making structure prior to October 1973 result in the assumption of power by a group of decision-makers who considered war as the best policy to pursue, and what role did this decision-making group play in 1973? and, (2) was the Sadat regime under domestic pressure to engage in war to prop up its declining legitimacy?

Although the Egyptian system of decision-making has been called "president-dominant," it took several rounds of internal purges for Sadat to recruit a small group of people who concurred with him on the feasibility and necessity of a limited war. The Egyptian case amplifies the contention that the conflict among elite groups, and who emerges from it as dominant actors, can influence what military response a state may take against its adversary in an asymmetric conflict. In the Egyptian case, to a certain degree, the response to external pressures might have been influenced by the orientations and value structures of the President and the struggle between him and his rivals.[69] Although all Egyptian decision-makers agreed on the need for military initiative, they differed on the timing and the type of action. A few advocated a large-scale operation to regain the major passes in

Sinai, but wanted to wait until Egypt attained full-scale capability to deter an Israeli counter-offensive in the interior. On the other hand, Sadat and several of his confidants believed that a war of limited aims was the only feasible option for Egypt to undertake.

Opposition to the limited war plans was strongly expressed by the then War Minister, General Mohammed Sadek and Vice President, Abdel Kader Hassan at a meeting of the Armed Forces Supreme Council on October 24, 1982. They feared that a limited offensive might develop into a full-scale war. According to Hassan, Egypt might succeed in the first phase of the attack, but the Israelis would eventually place the Egyptian forces on the defensive, which in turn would give them a much stronger position than they enjoyed before. In his view, the Israelis would still be in control of Sharm-el-Sheikh and most of Sinai, and might even claim rights to those areas. Israel might also step up air raids against the unprotected interior parts of Egypt.[70]

General Sadek and a powerful group of military elite opposed Sadat's limited aims strategy, designed to seize a small strip of land on the east side of the Canal as a prelude to political negotiations. To them, an all or nothing strategy was more appropriate, but until Egypt was able to attain enough capability for a major war, military operations should be postponed.[71] To Sadek, war made sense only when Egypt had acquired sufficient offensive weapons, such as MiG-23s and long-range missiles, so that the outcome of the conflict would be guaranteed in Egypt's favor. In his view, a limited operation would not bring any political or military benefits to Egypt. Sinai would not be liberated and Egypt would endanger its strong defensive position on the banks of the Canal.[72] Sadek was more interested in Egypt pursuing a defensive and deterrent strategy as he believed that the Israelis could not be removed from Sinai by limited military pressures.[73]

Sadat opposed their views and dismissed both Sadek and Hassan from office. In addition, he removed Abdel Khabir, commander of the army's central district, who had expressed opposition to taking the risk of a limited war without full mobilization. The Egyptian leader also dismissed the Deputy Minister of War, the Commander of the Navy, and the Director of Intelligence, all of whom had previously expressed skepticism about the proposed limited war plans. With these dismissals and with the appointment of General Ahmad Ismail as the new War Minister, Sadat succeeded in suppressing all opposition to the war that he and his supporters were about to embark on. General Ismail was willing to initiate a war with Israel with whatever weapons that Egypt possessed at that time. The new group of decision-makers agreed on the basic premise of a limited operation for political goals and was prepared to take a "calculated risk."

Were there other direct internal bearings related to the legitimacy of his regime in Sadat's calculations while taking the decision to launch an offensive in October 1973? One may argue that although Sadat managed to remove the Ali Sabri group from power and consolidate his position as President, his legitimacy and popularity were at risk as he failed to deliver his promise to liberate Sinai that he had made during 1971, "the year of decision." The Sabri group's demise helped Sadat to consolidate his hold on the Army, while the military strengthened its position among competing structures in the political system.[74] Despite this victory over his opponents, it has been argued that Sadat's legitimacy was still in doubt, given the lack of a strong civilian political base. His power base was confined to a selected group of friends and sympathizers in the military. The highly centralized decision-making system consisted of an inner cabinet with a handful of army officers, a few technocrats, Mohamad Heikal, a Cairo journalist, and the "chiefs of the four major security organizations."[75] The lack of a strong civilian base and the fear that the declining support among the masses and the army might erode his position were evident in Sadat's calculations in 1973. To many analysts, the search for legitimacy was clearly evident in the regime's policies before and after the war.[76]

The failure to take military action in 1971 ("the year of decision") undermined Sadat's domestic credibility. In a memorandum sent to Sadat in April 1972, ten prominent Egyptian politicians and public figures warned that the continued Israeli occupation of Sinai and the Egyptian inaction had almost resulted in the collapse of the internal political structure. They wanted Sadat to liberate the occupied territories with Egyptian resources alone. Most importantly, the memorandum said: "The formation of the latest Ministry and the unrest among the students has aroused some doubt among the people about the ability of the regime to deal with the current situation."[77] Internal disorder was slowly spreading throughout Egypt. In January 1972, students at Cairo University demonstrated violently, demanding immediate military action, and in November 1972 there were mass riots. According to one study, by the Summer of 1973 the Egyptian leadership had staked its political future on a successful surprise attack in Sinai. "A failure to go to war in October would almost certainly have brought the overthrow – probably by military coup – of the regime."[78]

For too long, Egypt had had nearly one million soldiers dug-in ready to confront the Israelis in forward positions, which was taking a heavy toll on the army's morale. The dissatisfaction had spread to the ranks

141

of the military, especially among junior and middle-ranking officers. Sadat knew well that the support of the military elite was crucial to the survival of his rule, as without it his regime would have been vulnerable to challenges by its opponents.[79] In the past, Sadat had received support from the military, especially in his purging of the leftist Free Officer faction. Sadat's victory over the Sabri group was largely due to his ability to gain the support or neutrality of the military, despite the alignment of the then War Minister, Muhammed Fawzi with the Sabri group.[80]

The continued Israeli occupation of Sinai and the diplomatic stalemate cost Sadat a good deal of sympathy from the military. Militant officers in the middle and lower ranks wanted to engage in a war with Israel. The Hussein Mosque incident and the participation of young officers in the 1972 street demonstrations were indications that dissatisfaction was spreading to the armed forces. Sadat also had to confront an army leadership, especially, War Minister Sadek, Air Force Commander Baghdadi, and several other senior officers who were proposing an all-out attack, while opposing plans for limited military operations.[81] On the economic front, Sadat had plans to restructure the economic and industrial base of Egypt. This entailed moving away from Nasser's restrictive policies and launching an open-door economic policy. According to one Egyptian scholar, to accomplish that objective, he needed "unquestioned legitimacy" from the Egyptian people and war was considered as a means to achieve that.[82]

Despite all these internal factors that seemed to have exerted pressure on Sadat, the external factors appear to have been more significant in the Egyptian leadership's calculations in launching an offensive in 1973. Internal factors, however, formed a secondary source of pressure on the Egyptian leadership. This conclusion is derived from the fact that without major changes in offensive capability and the possibility for a successful limited war, Sadat would still not have been in a position to launch an offensive in October 1973. A comparison between 1971, the year in which he planned an attack, and 1973 will attempt to substantiate this conclusion.

1971; the year of decision: why no attack?

In several statements, Sadat had declared 1971 as his "year of decision" and had made serious preparations for a war with Israel.[83] In a popular rally on January 4, 1971, he had warned that unless some serious steps were taken towards peace and a timetable was worked out for the Israeli withdrawal, Egypt would not renew the cease-fire.[84] He feared that if the cease-fire was further extended, the line of control in Sinai would transform into a fait accompli, and later on into political frontiers similar to the armistice lines of 1948.[85] On June 5, the anniversary of the 1967 War, Sadat declared, "the battle will end one way or other in 1971."[86] On July 7, 1971, the Egyptian leader repeated that 1971 would not end without the war being decided; he would not reconcile with a no-war, no-peace situation and Egypt was prepared to sacrifice one million casualties for the recovery of the occupied territories.[87]

The important question for this study is why did Sadat and his decision-making group fail to launch an attack in 1971 as promised? Which of the four conditions for war initiation were present and which were absent during that period? Sadat himself had acknowledged that the main reason for him not undertaking a war in 1971 was the lack of capabilities sufficient to make any impact against the Israelis. The Soviet unwillingness to provide offensive weapons as well as defensive cover for offensive operations has been attributed as an important factor in the Egyptian leadership's decision not to launch an attack, despite strong determination to do so. The Soviets refused to deliver the military materials that Egypt needed. In Sadat's words, "That is how it was in 1971 – the year that I said would be decisive – they kept me from unleashing hostilities by a very simple means: they refrained from honoring the arms contracts that had been made."[88] The Minister of Defense, General Mohammed Sadek concurred with Sadat by contending that the major reason for Egypt not launching a war in 1971 or in 1972 was the Soviet refusal to provide offensive weapons. In May 1972, he stated that the Soviets were not providing sufficient weaponry to liberate Sinai. If Egypt launched an attack, it would be out of munitions in less than ten days.[89]

General Shazly reveals that he and General Sadek had prepared two plans in 1971: one code-named Operation 41, the other Operation High Minarets. The first had envisioned a limited offensive to be launched to seize key Sinai passes, thirty to forty miles east of the Canal, with Soviet assistance. The second plan was aimed at a less ambitious penetration of forces; five or six miles into the east, on Egypt's own initiative. The request for a long list of arms to the Soviets was intended to execute the Operation 41 plan. Although the Soviets promised some weapons during the visits of Sadat and Sadek to Moscow in October 1971, those weapons were not sufficient to launch an attack based on this plan. According to Shazly, despite the 100 MiG-21 FMs and the brigade of mobile SAM-6s the Soviets promised, it was still not sufficient to repel Israeli air strikes if the Egyptian forces advanced eastward beyond the umbrella of its static SAMs.[90] Clearly, the Egyptian leadership had to abandon the proposed operation in 1971.

Apart from the refusal to supply offensive weapons required for military operations, the Soviets also opposed the idea of an Egyptian offensive as they were eager that Egypt would not fight another losing war. The Soviet leaders feared that if the Egyptians lost the next round too, the USSR would lose its credibility both as a super power and as a weapons supplier. The Egyptian failure to use Soviet weapons properly, both during the 1967 War and the War of Attrition, confirmed the USSR's fears that the Egyptians were incapable of employing these systems in the right manner. Therefore, for over two years they kept the Egyptians under suspension, by promising offensive weapons but by supplying only defensive systems. After the Israelis began to raid deep inside the Egyptian interior and jam the latter's SAM-2 missiles with their newly acquired electronic counter-measures (ECMs), "the Soviets were even less anxious to risk their most advanced armaments on Egyptian soil."[91] Moreover, in 1971, the Soviets opposed Egypt taking the offensive and refused to discuss operational plans with the Egyptians.[92]

Explaining the war in 1973

Although all the four factors seem to have been present in 1973, in their relative importance the strategic calculations, offensive capability, and alliance support appear to be more influential than domestic pressures or regime insecurity. Since its defeat in the 1967 War, the Egyptian strategy had been evolving from attrition to limited aims. Egypt's failure to achieve its goals in the War of Attrition prompted President Sadat and his close military commanders to devise a new strategy based on limited objectives. Thus by 1971, the new strategic conception had almost fully evolved, yet the Soviet opposition prevented the operations. By 1973, however, the Soviets had changed their policy and were willing to provide sufficient offensive and defensive systems for a limited war fought for limited political and military objectives. The expulsion of Soviet experts strengthened Sadat's ability to make his own decisions as the Soviets could no longer veto his war plans. Henceforth, they were rather persuaded to support the Egyptians in their military initiative. Although the threat to the legitimacy of the regime appears to be significant in Sadat's calculations, it does not seem as critical as the external conditions resulting from changes in alliance support and acquisition of offensive capability. Sadat was still popular among the Egyptian masses, although disaffection was slowly spreading to the elite and the armed forces. It seems that the Egyptian leader was under time pressure for domestic reasons to do something as drastic as going to war to break the stalemate resulting from the continued occupation of Egyptian territory by Israel. This could have been a secondary consideration in his choice for war in 1973.

The main conclusion of this chapter is that the decision to launch an offensive in the Sinai in 1973 was greatly influenced by the expectation of the Egyptian leadership that it was possible to wage a limited, fait accompli war, confined to the occupied territories, for political and limited strategic objectives. The weapons that Egypt acquired by 1973 permitted such a war, while the expectation of support from the USSR and Arab countries made its success a probability in Egypt's estimation. This case strongly confirms three of the hypotheses presented in chapter 2 while modestly confirming the fourth one. It shows that a weaker challenger's expectations regarding a successful limited aims/fait accompli strategy could be a determining factor in explaining asymmetric war initiations. In the Egyptian case, the short-term offensive capability that Cairo acquired by October 1973 and the changes in Soviet position regarding a limited war acted as two critical factors contributing to the choice for war. The shifts in domestic power structure and the emergence of a militaristic group of decision-makers also occurred in this case, although President Sadat still had the final say.

The strategic choices of the stronger power, i.e. Israel, helped to strengthen Egypt's resolve to go to war. The Israeli leaders did not anticipate a limited war for limited objectives to be launched by a weaker adversary. While deterrent threats were made, few precautionary measures were taken against a surprise offensive. Politically, a policy of reassurance would have probably dampened the Egyptian resolve to go to war. However, neither active deterrence nor credible reassurance characterized the Israeli strategy in 1973. The Israeli failure to deter Egypt also shows that a determined challenger can transcend a stronger defender's deterrent threat by opting for a limited aims/fait accompli strategy.

8 THE ARGENTINE INVASION OF THE FALKLANDS/MALVINAS, 1982

The South Atlantic War of 1982, sparked off by the Argentine invasion of the Falklands (Malvinas) Islands, is an asymmetric conflict in which the weaker side initiated the war. The balance of capabilities in 1982 was clearly in favor of Britain, the defending state in this conflict. In manpower alone, Britain held a major advantage, as its fighting forces comprised professionally trained volunteer soldiers, while that of Argentina's consisted of conscripts, who were mostly below twenty years of age.[1] Britain's military expenditure was six times higher than Argentina's, allowing it to have superiority in firepower, technology, and training.[2] The Argentine military's heavy involvement in internal politics and the intra-service rivalries resulted in the development of a force structure less cohesive than that of Britain. Several Argentine commanders were political appointees whose promotion to higher echelons was not always based on their professional competence. Although prior to the arrival of the British task force in the South Atlantic, Argentina held limited tactical advantages in the theater due to its proximity to the Islands, this proved to be of short-term value as Buenos Aires lacked comparable landing facilities, such as aircraft carriers, that Britain possessed. Being over 400 miles away from the mainland, the Islands were at the outer limits of the combat radii of the Argentine aircraft that had to fly from home ports for military missions, thereby greatly diminishing their weapon-carrying capability.[3] The sole aircraft carrier, *Vienticino de Mayo* was stationed in home waters most of the time which curtailed the effectiveness of Argentina's bombing ability and capability to counter the British naval forces seriously.[4]

Argentina's disadvantages were all the more glaring in electronic warfare. Unlike Britain, Argentina possessed no electronic countermeasures (ECMs) or other sophisticated defensive capabilities. The British had the advantage of having some of the most modern surface-to-air missiles, fire control systems, and the carrier-based Harrier aircraft. These systems enabled Britain to provide defense in-depth to its naval fleet during its operations in the South Atlantic.[5] Argentina's inferiority in intelligence and tactical warning capabilities also acted as a constraint on its forces' ability to conduct effective offensive and defensive operations. Britain had such an overwhelming advantage in this respect that all major missions of the Argentine forces were known to its military command in advance. Additionally, because of lack of sufficient number of helicopters, Argentina could not provide adequate logistical supplies to the troops in the Malvinas.[6] Despite these constraints, the Argentine leadership decided to go forward with the invasion plan which its navy had been developing for several years. In this chapter, I address the question of why the Argentine Junta opted in March 1982 to engage in a conflict with a more powerful adversary which was also a nuclear-weapon state even though its members were fairly well aware of Argentina's vulnerabilities vis-à-vis Britain.

The dispute over the control of the Falklands dates back to 1833 when Britain occupied the islands, unseating the Spanish settlers and thereby ending the control of the United Provinces of Rio de La Plata (which later became Argentina) over them. Generations of Argentines have maintained that the British annexation was an illegal act that was never recognized by the South American nation. In the post-World War II decolonization era, the Argentine claim received special international attention, especially in 1964, when the dispute was taken up by the United Nations Sub-Committee on Small Territories.[7] Argentina and Britain held ambassadorial-level talks in 1966, with London attempting to limit the nature of the dispute and Buenos Aires demanding return of sovereignty. There were some hopeful signs of a peaceful settlement as during the initial negotiations Britain promised eventual ceding of sovereignty. But by 1968, the lobbying group for the Islanders in the British Parliament, the Falklands Islands Committee, became a critical factor as it began to obstruct the progress toward a settlement that would give sovereignty to Argentina.[8]

However, negotiations after 1969 led to the Communications Agreement of July 1971, following which air and sea links between the Islands and Argentina were inaugurated. This agreement also permitted the Falkanders freedom to travel in Argentina.[9] In March 1977, Britain resumed negotiations with Argentina and conveyed its willingness to cede sovereignty, provided the Islanders' (Kelpers') interests were safeguarded. These negotiations reached a new turning point, with the British Junior Minister of Foreign Affairs, Nicholas Ridley, proposing leaseback of the Islands to Argentina. However, it was received with hostility by the British Parliament and the Islanders alike. When Ridley visited the Islands in November 1980, he was forced to accept participation of representatives of the Islanders in all future negotiations and to freeze the sovereignty question, which further complicated an already entangled negotiation process.[10] In February 1981, a new round of negotiations was conducted in New York, and at this time, representatives from the Islands took part in the talks. The last round of negotiations, held in New York in February 1982, also failed to produce any tangible results as the Argentine regime could not accept the working agreement reached between its representative, Enrique Ros and his British counterpart, Richard Luce. At that meeting, both sides had agreed to establish a permanent negotiating commission to "accelerate progress towards a peaceful and comprehensive solution of the dispute."[11]

Despite these failures in finding a negotiated settlement, it is not apparent why military action became the dominant strategic option for Argentina in 1982. Moreover, negotiations between Argentina and Britain had been continuing for years without producing any tangible results. Several times in the past the Argentine military, especially the navy, had made preparations for the occupation of the Islands. What were the specific pressures that the Argentine leadership experienced in March 1982, making war with a militarily superior adversary a reality? What specific external and internal factors arose by this time that might have facilitated a surprise Argentine invasion of the Islands? I seek an answer to these questions by looking at the strategic calculations of the defender and the initiator, and changes pertaining to the initiator's alliance relationships, capability, and domestic power structure.

The British strategy prior to the war

To begin with, what was the British strategy on the eve of the war vis-à-vis Argentina and for the protection of the Islands? While the Falklands/Malvinas issue received top billing in the Argentine leadership's foreign policy priorities, there is general consensus among scholars that, before 1982, it attracted limited interest from successive British governments. Many times these governments gave contradictory signals to Argentina, one of which was a willingness to discuss the sovereignty issue, but without providing a realistic timetable or a plan on how to implement the vague promises. Britain also did not unequivocally commit its forces to protect the Islands against a possible invasion by a disgruntled Argentine regime. Prior to 1982, the British decision-makers generally believed that the Argentines would not use force to recover the Islands. The prolonged nature of the dispute, the previous false alarms, Argentina's tough posture in negotiations, and the constant rhetoric from Buenos Aires, all provided evidence to Britain that this time too an outright invasion was unlikely. The British Foreign Office thought that even if Argentina resorted to force, it would be by gradual escalation, as opposed to a quick fait accompli action.[12] To the British, a country would go to war only when sufficient military forces were available to it to achieve its politico-military objectives.[13] Similar to other stronger powers in asymmetric conflict situations, the British leaders also seemed to be unable to visualize how a poorly equipped Argentina would embark on a military operation which it was likely to lose.

The British strategy towards the South Atlantic thus remained generally ambivalent prior to the war. At times, it showed elements of a lack of determination to protect the Islands while at the same time not offering the Argentines any serious propositions to resolve the conflict. As with most status quo powers, Britain followed a strategy of prolonging the negotiations without actually making any major concessions to the challenger. Various British governments had conducted negotiations with their Argentine counterparts and had signalled the possibility of ceding control of the Islands, but the question of sovereignty was eventually withdrawn from the negotiating table. For instance, in 1977, the Labour Government had conveyed to Argentina that sovereignty was a topic for negotiation and that transfer of sovereignty with leaseback option was its preferred policy position.[14]

The ambivalence of the policies being pursued by different British governments was due largely to internal reasons. These governments feared loss of public support if they complied fully with the Argentine demands. Opposition in Parliament was strong, especially after the pressure group, the Falklands Islands Committee, began its active campaign in London. At the same time, the British leaders wanted to continue their contacts with the Argentines as they feared the latter breaking off the Communications Agreement of 1971 would force Britain to make huge investments for the resumption of those services which Argentina was providing to the Islanders. Budgetary constraints did not allow Britain to make major investments in a region which many considered as peripheral to the country's interests, other than for emotional reasons.[15]

Even the most strident Conservative Government in recent British history viewed the Falklands as a matter of little importance, as evidenced in the Thatcher Government's decision to withdraw the only major British military presence, the ice-patrol ship, HMS *Endurance*, from the South Atlantic. As per the recommendations of the Defence

Review Committee, in June 1981 Britain decided to withdraw the icebreaker at the end of its 1981–82 tour. The decision was the result of budget cuts which generally affected non-NATO defense expenditures, of which the South Atlantic was considered of least importance and, therefore merited the saving of over two million pounds. This seemed to have signalled to Argentina Britain's waning commitment toward the South Atlantic region. Other steps, such as the refusal to grant full British citizenship to the Islanders in the British Nationality Bill and the proposals to close down the British Antarctic Survey Base at Grytviken in South Georgia, were also evidence of the declining British interest in the region.[16] The Thatcher Government's approach to the Falklands question was one of maintaining the status quo, while giving the appearance to the Argentines that Britain was interested in negotiations. This was especially the case after the visit of Junior Minister Nicholas Ridley to the Islands, when the Islanders were asked to choose among four options. They were: ceding sovereignty to Argentina, leasing back the territories from Argentina after giving it sovereign rights, freezing the status quo for twenty-five years, and ending negotiations. The Islanders chose freezing the status quo as their favorite option.[17] From then onwards, Britain started to include the Islanders in the negotiations, making it difficult to extend any major concessions to Argentina, as the Islanders overwhelmingly clamored for maintaining British control over the territory.

In strategic interaction terms, the defender and the challenger thus held dissimilar assumptions which resulted in incompatibility in their implementation as well. The British expected no major military challenge and therefore did not make an immediate deterrent threat or show a willingness to resolve the underlying dispute with concessions that would have been sufficient to reassure Argentina. Neither effective deterrence nor reassurance characterized the British strategy towards Argentina on the eve of the war. It was rather "strategic ambivalence," a situation in which the defender's policy does not provide an unequivocal statement of intent to protect the status quo or provide concessions that can satisfy a challenging state's territorial ambitions. As we shall see, in the Argentine military leadership's strategic calculations, the political options were few and a limited aims/fait accompli strategy held prospects for attaining sovereignty over the Islands.

Argentina's strategic assumptions

In launching the invasion on April 2, 1982, the Argentine leadership held several strategic assumptions. The primary strategic objective behind the invasion was to create a politico-military fait accompli which Britain would not be able to alter without incurring major costs. The Argentine calculations were based on an expectation that Britain would not respond militarily to their action, and even if it did, the war would remain limited. Before the Junta ordered the invasion, Foreign Minister Costa Mendez sought advice from the Argentine missions in London and New York regarding the possible response from Britain. They reported that Britain would most likely sever diplomatic relations and impose trade and economic sanctions, but would refrain from military counter-actions.[18] The Argentine Foreign Minister, in subsequent writings, revealed that the signals that were sent by Britain regarding its intentions to protect the Islands militarily were confusing to the Argentine decision-makers. Past British behavior had shown a lack of clear-cut determination to keep the Islands permanently in British hands. He cited the British willingness to let the Islanders and Argentina develop closer relations, the acceptance of the installation of an Argentine naval base on the Thule Islands, and the condoning of Argentina's chasing of Bulgarian and Russian fishing boats from South Atlantic waters as evidence of a declining British interest in keeping the Islands. Additionally, the drastic reduction of the Royal Naval Fleet in the Atlantic – especially the decision to remove HMS *Endurance* from South Atlantic waters – and the decision to evacuate the British Antarctic Mission from South Georgia confirmed the Junta's expectation that the British would not "deploy major forces to protect the Islands."[19]

The lessons that Argentina had learned from past British behavior, especially from the low-key response to the Thule incident, gave them assurance that Britain would not be keen on fighting a large-scale war in the South Atlantic. The incident occurred in late 1976 when Argentina succeeded in sending fifty technicians to South Thule in the South Sandwich group of Islands without incurring any major reprisals from Britain. In May 1978, the Callaghan Labour Government rejected proposals for sending marines to forcefully re-occupy the Islands.[20] The behavior of Britain in other past international crises also provided learning experience and reinforced the Argentine expectation regarding no military counter-actions by the defender. For instance, in the Suez Crisis in 1956, the then British Government had accepted a cease-fire while an invasion of Egypt was in progress, largely due to American pressure. This historic instance further reinforced the Argentine expectations that the British leaders were pragmatic and that they would not engage in a war with Argentina in the South Atlantic for such a strategically and economically insignificant piece of territory as the Falklands. The Argentine military leadership considered the Suez analogy seriously while hoping that the situation was almost akin and that the US might hold the same attitude towards the South Atlantic crisis and prevent the British from escalating it.[21]

The Junta also considered the chances of Britain using its nuclear forces against Argentina, in the event of its losing the conventional battle. Such a contingency was viewed as highly improbable as the US and the USSR would have prevented it if the British threatened to use nuclear weapons in a small conventional theater. Moreover, Britain would have incurred the world's wrath by breaking the "nuclear taboo," i.e., the use of nuclear weapons against a non-nuclear state.[22]

The strategic framework for the operation was derived from the naval training exercises conducted since 1942 and the plan that was refined by Admiral Jorge Anaya in 1977. A task group, headed by Juan Jose Lombardo, reformulated it in January 1982. Code-named, "Operation Azul," it envisioned the landing of about 3,000 troops in a surprise invasion that would cause minimal bloodshed among the token contingent of Royal Marines on the Islands. In a fast-moving operation, these troops would capture the Island Administration and take over Port Stanley and adjacent areas so that the Islanders would not be able to initiate a protracted armed struggle against the occupying forces. Argentina would withdraw the bulk of this force in forty-eight hours, leaving a military governor and about 500 marines to maintain the "symbolic assertion of Argentine sovereignty and await Britain's diplomatic surrender to a fait accompli."[23] The primary motive of the original military action was thus not an outright military victory in a war with Britain, but to create a fait accompli situation, and thereby force the defender to resume negotiations, with the purpose of ceding sovereignty of the Islands to Argentina. "Occupy to negotiate" was the key objective of the invasion.[24] War was also conceived as a means to "maintain the international credibility" of Argentina's claims over the Islands, and to avoid a "definitive freezing of negotiations."[25] As characterized by the then Argentine Foreign Minister, the strategic objective was to "corner Britain diplomatically and militarily" and compel it to cede sovereignty of the Islands.[26]

Surprise was a key element of the Argentine strategy, which was further intended to preclude a pre-emptive military response or the fortification of the Island group by the superior British forces. The Junta's decision to carry out the invasion in early April was partially motivated by its recognition of the need for surprise for the success of the operation.[27] The Argentine strategists calculated that with surprise and a favorable local balance they could resist a British counter-attack in the short run. In their estimation, a well-entrenched force of 5,000 men in defensive positions could protect the Islands against an attack by a British force three times larger.[28] The Argentine leadership expected that Britain would not fight a large-scale war, even after the task force had started sailing from British ports. This was evident in the Argentine failure to make any efforts to extend the runway at Port Stanley in order to enable its larger aircraft to land and conduct operations from there. Had the runway been lengthened, Argentina would have been able to deploy its Skyhawks and Etendards there, instead of flying them from the mainland.[29]

The Rattenbach Commission, appointed by President Reynaldo Bignone to inquire about the Argentine conduct of the war, concludes that the occupying marines under General Mario Menendez spread their forces thinly around the Islands while assuming a static defensive position. The Junta neither instructed him to maintain mobility nor supplied him sufficient numbers of marines, helicopters, and close air support.[30] The Argentine troops assumed fixed positions while awaiting the arrival of the British forces, thereby leaving the initiative to the British Navy while failing to launch a counter-offensive.[31] Argentina also kept its best winter-trained troops in the mainland on the Chilean border expecting an offensive from that country.[32] The Argentine expectation of a limited engagement was also evident in its failure to develop a coherent air strategy before the war. The air strategy relied heavily on frontal attacks on the British Fleet by courageous aircrew which in turn helped the Royal Navy to play on its strengths.[33] The three Argentine services, in fact, failed to coordinate their operational plans, resulting in each fighting its own war. Both the air force and the navy were reluctant to commit their forces, fearing that they would become marooned. The Rattenbach Commission was especially critical of the air force chief who worked on his own without developing and taking part in a coherent strategy.[34] The Argentine Navy was especially reluctant to use its hardware, despite its strident policy position to conquer the Islands, and according to one analyst, "they sent planes that could easily be replaced."[35]

In the Argentine planning, the best time for invasion was considered to be between June and October 1982, when Britain would have sold its aircraft carriers and withdrawn its only naval presence in the region – the icebreaker, HMS *Endurance*. Britain was also planning to close down its Antarctic survey station in South Georgia and the retirement or the sale of its aircraft carriers, HMS *Hermes* and HMS *Invincible* because of a budget crunch. On the other hand, Argentina would have received all the major weapons it had ordered, especially the French

153

Super Etendard aircraft and Exocet missiles, and would have inducted them into its forces. Why did the military regime advance the date of invasion by four to five months to a less propitious time? The available evidence suggests that the political preconditions for war had arrived following the British attempt to evacuate forcibly the scrap-metal dealers under Constantino Davidoff from South Georgia. Davidoff and his workers, after informing the British Embassy in Buenos Aires, had gone to South Georgia to collect scrap metals from an abandoned whale station at Leith. On their arrival at Leith, the workmen hoisted an Argentine flag which was presumed by the British authorities to be an attempt by the military rulers, with the connivance of the Argentine Navy, to proclaim sovereignty over the Islands. Having been informed of the Argentine presence by the British scientists working nearby, the Thatcher Government put tremendous pressure on Argentina to evacuate the workmen from Leith. When Argentina refused to do so, the British Government announced that it was sending the *Endurance*, the *Briscoe*, the *Bransfield*, and a nuclear submarine to the South Georgia waters to forcefully evacuate the traders.[36]

Although Britain was attempting to deter future Argentine actions by giving a warning signal, the Argentine military leadership perceived the action as an overtly aggressive and provocative move, and as a sign of the British determination to use force against Argentina's citizens who had gone to an island that it considered as its legitimate territory. The immediate reaction in Buenos Aires was that Britain had broken international law enshrined in the UN Charter and that Argentina, by responding militarily, was in a legitimate position to bring the British action to international attention.[37] The Junta viewed the British response as the beginning of a greater military commitment to the region, threatening Argentina's military position vis-à-vis the Malvinas. Its already laid out limited aims/fait accompli strategy heavily relied on surprise and on taking the initiative before the defender could mobilize. The strategic and tactical surprise would be completely lost if the defender already had its forces on the alert in the theater of operations. If Britain went ahead with the deployment of larger forces and the fortification of the Islands, then Argentina might not be able to carry out its planned limited operation, slated to begin in a few months time. There was also a belief that the British had only eighty or so marines on the Islands at that moment. Before Britain beefed up its forces, Argentina should make use of its local advantage and pre-empt any British plan to permanently station a large contingent of marines on the Islands.[38]

The Argentine military leadership was thus under intense time pressure to launch their invasion before the British arrived in the theater. According to Carlos Busser, the commander of the task force that conducted the first invasion, the dilemma was that if Argentina accepted the British ultimatum and evacuated the scrap-metal dealers on its own, then it would be conceding British sovereignty over the Islands. On the other hand, if it permitted Britain to send its forces to forcibly evict the workers, that would also be tantamount to accepting British sovereignty without resistance.[39] The furore the incident caused in the British Parliament and the open support in Whitehall for protecting the Islanders' territorial rights, the growing public opposition to the transfer of sovereignty to Argentina, and the demands for sending a task force, all compounded the fears of an insecure military regime that time was running out for it to act.[40] The alternative to military response, i.e. raising the issue at the UN Security Council, was considered but rejected, especially at the insistence of Admiral Anaya, because the military leadership "desperately needed victory" for domestic reasons.[41] The Junta also feared that if it did not respond militarily, Argentina would not receive any global recognition for its claim over the Malvinas. According to Costa Mendez, the Argentine decision-makers were under intense pressure to do something in support of their citizens in South Georgia.[42] More than anything else, the Argentine leadership was afraid of the domestic price to be paid for inaction, especially since they were already unpopular because of the economic downturn and internal repression. It seemed like victory was desperately needed for the Junta to continue its rule.[43] Therefore, the strategy to pre-empt and "put Britain into a corner" became attractive to the Argentine decision-makers.

The strategy that Argentina had adopted played an influential role in its choosing war in April 1982. It was a classic case of limited aims/fait accompli, the success of which required taking surprise military action before the defender recognized the threat and mobilized its forces. The weaker initiator expected to use a limited military takeover for establishing sovereignty; a fait accompli once achieved would not be easily reversed. It acted under a belief that the defending power would not use overwhelming force or retaliate massively because of political and diplomatic constraints.

Weapons in Argentina's calculations

What role did military capability play in the Argentine calculations? Did the possession of offensive capability provide incentive to the Argentine leadership to resort to military means? One may argue that

155

the arming of Argentina had been going on at a fast pace ever since the military assumed power in 1976. The military regimes from 1976 to 1982 had increased substantially the budget for the armed forces in general and weapons acquisitions in particular. According to one estimate, the military had spent about $20 billion from 1976 to 1980 for defense purposes. By 1980, the military's share in the national budget grew by over 200 percent from the 1972 level. Additionally, the defense allocations of the military regimes since 1976 accounted for 8 percent of the GDP as compared to the less than 3 percent level under previous regimes.[44] This extraordinary spending on defense made Argentina, during the 1976–83 period, the largest arms purchaser in Latin America. A third of the $40 billion foreign debt accrued up until 1983 was the result of arms purchases. These purchases were largely financed by short-term credit that carried high interest rates, thereby contributing to the worsening economic woes of Argentina.[45] The spending on arms increased considerably during the period when Admiral Emilio Massera was the naval chief, mainly because of his militaristic posture on the Falklands question and Argentina's dispute with Chile over a group of islands in the Beagle Channel. In order to beef up its strength in the South Atlantic, the Argentine Navy had ordered four Type 1700 and four Meko-360 destroyers from West Germany, fourteen Super Etendard fighter aircraft and MM-38 Exocet missiles from France, eight Lynx helicopters from Britain, and sixteen Mirage-3 fighters and two patrol boats from Israel. The air force purchased forty A-4 Skyhawks and five Chinook helicopters from the US and forty-two Daggers from Israel. The army ordered artillery, armored personnel carriers, and missile systems from supplier countries such as Austria, Switzerland, and the US.[46]

From 1980 to 1981, the Junta spent $13 billion on arms acquisitions from abroad in addition to the domestic production of weapon systems, such as TAM tanks, Pucura aircraft, and light and heavy firearms.[47] By March 1982, Argentina was slowly acquiring some sophisticated weapon systems such as the French Super Etendard and the Exocet missile. It had just received a limited number of these systems, but was waiting for further shipments. By October 1982, it would have received all those orders. In addition, the navy was yet to refit many of its vessels, while the installation of the already acquired Super Etendard–Exocet missile system was not complete.[48] An invasion at a later date carried a better chance of success as Argentina would have been able to use those weapons in battle. Therefore, it seems the factor of offensive capability had a rather limited impact on decision-makers as their timing of invasion was not the best in terms of

Argentina's acquisition of maximum military capability. Part of the reason why offensive or defensive military capability did not figure in the calculations of the Junta was that it was not expecting a major military response from Britain. A limited engagement would not require major forces, while Argentina's existing capability was considered sufficient to engage in a fait accompli operation; the final outcome of which would be determined through the political process.

Alliance relationships

Although the military balance was given limited consideration by the Junta, alliance support was a critical factor in its calculations. The timing of the invasion seems to have been partially influenced by the Argentine leaders' expectation that the US would, at a minimum, provide political support to their cause or remain neutral in the conflict involving its two allies. In the words of Costa Mendez: "We expected that the US Government would act as a real go-between, a real neutral friend of both parties interested in the full implementation of the UN Charter," or that they would at least attempt a peaceful settlement, and there were some signs of this happening before the war.[49] There was also an expectation that given the American and British commitments to NATO and European security, the US and other European allies would impress upon Thatcher not to divert British forces to a peripheral region like the South Atlantic.[50] A neutral American position would also be helpful to Argentina as the British would not be able to use the strategic or intelligence facilities of the US in the Atlantic, a prerequisite for its naval assault on the Argentine forces in defensive positions on the Falklands.

These expectations were reinforced by a number of signals being sent by various Reagan Administration officials, especially by the US Ambassador to the UN, Jeane Kirkpatrick.[51] Kirkpatrick had expressed her sympathies for the Argentine cause, although she was against the use of force by either side. In a 1989 article on the war, Kirkpatrick contended that she had in fact argued for the US to take a neutral position which was opposed by, among others, Secretary of State Alexander Haig. In her view, the US should attempt mediation and if that failed, must declare neutrality "because the US had a continuing interest in good relations with Latin America as well as with the UK."[52] Some other Reagan Administration officials had also sent signals which were interpreted in Argentina as equivalent to America's support for its quest for sovereignty over the Islands. During his visit to Buenos Aires in March 1982, Assistant Secretary of State for Latin

American Affairs Thomas Enders suggested that the US would pursue a "hands off policy" with respect to the Falklands dispute. Enders made this comment in response to Foreign Minister Costa Mendez's concern that the Anglo-Argentine negotiations were thus far futile and that the Argentine military was getting restless. Costa Mendez was in fact testing the US diplomat on the American policy in the event of a military confrontation.[53] It is not surprising that given the Reagan Administration's preoccupation with the Soviet Union and the perceived Communist threat from Latin America, an issue such as the Falklands dispute involving two of its allies received little attention in its global policy. The chill of the Carter years in US–Argentine relations had vanished with the arrival of the Republican President. In the early 1980s, Buenos Aires witnessed many important American officials visiting and courting this once-detested human rights violator in Latin America. The visitors included Kirkpatrick and former Secretary of State Henry Kissinger.[54]

The Argentine military regime had received special friendly gestures from the Reagan Administration during its intensification of covert operations in Central America. According to one estimate, Argentina had sent 500 soldiers to Honduras for the purpose of sabotage raids inside Nicaragua. The Argentine military had also trained death squads in El Salvador, Guatemala, and Honduras.[55] The Junta's support for the secret operations in Bolivia and Nicaragua convinced the military leaders that the Reagan Administration would reciprocate its support by sympathizing with Argentina's struggle against Britain for the Malvinas. Some military leaders even developed a belief that Argentina was a "privileged ally" of the United States, as a result of its championing the counter-revolutionary alliance in Central America. Argentina indeed held a special status in the Reagan strategy for Latin America, since it was the only major power in the region that supported the US covert operations.[56] The administration lifted the Humphrey–Kennedy Amendment, which had imposed arms embargoes on human rights violators such as Argentina, as part of its new global strategy of containing Soviet influence. This policy posture effectively belittled human rights violations by right-wing dictatorships as being of little significance in US foreign policy. The impression that Argentina played a key role in the fight against Communism in the American strategy was reinforced by the US Navy's promotion of the idea of making the annual UNITAS exercise a permanent military pact.[57]

Thus, the contours of the changing Argentine–US relationship exerted a major influence on the Junta's timing of operations. The military leaders also hoped that the spirit of the Monroe doctrine and the Rio Pact made it binding on the US to support Argentina against the onslaught of a non-hemispheric power.[58] In the Junta's estimation, the US would "either lean towards it in the conflict or remain strictly neutral, in either case this would have made it impossible for Britain to mount a credible military reaction."[59] The general expectation in Buenos Aires was that like its action during the 1956 Suez Crisis, when the US opposed the Anglo-French-Israeli attack on Egypt, in this case too, Washington would block a military response by Britain.[60] The Junta chief, General Leopoldo Galtieri, himself stated in interviews after the war that if he had known that the US would oppose Argentina and support Britain, he would not have gone for the military action.[61] Costa Mendez confirms the Argentine expectation that the US would remain neutral and would show great interest in ending the conflict before it escalated. The Junta, according to him, could never visualize an American veto against Argentina in the Security Council for an end to the conflict, before Argentina achieved its objectives.[62] Enders' "hands off gesture," and Kirkpatrick's supportive statements, as well as the negative repercussions of past American interventions in Latin America, all strengthened the leaders' belief that the US would attempt mediation and that the British would be willing to listen to an American call for negotiated settlement.[63]

Domestic politics and the timing of the invasion

Apart from the external factor of changes in alliance support, what role did domestic politics play in the Junta's decision to go forward with the invasion plan? A key factor in the Argentine decision to invade the Islands may be sought in the domestic politics of the country prior to March 1982. The resumption of military rule in 1976, especially the coming into power of the Junta under Galtieri in December 1981, seems to have had a major impact on the timing of the invasion in 1982. The military rule since 1976 was more authoritarian than that of the previous Peronist regime (1973–75), the first military regime (1966–72), and certainly the democratic governments that ruled the country from 1961 to 1965. The "security first approach" of the post-1976 regimes was evident in their outspending all predecessors on the armed forces.[64]

Although the Galtieri regime took power with the declared policy of economic recovery, by 1982 the situation had worsened considerably, with the economic programs of the previous military regimes under Jorge Videla and Roberto Viola, and that of the new Economy Minister Roberto Alemann, deepening the crisis. The country's economic

159

troubles were clearly manifested in the massive capital outflow during the period between 1979 and 1982, which stood at over $20 billion. Domestic investment in 1981 had dropped by 27 percent, and the already meager foreign investment by 13 percent.[65] In 1976, the then Economy Minister Jose Martinez de Hoz had launched his "new political economy" program. This plan had envisioned IMF-type reforms, such as the opening up of Argentina to international market forces, elimination of subsidies, reduction of real wages, removal of export taxes on agricultural products, and liberalization of foreign exchange markets. By 1977, these measures proved largely ineffective. In June 1977, in the next phase of economic policies, several financial reforms, such as linking the banking system with short-term capital markets and lifting controls over interest rates, were announced. The result was a major jump in inflation. More measures were adopted in May 1978 in an effort to control inflation and in December 1978, devaluation of the peso was held below the level of price increases. When the next Junta under General Viola took office in March 1981, Argentina's economic conditions were the worst since the military takeover of 1976, with the colossal capital outflow from the country continuing unabated.[66]

By June 1981, the economic crisis had reached new heights and Viola's Finance Minister Sigaut's attempts to counter it also proved ineffective. The Viola regime was forced to free-float the peso which further aggravated the crisis. Viola was ousted in December 1981 and the new military regime under Galtieri assumed power. In January 1982, Galtieri's Economy Minister, Alemann launched a major austerity program, under the catchwords, "deflate, deregulate, denationalize." The program envisioned floating the exchange rate, freezing public wages, and hiking indirect taxes.[67] Alemann was desperately attempting to impose strict monetary policies in order to arrest the falling GNP, industrial production, and real wages. His measures included ending the two-tier exchange rate system, the introduction of a 10 percent export tax, freezing public employee salaries, and raising taxes.[68] These measures resulted in further economic misery for the Argentine people. The deepening economic and political turmoil convinced the popular daily, La Prensa in February 1982 to suggest: "The only thing that can save this government is a war."[69]

Additionally, it seems war was considered by the regime and the military leaders who supported it as a way to exonerate themselves from the crimes committed against internal opposition during the "dirty war," when several youngsters disappeared from the streets for their alleged leftist activities. The military seemed to have calculated that;

"from being an Army of the 'dirty war,' they would turn into patriots bent on recovering for the nation a portion of territory under imperial occupation."[70] There was also an expectation that a popularly elected government in the future would "witch hunt" the culprits of internal repression and that the best way to avoid such a possibility would be to project the armed forces as the liberators of a national dream long denied by Britain. This seems to have been felt especially after the Galtieri regime's failure to attract much popular sympathy for a pro-regime centrist political party that it organized. The party could muster barely 10 percent of electoral support, while the multi-party agreement of Peronists, Radicals, and other smaller parties was expected to have the support of over 80 percent of the electorate.[71]

The most important change that occurred in the decision-making structure prior to war was the arrival of the Galtieri regime, with the navy chief Admiral Jorge Anaya as a key member of the triumvirate. Even when he was a captain in the navy in 1968, Anaya had drawn up a plan for the occupation of the Islands with minimum bloodshed. Anaya's plan was accepted by Admiral Emilio Massera who was the naval chief under Juan Peron in 1973 and who had revised it to include a bloodless occupation of the Islands similar to the Indian takeover of Goa, a former Portuguese colony, in 1961. Code-named, "Plan Goa," it had envisioned the surprise landing of Argentine marines on the Islands and the removal of its population, to be replaced by Argentine settlers. The plan never took off because of the apparent difficulties in sustaining a small number of troops there.[72] The golden opportunity for the implementation of his plans came when Galtieri became President and Anaya joined him as one of the three members of the Junta in December 1981. In fact, Anaya was a key accomplice of Galtieri in the removal of the Viola regime. Anaya supported the Galtieri takeover on the condition that the new President would take up the Malvinas question as a top priority item on the regime's agenda and support the navy's long-standing plans for an invasion of the Islands. Anaya convinced Galtieri of the feasibility and the need for invading the Islands before the 150th anniversary of its occupation by Britain in January 1983.[73]

For Anaya and other naval commanders, the fate of the Argentine Navy was linked to regaining the Malvinas. Argentina lost its bid to possess the islands south of the Beagle Channel when in 1978 the Pope awarded the territory to Chile. Argentina's counter-claim also looked unlikely to alter the pontiff's previous decision. In addition, the possibility of Argentina reinforcing its position in Antarctica was non-existent as the 1959 Antarctica Treaty forbade such an action. Thus, with the impending settlement with Chile, the naval commanders had strong reason to be concerned about the lack of an operating base in the southern waters, where it feared that Argentina's security was threatened, especially by Chile. The sole remaining base was the Port of Ushuaia in Tierra del Fuego whose access could be obstructed by Chile during a time of crisis. There were also fears that Chile would gradually strengthen its relations with Britain and together they could build a formidable maritime presence in the South Atlantic. Admiral Anaya had thus viewed the possession of the Malvinas as the key to the Argentine Navy's southern operations.[74]

The Galtieri regime's ascendance into power in December 1981, increased the tempo for military action as the slow negotiation process was not acceptable to the new military rulers. Galtieri's predecessor, General Viola, had reportedly favored a negotiated settlement on the basis of the British proposals. However, with the arrival of Anaya and Basilio Lami Dozo as heads of the navy and the air force, he found himself without support for his approach. Viola's soft-line approach toward the dispute seemed to have played a crucial role in his removal from power.[75] Viola had the support of moderate naval chief Armando Lambruschini for a negotiated settlement. But when Anaya succeeded Lambruschini on September 11, 1981, he brought along plans for a military recovery of the Islands.[76] Shifts in the domestic power structure thus exerted a powerful role in this case of asymmetric war initiation. The rise of the most outspoken proponent of invasion, Admiral Anaya, in the triumvirate that came to power in 1981 increased the chances for Argentina taking military action as such a course was one of the conditions for the Navy supporting Galtieri's bid for power. A forceful takeover of the Islands was also considered by the military leadership as the best way to strengthen its domestic power base and continue its rule for an indefinite period. The economic crisis and negative effects of internal repression further increased the determination of the Junta to recover the Islands so as to exonerate the military from its misdeeds of the past decade.

Why no invasion before 1982?

A comparison of 1982 with previous periods when war was considered will provide clues to the specific factors behind the timing of invasion. Although the plan for the invasion had been in existence since the 1940s, three major occasions stand out when Argentina seriously considered the use of force to re-occupy the Island group. The first was on February 5, 1976, a few weeks before the military coup, when the

Argentine military fired across the bows of the British scientific research vessel, R.R.S. *Shackleton*, in the expectation that Lord Shackleton would be on board. Shackleton was expected to visit South Georgia to investigate the economic prospects of the Falklands and their dependencies and make proposals on the possibility of the Islanders achieving limited self-determination. The Argentine opposition to the visit was upheld by the UN and the Organization of American States, despite British reservations.[77] Protesting the visit, the Argentines recalled their ambassador from London and Britain followed suit by recalling its ambassador from Buenos Aires.[78]

The Argentine military's intention was clearly to take over the ship and force the British to come up with a proposal for ceding sovereignty. Isabella Peron, who was shortly to be overthrown (March 23, 1976) in a military coup, was persuaded by her military advisers to escalate the incident. She rejected their advice and the military decided not to proceed with its invasion plan. Apparently, the military did not want to give credit for the recovery of the Islands to the civilian regime. The incident failed to escalate into an armed conflict partly because the British agreed to resume negotiations in February 1976. In the words of the Franks Committee, with the British decision to resume negotiations, including "discussion of sovereignty, the threat of military action receded."[79]

The second incident occurred in December 1976, when Argentina took control of the South Sandwich Island of Southern Thule, with the declared intent of establishing a scientific station there. The British reaction was confined to diplomatic protests. The Argentines had made contingency plans to respond militarily if Britain attempted to retake the Island by force. If Britain reacted militarily and captured the Argentine personnel, Argentina was prepared to take over the British Antarctic Survey Party on South Georgia. The Junta had carefully planned an operation to invade the Falklands coupled with a renewed diplomatic effort at the UN to obtain legitimacy for its action. The objectives were to demonstrate the Argentine sovereignty over the Island groups, to place the UK in a defensive and reactive position, and to achieve a strong bargaining position in the forthcoming negotiations. British intelligence reported to the government that the Argentine Navy shelved its invasion plan largely because of internal reasons and due to an expectation that Argentina might not receive support for its action from the international community, especially from the Third World and the Eastern-bloc nations at the United Nations.[80]

Again in November 1977, the Argentine Navy made moves to establish a base on an island in the South Sandwich group. British naval intelligence detected the possibility of an impending invasion. By then, relations between the two countries had deteriorated, with the Argentine decision to disrupt fuel supplies to the Falkland Islanders. The Callaghan Government secretly dispatched two frigates and a submarine from the Caribbean. The British were determined to prevent another occurrence such as the Thule incident. In the meantime, the Argentines had decided to cancel their plans.[81] The British decision to deploy a nuclear-powered submarine and two frigates was taken secretly and according to the Franks Committee Report, there had been no clear evidence on whether the Argentine Government was aware of the British move.[82]

Explaining the Argentine decision

It is the conclusion of this chapter that the advent of the Galtieri regime in December 1981 changed the Argentine approach towards the settlement of the Malvinas question. The new regime accorded a higher priority to the resolution of the dispute than its predecessors and a limited military action was an attractive option for the Junta from its very inception, mostly for domestic reasons. Even when its predecessor regimes contemplated military action off and on, proponents of invasion had never gained full control of the decision-making structure. But by December 1981, the regime was dominated by navy chief Anaya, the chief proponent of invasion, General Galtieri, and Brigadier Lami Dozo, two supporters of military action. This change had a significant impact on what course Argentina would take in the coming months. The Galtieri regime was under intense domestic pressure to remove threats to its legitimacy and continued existence, arising largely from failed economic policies and the trampling of human rights during the "dirty war" against suspected leftist sympathizers. War seemed like the best means to allow the Junta to gain legitimacy in the eyes of the people. Of the three other factors, the expectations regarding a successful limited aims/fait accompli strategy seem to have been a second key determinant in the decision process. A limited military takeover followed by stationing of troops on the Islands for defensive purposes formed the core of this strategy. Such a takeover was expected to raise Argentina's prospects for recovering sovereignty through negotiations as Britain would be reluctant to use massive force against Argentina. The Argentine leadership feared that with the Thatcher Government's decision to send reinforcements to forcibly evict its citizens from Leith, the British commitment to the

Islands would also increase, thereby affecting its strategic plans for a later-date invasion. In March 1982, on the other hand, it saw a window of opportunity for a quick, fait accompli operation that would receive minimal adverse response from Britain.

The expected political support from the US, largely in terms of extending its good offices to prevent a British counter-attack also played a key determining role in the Argentine calculations. A low-key British military response would be possible if the US declared neutrality and did not allow its bases and other facilities to be used by the British Navy. The condition of short-term offensive capability seems to have exerted negligible impact on the decision as the Argentines would have been better off had they waited a few more months. By July 1982, the regime was expected to receive all the weapons that Argentina had ordered, especially the French Super Etendard aircraft and Exocet missiles. The limited response it expected from Britain, the fait accompli strategy, and the anticipated support from the US were viewed as factors that would compensate for Argentina's weaknesses in military capability to wage a war with Britain.

This case illustrates that a weaker challenger in an asymmetric conflict relationship may undertake offensive operations if it expects that the stronger power will be reluctant to retaliate militarily. Although Britain did not mount any immediate deterrent threat, the overwhelming British superiority in conventional and nuclear capability should have acted as a general deterrent against Argentina's military initiative. It shows that political factors, both domestic and international, often play a more significant role in a weaker challenger's strategic calculations than the fear of a stronger defender's raw military capability.

CONCLUSION

In Chapter 2, I outlined the major hypotheses pertaining to war initiation in asymmetric conflicts. The hypothesized relationships between war initiation and the four variables – strategic calculations of the belligerents, changes in short-term offensive capability, great power alliance relationships, and domestic power structure – were also elaborated. The arrival of these factors has been hypothesized to have causal connection to the choice for war by states that hold inferior aggregate capability vis-à-vis their opponents.

In subsequent chapters, these hypotheses were tested in the light of six historic cases of asymmetric war initiations. The following matrices show the approximate level of presence of the variables for the chosen cases at the time when war was being considered. Table 1 rates the presence of these factors in cases when war initiation actually occurred. Table 2 similarly rates the variables when war initiation was considered but did not take place. The variables are rated for each case on a numerical scale of 0 to 10, where 0 indicates no presence of that variable and 10 denotes a very strong presence.

In the six cases that I have explored in this study, the first factor – strategic calculations, based on a limited aims/fait accompli strategy – seems to be of major significance in explaining the phenomenon of asymmetric war initiations. As shown in table 1, the initiators of asymmetric wars overwhelmingly expected a successful limited aims/ fait accompli strategy. This factor is strongly present in all the cases except that of China, whose leaders followed a strategy that combined elements of limited aims and attrition, but with the objective of achieving limited territorial and political gains.

In 1904, the Japanese leaders believed that if Japan could make tactical and strategic gains in Korea and Manchuria through a surprise attack, the Russian presence in those territories could be effectively removed. A peace settlement was possible through US mediation, thus making Japan's territorial and political gains permanent faits accomplis. Prior to Pearl Harbor, the Japanese leadership believed that a

Table 1 · *Positive cases*

Case	Variable			
	Limited aims strategy	Short-term capability	Great power support	Domestic structure
Japan/Russia, 1904	10	10	10	9
Japan/ US, 1941	10	10	10	9
China/US, 1950	9	3	9	9
Pakistan/India, 1965	10	10	10	9
Egypt/Israel, 1973	10	10	9	8
Argentina/UK, 1982	10	5	8	10

Table 2 *Negative cases*

Case	Variable			
	Limited aims strategy	Short-term capability	Great power support	Domestic structure
Japan/Russia, 1895 & 1901	2	2	2	6
Japan/US, 1936–40	6	6	6	7
China/US, 7/1950–10/1950	6	3	6	7
Pakistan/India, 1962	5	6	4	6
Egypt/Israel, 1971	5	4	4	7
Argentina/UK, 1976 & 1977	7	4	2	5

surprise attack on the US Pacific Fleet would make the opponent unable to mobilize for a year and during this period Japan could advance to the southern areas unhampered. They also expected that the US would eventually concede to Japan's occupation of the territories. The Chinese leadership in 1950 calculated that their surprise intervention in Korea would achieve a military and political fait accompli through which the North Korean buffer could be re-established. The Chinese strategy had elements of limited aims as well as Mao's guerrilla warfare, based on attrition, although the avowed Chinese objective remained limited, i.e., denying the US and South Korea their goal of reunifying Korea under Seoul's auspices. In the Pakistani case, its leadership expected that in a limited war confined to

Kashmir, Pakistan could make tactical gains, while making the Indian control of the state tenuous. Likewise, in 1973, the Egyptian leadership believed that a surprise offensive in Sinai would force Israel to accept negotiations for the ceding of the occupied territory. The Argentines also pursued a limited aims strategy, believing that their surprise invasion of the Falklands would force Britain to concede sovereignty of the Islands.

The strategic calculations of the initiators, based on limited aims, were facilitated by offensive–defensive military doctrines. Initiators of all these wars, including China, held offensive–defensive doctrines which entailed quick offensive operations followed by defensive postures that were intended to create politico-military faits accomplis. Initiators in all the cases, except Argentina, also expected limited wars or limited retaliation by their adversaries. They anticipated little prospects for waging a war of attrition and the stronger opponent would not be politically able to launch such a war. In five of the cases, massive retaliation by the stronger power was also ruled out by these weaker initiators who believed that their great power ally would defend them in such a contingency. However, in the case of Japan in 1941, the initiator expected that the defender would be preoccupied with Europe and that the prospects of waging a two-ocean war would reduce its will to fight. In the case of Argentina, the expectation was that the stronger power might not retaliate, and that even if it did decide to retaliate, the response would be limited to economic and diplomatic sanctions rather than military action.

The Japanese in 1904 believed that once the Russian naval presence in the Pacific was curtailed, Russia would not be in a position to retaliate against Japanese territory in the short-run and that the war could be concluded in Japan's favor, before Russia brought in overwhelming forces from the European theater. The British defensive support would also reduce the Russians' incentives to engage in a long, bitter war. In 1941, Japan also calculated that the US would lose its will to fight if Japan achieved its strategic goals in the initial phase of the war. In the case of China, although there were discussions of the possibility of a US nuclear attack, the Chinese leaders calculated that if they could arrest the US advance near the 38th Parallel, they could limit the war to the Korean peninsula and thereby prevent an attack on China. The Soviet nuclear capability was also viewed as a deterrent against such an attack. In 1965, the Pakistani leaders were convinced that their limited action in Kashmir would not lead to retaliatory attack by India on the international border. The Pakistani leaders anticipated the intervention by China in the event that their nation's survival was

169

in great danger. In 1973, Egypt calculated that the super powers would restrain Israel from escalating the war deep into Egypt proper and that if it confined the operations to Sinai, Israel might follow the same moderation.

The stronger powers in all the cases anticipated that their overall superiority in power capability would act as a general deterrent preventing their weaker opponents from engaging in war. The US in 1941 and Israel in 1973 did make strong deterrent threats and had deployed forces for the purpose of immediate deterrence. The US in 1950 and India in 1965 had made limited retaliatory threats against their weaker opponents. Yet neither these threats nor the overall superiority in capability prevented the weaker powers from initiating wars. The case studies robustly support the hypothesis that the strategic assumptions leaders hold can have an important bearing on decisions regarding the timing of war initiation by weaker powers in asymmetric conflicts. In the case of the challenger, the choice for the use of military force is heavily dependent on its adopting a limited aims/fait accompli strategy and a realization of the possibility of waging a limited war confined to a small theater of operations. The anticipation regarding the defender's inability to wage, or disinterest in waging, an attrition style warfare also influences the calculations of a weaker challenger.

In four of the six cases, short-term offensive capability was a determining factor in war initiation. As table 1 shows, the changes in short-term offensive strike capability appeared to have profoundly influenced the Japanese decision to go to war against Russia in 1904 and the Japanese decision to strike Pearl Harbor in 1941. By 1904, Japan had acquired sufficient offensive capability for a limited war, while waiting would have resulted in Russia strengthening its position in the Pacific. In 1941 also, Japan had acquired the required offensive capability for waging a short war in the Pacific, while the US was still building up its forces.

The capability factor seems to have been of minimal impact on both the Chinese decision to intervene in Korea and the Argentine decision to invade the Falklands/Malvinas in 1982. In both the Pakistani and the Egyptian cases, the possession of short-term offensive capability played a crucial role in the timing of war initiations by these states against their stronger opponents. Pakistan had acquired aircraft and tank capability, sufficient for a limited offensive in Kashmir, while waiting would have seen India negating the limited advantage in weapons through its defense modernization program. By 1973, the Egyptians also had acquired sufficient offensive and defensive capability for a quick tactical advancement to the Sinai. The general

170

conclusion that is derived from these cases is that short-run offensive dominance has a modest influence in the war decisions of weaker initiators and therefore, in the explanation of the phenomenon of asymmetric war initiations it may be viewed as playing a moderate role.

Anticipated defensive support from a great power was crucial in all the six cases. The Japanese decision in 1904 was greatly facilitated by the support extended by Britain, while in 1941 Japan's war choices were influenced by Germany and its successful moves in Europe. As for the Chinese case, it is reasonable to conclude that the anticipated favorable Soviet position had exerted a significant influence on Mao and his decision-making group's choice to intervene in Korea. Likewise, Pakistan in 1965 expected China's alliance support, and Egypt in 1973 anticipated assistance from the Soviet Union prior to launching their offensives. The Argentine leaders also expected diplomatic support from the US which acted as an important factor in their decision to invade the Falklands/Malvinas in March 1982. The Reagan Administration's attempts to befriend Argentina for its anti-Communist operations in Latin America gave sufficient assurance to the Argentines that the administration would either support its sovereignty bid or remain neutral and thereby help facilitate a diplomatic settlement of the conflict after their occupation of the Islands.

Thus the hypothesis that the anticipated support from a great power considerably influences the choice for war by a weaker challenger is strongly upheld. As shown in a majority of these cases, the ally not only acted as a last bastion of defensive support, but as an anticipated source for facilitating a weaker power to achieve its limited territorial or military aims. Without the arrival of the alliance factor, one may have to conclude that Japan, China (to a certain extent), Pakistan, Egypt, and Argentina might not have gone to war against their more powerful opponents.

The condition of changing domestic decision-making structures was critical in the cases of Japan (on both occasions) and Argentina and exerted modest influence in all the other cases. Regime changes occurred prior to war in the cases of Japan (in both instances) and Argentina, while in all the other cases, the shifts were within the regime, especially the key decision-making unit surrounding the head of government. In other words, these were changes in the domestic balance of power in which more militaristic groups gained control of decision-making by becoming key decision-makers themselves or by assuming the role of powerful advisers to the head of government. The Katsura Cabinet's assumption of power in 1903 and the decline of the Genro's role in decision-making seemed to have increased the Japanese time pressure to go to war with Russia. Likewise, the rise of Tojo and the army's "Control Group" faction led to quick reappraisals of national strategy, especially towards the US, and the choice for war.

In the case of China, the new revolutionary regime under Mao was consolidating its power in the vast country and the US successes in Korea were considered as serious threats to its very survival. The key decision-making group underwent changes prior to the war, with the supporters of military action, Mao and Peng Dehuai, gaining influence in the decision process while opponents, such as Lin Biao and Ch'en Yun, gave up their opposition to the plans for intervention. In the Pakistani case, the ascendence of Zulfikar Ali Bhutto as a key decision-maker in 1963 resulted in major changes in Pakistan's approach towards the Kashmir question. It was Bhutto and a small group of civilian and military officials who convinced President Ayub Khan to order a limited operation in Kashmir. In the Egyptian case also there were some internal changes within the regime, although Sadat remained the key decision-maker during this period. Opponents of limited war – War Minister Sadek and Vice President Hassan – lost their positions in the government in 1972, while supporters of a limited war – General Ismail and General Shazly – were elevated to key jobs. Thus to some extent, the choice for war became more acceptable to Egypt with the arrival of the new decision-makers. In the Argentine case, the arrival of the Junta headed by General Galtieri and the most important proponent of war, Admiral Anaya, in December 1981, had a major impact on the timing of the operations. The general conclusion that is derived from these case studies is that domestic power shifts have a moderate to strong significance in explaining the phenomenon of asymmetric war initiations.

Finally, the hypothesized relationship of time pressure as an intervening variable that runs between the causal variables and the outcome variable – war initiation – is proved to be valid in all the cases. Decision-makers in all the instances felt the need to go to war without delay because they believed a successful limited aims/fait accompli strategy warranted quick military action. Time pressure was felt by decision-makers in all the cases, in terms of making use of their great power alliance support and, in four of the cases, with regard to their short-term advantages in offensive capability as well. Time pressure was also felt by the militaristic decision-making groups that emerged prior to the wars in almost all of these cases. These decision-makers generally believed in the virtue of quick military action for the resolution of disputes with their stronger opposing states in order to fulfil their domestic or international objectives.

172

In terms of the relative significance of factors in explaining asymmetric war initiations (as shown in tables 1 and 2), the two most compelling ones relevant to a majority of cases are the limited aims/fait accompli strategy and the alliance support from a great power. The condition of short-term offensive capability is third in significance, while the changes in domestic decision-making structure are fourth, in terms of their application to the cases studied.

Theoretical implications

The case studies and the theoretical arguments presented here have implications with respect to theories of war initiation, especially to systems level theories such as balance of power and power transition. They also have ramifications for decision level theories such as deterrence and expected utility. In addition, the findings in this study are somewhat relevant to polarity, capability diffusion, and international conflict theory in general. First, this study has significant implications for deterrence theory and policy, especially relating to general deterrence. It highlights some important but neglected elements of the deterrence calculus of defenders and challengers. In all these cases, the calculations of the initiators were more complex than is predicted by deterrence theory with respect to challengers who confront powerful opponents. The case studies prove that initiators can hold considerations other than victory and defeat, prior to launching an attack. Partial gains may matter to a weaker initiator who can stand to lose everything in dispute without military action. Such states may conceive war as a means to resolve uncertainty, to change an unbearable status quo, or to obtain sympathy for a cause from third parties. The case studies highlight the significance of factors such as strategy, short-term capability, alliance support, and domestic changes in the deterrence calculations of war initiators.

Consistent with George and Smoke, this study concludes that a determined challenger can design around deterrence with strategies such as limited aims/fait accompli.[1] The case studies also prove that gross capabilities are not sufficient to deter an adversary who is highly motivated to change the status quo. Clearly, to explain deterrence failures and successes, the strategies and doctrines that initiators and defenders hold prior to war need to be taken into consideration. Although this study concurs with Mearsheimer that the strategies a state adopts may determine the timing of war initiation, it does not fully agree with his argument that conventional deterrence is simply a function of battlefield capability to deny victory to a potential initi-

173

ator.[2] As the case studies exemplify, battlefield victory does not always constitute the motive for war by a weaker initiator in an asymmetric conflict situation. These case studies show that deterrence is difficult to obtain in an intense asymmetric conflict, when a dissatisfied challenger holds limited war expectations and strategies such as limited aims/fait accompli. Such strategic calculations can allow a state to engage in a short war even with a more powerful adversary, without anticipating a massive military retaliation. Short-term capability and alliance factors also play key roles in these calculations. In the cases that I examined, the status quo powers (in these instances, the stronger powers) expected that their preponderance in overall capability would deter the weaker states. The weaker challengers' possible strategies to circumvent their inferior capability was given little attention by the stronger defenders.

Another conclusion derived from this study for deterrence theory is that a weaker power can engage in war initiation, knowing very well that it may lose the war militarily but may gain politically. Thus, on the eve of war, a weaker power may hold the well-known axiom: "One may lose the battle but not the war." A weaker state may go to war willing to bear the costs of an indecisive defeat. For some such states, the prospect of a limited defeat is better than living with an unbearable status quo. The calculations of Japan in both instances and Egypt in 1973 attest to the validity of this conclusion. Even if the threat of massive retaliation is evident, a weaker power can still believe that such threats are seldom carried out. Rarely does international and domestic opinion support the total obliteration of a country unless the stronger power's own national interests are severely affected. Deterrence theory assumes that a potential initiator may back down if confronted with overwhelming force. In some of the cases that were examined, retreat was not considered by the decision-makers for political reasons, even when they knew they were confronting superior adversaries and that the chances of their military victory were fifty-fifty or less. This conclusion has some relevance to compellence and coercive diplomacy as well. Thus, in 1991, the Iraqi regime under Saddam Hussein refused to back down from its invasion of Kuwait, despite a very credible compellence attempt by a militarily superior international coalition, led by the US. It may be argued that an unconditional withdrawal would have been considered by Baghdad a highly unpalatable option even when it had to confront adversaries several times stronger in technological prowess, military capability, and economic power.

The inability of the stronger powers to deter attacks against them

174

also coincided with their unwillingness to provide major concessions that would possibly have decreased in at least some cases the incentives of the weaker initiators to challenge the status quo militarily. Although this would have been tantamount to appeasement in cases like Pearl Harbor; in others, such as the Japanese (1904), the Chinese, the Pakistani, the Egyptian, and the Argentine cases, concessions by Russia, the US, India, Israel, and Britain respectively, would have probably made some difference in the prevention of wars. The policy conclusion here is that general deterrence is highly difficult to obtain by military means alone. As long there are windows of opportunity for limited action, superior capability of the defender may not deter a determined adversary. Reassurance and concessions are not always wrong policies to pursue, if the status quo power desires to avert war. Especially if these states are willing to eventually give up their control over the issue in dispute – e.g. territory – the correct timing of such concessions could reduce the incentives of those challengers who are interested only in gaining their limited objectives from going to war. Thus, war could probably have been averted in 1904, 1941, 1950, 1965, 1973, and 1982, had the defenders engaged in credible reassurance policies and had made the concessions which they had promised at one time or another prior to the wars. This study thus takes exception to the argument in deterrence theory that concessions can be viewed as weakness and that a tough posture is required to signal a credible deterrent threat. Such posturing could be counter-productive to war prevention in many situations of asymmetric conflict, averting war being the key objective of deterrence policy itself.

This study also points to the limited utility of nuclear weapons in asymmetric conflicts. Contrary to the Neo-realist position, as represented by Waltz, that nuclear weapons have major utility in preventing wars, this study suggests that they tend to have a limited role in averting a conflict between a "nuclear have" and a "nuclear have not."[3] The possession of nuclear weapons by the US, presumably by Israel, and by Britain did not prevent their weaker adversaries from launching military actions against them. The leaders of China, Egypt, and Argentina calculated that the chances of the use of nuclear weapons against a non-nuclear state were very low. The "nuclear taboo," which ordains that nuclear weapons shall not be used in a war against a non-nuclear state, seemed to have provided sufficient assurance to the decision-makers of these states that the possibility of their use was extremely slim. The implication here is that the mere possession of nuclear capability and an ambiguous threat of use do not provide sufficient deterrent against a challenger without nuclear weapons. The nuclear policies of countries like India and Israel, based on "opaqueness" or "bomb in the basement," need not prevent wars against these states by their weaker regional adversaries. This was clearly evident during the 1991 Persian Gulf War when Iraq attacked Israeli population centers with Scud missiles, even when they knew Israel held sufficient nuclear capability to destroy Iraq several times.

For systems level theories, the study finds that neither parity nor preponderance has proven to be an adequate condition of peace preservation. Although one may conjecture that overwhelming preponderance in the immediate theater might have prevented some of these wars, parity in capability between the adversaries seems less likely to have averted the outbreak of war. Thus the balance of power theory's contention – "parity preserves peace" – at best is tenuous in the conventional realm, if a weaker state can engage in war against a stronger opponent. A state with better strategy, tactics, and willingness to make use of windows of opportunity can go to war even when it has less relative aggregate military capability. As the case studies show, the timing of war is greatly affected by a weaker state's strategic assumptions and its assessment of the loopholes in the opponent's strategy and tactics.

As for expected utility theories, the study finds that war initiators' expected utility can be positive even when aggregate capabilities are not. Decision-makers can have a higher expected utility in waging wars even when victory is not an assured outcome. This implies that an initiator's utilities are not singularly shaped by calculations of victory and defeat, but by other considerations such as strategy, tactics, and domestic politics. Decision-makers may also engage in wars due to time pressures and such pressures may result from considerations of short-term advantages and changing alliance relationships. In order to be more accurate and comprehensive, expected utility models need to incorporate the strategic and political calculations of decision-makers, short-run shifts in offensive capability, and changes in domestic balance of power. These factors are important in understanding processes as well as outcomes and in explaining what goes on inside the decision-making black box. Changes in conditions over time and choices made out of time pressure are not adequately factored into existing expected utility models. This study highlights the importance of incorporating theses factors into the expected utility framework.

With respect to polarity, the main conclusion here is that conditions of extreme multipolar and bipolar competitions may not preserve sub-systemic peace. As shown in the case studies, initiators of asymmetric wars invariably expected support from great power allies prior to their launching of the wars. If one can agree that extreme multipolar competition was the prevailing condition during the early part of this century and prior to World War II, one may contend that Japan's war decisions in 1904 and in 1941 were greatly facilitated by anticipated support from other great powers that shared its territorial and military objectives. In the post-World War II cases, when bipolarity was prevalent, the support of a great power, especially a super power, was a crucial determining factor in a weaker initiator's calculations. These cases point out that during periods of intense bipolar competition, smaller powers can expect support from their super power patrons, especially if they are fighting an opponent who is non-aligned or who belongs to the other side of the bipolar equation. This is further evident in the number of cases of asymmetric war initiations in the 1970s and early 1980s (as cited in chapter 1). A policy implication in this respect is that great power competition increases conflict among smaller allies. Great powers, on the other hand, can help reduce the probability of asymmetric war initiations if they act as mediators as opposed to allies of belligerents. Alliance support can encourage lesser powers to engage in conflict with their opponents, after anticipating backing from their great power ally. In this sense, extreme forms of bipolar or multipolar competition are not necessarily conducive to regional peace. To some extent this study questions the utility of defensive alliances as peace preserving mechanisms. In many historic instances they served as camouflage for the offensive intentions of war-prone states in regional conflicts.

The relevance of this study for capability diffusion is that although proliferation of advanced weaponry may reduce the incentives of the bigger powers to take military actions against their smaller opponents, initial phases of such an arms race may provide windows of opportunity in a theater of perpetual conflict. A weaker state in possession of some quality weaponry, such as nuclear arms, may feel the time pressure to act militarily before a window closes. Mutual incentives may decline over time if the arms race ends up in a more stable equilibrium and does not result in rapid changes in the capability distribution of a region. Thus, the diffusion of advanced offensive weaponry such as precision guided munitions (PGMs) and weapons of mass destruction, like nuclear and chemical arms, may reduce the incentives of bigger powers to attack smaller adversaries. However, the possession of such capabilities by a weaker challenger who is in conflict with a stronger adversary may encourage its decision-makers to go to war if they feel these capabilities have only a short-term offensive value in changing a military or political situation in their favor. They may view such force-in-being as sufficient to make limited tactical or strategic or political gains.

Finally, this study also has some implications for international conflict theory and defense policies of states. The conditions and factors that I discussed have significance in predicting and explaining the timing of war among asymmetric dyads that are engaged in conflict relationships. We need initiation theories at different levels of conflict for a comprehensive understanding of the dynamics of war. This study is a modest attempt to explain conflicts at the asymmetric level. At the policy level, the study shows that military power alone, both potential and present, is not sufficient for war prevention and that leaders make choices for war and peace not exclusively on the basis of capability considerations. In 1991, the Persian Gulf War brought forth that stark reality when a superior coalition had to go to war to compel a weaker adversary to retract from its annexation of a small neighboring state.

NOTES

1 Introduction: war initiation in international relations theory

1 For these cases, see Edward N. Luttwak, *The Grand Strategy of the Roman Empire: From the First Century AD to the Third* (Baltimore and London: The Johns Hopkins University Press, 1976), p. 147.

2 For brief descriptions of these wars, see John Laffin, *Brassey's Battles* (London: Brassey's, 1986).

3 Carl von Clausewitz, *On War*, Vol.I, trans. Col. J.J. Graham (London: Routledge & Kegan Paul, 1962), p. 35.

4 For a comparison of the power capabilities of these states, see Zeev Maoz, "Power, Capabilities, and Paradoxical Conflict Outcomes," *World Politics*, 41 (January 1989), 239–66.

5 In the case studies section, six of these wars will be explored in detail.

6 An initiator in such a crisis challenges its opponent's commitment with the expectation that the adversary will back down rather than fight. Richard Ned Lebow, *Between Peace and War: The Nature of International Crisis* (Baltimore and London: The Johns Hopkins University Press, 1981), pp. 57–97.

7 Examples of asymmetric colonial wars in which the weaker liberation armies won include Indonesia against The Netherlands (1949); Viet Minh against France, especially in Dienbienphu (1954); Cyprus against Britain (1960); Algeria against France (1962), Aden against Britain (1967); and Vietnam against the US (1973). Cases of superior military powers withdrawing from their interventions abroad include Israel and the US from Lebanon (1982 and 1983); USSR from Afghanistan (1989); and India from Sri Lanka (1990). This study does not cover these types of wars.

8 For instance, William R. Thompson, *On Global War: Historical-Structural Approaches to World Politics* (Columbia: University of South Carolina Press, 1988); Robert Gilpin, *War and Change in World Politics* (Cambridge: Cambridge University Press, 1981). For system structure, see Kenneth Waltz, *Theory of International Politics* (New York: Random House, 1979), chs. 5 and 8. To structural and system theorists, war initiations by weaker powers do not seem significant occurrences worth theoretical explanation. These states are expected either to succumb to the wishes of their stronger adversaries or to affiliate themselves with states that are strong enough to offset their more powerful opponents. "Each is a policy of submission; in either case can the weak state act on its own." Michael Mandelbaum, *The Fate of Nations* (Cambridge: Cambridge University Press, 1988), p. 195.

9 See, for instance, Nazli Choucri and Robert C. North, *Nations in Conflict* (San Francisco: W.H. Freeman, 1974).

10 Taylor presents the analogy of road accidents to explain general vs. particular causes of wars. Every road accident is caused by two general factors: the invention of the internal combustion engine and the human desire to travel. However, other specific factors such as excessive speed, drunkenness, or bad roads are the more compelling immediate causes. "So it is with wars. International anarchy makes war possible; it does not make war certain" A.J.P. Taylor, *The Origins of the Second World War*, 2nd edn. (Greenwich, Conn.: Fawcett Publications, 1961). See also John A. Vasquez, *The War Puzzle* (Cambridge: Cambridge University Press, 1993, pp. 293–97), for distinction between underlying and proximate causes.

11 David J. Singer (ed.), *The Correlates of War, Vol.I Research Origins and Rationale* (New York: The Free Press, 1979); John A. Vasquez, "The Steps to War: Toward a Scientific Explanation of Correlates of War Findings," *World Politics*, 40 (October 1987), 108–145.

12 For a discussion, see Randolph M. Siverson and Michael P. Sullivan, "The Distribution of Power and the Onset of War," *Journal of Conflict Resolution*, 27 (September 1983), 473–94; J. David Singer, et al., "Capability, Distribution, Uncertainty, and Major Power War," in Bruce Russett (ed.), *Peace, War and Numbers* (Beverly Hills: Sage Publications, 1972); Wayne H. Ferris, *The Power Capabilities of Nation States* (Lexington: Lexington Books, 1973).

13 For various meanings of balance of power, see Ernst B. Haas, "The Balance of Power: Prescription, Concept or Propaganda?" *World Politics*, 5 (July 1953), 442–77.

14 Inis L. Claude, *Power and International Relations* (New York: Random House, 1964), p. 56; Ferris, *The Power Capabilities of Nation States*, p. 15; Singer et al., "Capability, Distribution," pp. 23–24. The "parity preserves peace" argument is also the basis of nuclear strategies such as mutual assured destruction.

15 Dina A. Zinnes, et al., "Capability, Threat and the Outbreak of War," in James Rosenau (ed.), *International Politics and Foreign Policy: A Reader in Research and Theory* (New York: Free Press, 1961), p. 470.

16 George Liska, *International Equilibrium: A Theoretical Essay on the Politics and Organization of Security* (Cambridge, Mass.: Harvard University Press, 1957), pp. 34–41; Stephen M. Walt, "Alliance Formation and the Balance of World Power," *International Security*, 9 (Spring 1985), 3–43; Stanley Hoffmann, "Balance of Power," in David L. Sills (ed.), *International Encyclopedia of the Social Sciences*, Vol.I (New York: Macmillan, 1968), p. 507.

17 Waltz, *Theory of International Politics*, p. 127. It should be noted that the focus here is not on balancing behavior of states per se, but the theory's conception of war initiation.

18 Siverson and Sullivan, "The Distribution of Power..."

19 Unlike balance of power, the power transition theory places the onus of war initiation on rising powers who have almost reached parity in power terms with their great power adversaries. The challenging nation may eventually surpass the dominant power, but in order to quicken passage, it prematurely indulges in war. A.F.K. Organski, *World Politics*, 2nd edn.

(New York: Alfred A. Knopf, 1968), pp. 364 and 366; A.F.K. Organski and Jacek Kugler, *The War Ledger* (Chicago and London: The University of Chicago Press, 1980).

20 Claude, *Power and International Relations*, p. 56.

21 Klaus Knorr, *The Power of Nations: The Political Economy of International Relations* (New York: Basic Books, 1975), p. 10. Often the rationale for arms buildups has been that the "weak are induced to give way to the strong without a fight." Edward N. Luttwak, *Strategy: The Logic of War and Peace* (Cambridge, Mass.: The Belknap Press of Harvard University Press, 1987), p. 3.

22 For instance, Erich Weede "Overwhelming Preponderance as a Pacifying Condition among Contiguous Asian Dyads, 1950–69," *Journal of Conflict Resolution*, 20 (September 1976), 395–411.

23 Michael D. Wallace, "Armaments and Escalation: Two Competing Hypotheses," *International Studies Quarterly*, 26 (March 1982), 37–56.

24 William W. Kaufman, "The Requirements of Deterrence," in William W. Kaufman (ed.), *Military Policy and National Security* (Princeton: Princeton University Press, 1956), p. 19.

25 Patrick M. Morgan, *Deterrence, A Conceptual Analysis* (Beverly Hills: Sage Publications, 1983), p. 30; Paul Huth and Bruce Russett, "General Deterrence between Enduring Rivals," *American Political Science Review*, 87 (March 1993), 61–73.

26 Glenn H. Snyder, *Deterrence and Defense: Toward a Theory of National Security* (Princeton: Princeton University Press, 1961), pp. 14–15.

27 John J. Mearsheimer, *Conventional Deterrence* (Ithaca and London: Cornell University Press, 1983), p. 15.

28 See Paul Huth and Bruce Russett, "What Makes Deterrence Work? Cases from 1900 to 1980," *World Politics*, 36 (July 1984), 496–526, for an examination and critique of these hypotheses; and Robert Jervis, "Deterrence Theory Revisited," *World Politics*, 31 (January 1979), 289–324 on the three waves of deterrence theorists.

29 This is implied in the writings of early deterrence theorists such as Herman Kahn, *On Thermonuclear War* (Princeton: Princeton University Press, 1961); Glenn H. Snyder, "Deterrence and Power," *Journal of Conflict Resolution*, 4 (June 1960), 163–81; Snyder, *Deterrence and Defense*. It is assumed that a challenger will not go to war if it is confronted by an opponent that is militarily its equal or superior. Paul F. Diehl, "Arms Races to War: Testing Some Empirical Linkages," *Sociological Quarterly*, 26 (1985), 331–49.

30 Jack S. Levy, "Review Article: When Do Deterrent Threats Work?" *British Journal of Political Science*, 18 (October 1988), 485–512.

31 Huth and Russett, "What Makes Deterrence Work?" p. 501.

32 Christopher H. Achen and Duncan Snidal, "Rational Deterrence: Theory and Comparative Case Studies," *World Politics*, 41 (January 1989), 143–69.

33 As Lebow and Stein contend, in the annals of military history, many credible commitments have been challenged by initiators while many vulnerable commitments have never been challenged. Richard Ned Lebow and Janice Gross Stein, "Beyond Deterrence," *Journal of Social Issues*, 43 (1987), 5–71.

34 Alexander L. George and Richard Smoke, *Deterrence in American Foreign Policy: Theory and Practice* (New York: Columbia University Press, 1974), pp. 520–32.

35 Major efforts include, Robert Jervis, *Perception and Misperception in International Politics* (Princeton: Princeton University Press, 1976); Robert Jervis et al. (eds.), *Psychology and Deterrence* (Baltimore and London: The Johns Hopkins University Press, 1985); John Steinbruner, "Beyond Rational Deterrence: The Struggle for New Conceptions," *World Politics*, 28 (January 1976), 223–45.

36 See for instance, George and Smoke, *Deterrence in American Foreign Policy*; Alexander L. George and Richard Smoke, "Deterrence and Foreign Policy," *World Politics* 41 (January 1989), 170–82; Lebow and Stein, "Beyond Deterrence."

37 Bruce Bueno de Mesquita, *The War Trap* (New Haven and London: Yale University Press, 1981), pp. 46–47.

38 Ibid., pp. 34 and 36.

39 On the static nature of the model, see James D. Morrow, "Moving Forward in Time: Paths toward a Dynamic Utility Theory of Crisis Decisions," in Urs Luterbacher and Michael D. Ward (eds.), *Dynamic Models of International Conflict* (Boulder: Lynne Rienner, 1985), p. 119; Patrick James, *Crisis and War* (Kingston and Montreal: McGill–Queens University Press, 1988), chs. 2–3.

40 Joseph S. Nye, "Old Wars and Future Wars: Causation and Prevention," *Journal of Interdisciplinary History*, 18 (Spring 1988), 581–90.

41 Two of the variables that I use in chapter 2 for explaining asymmetric war initiations have some similarities with those of BDM's on relative capability and third party support. However, the variables in this study are more specific – the first one being limited offensive capability, and the second, the defensive support from a great power. Additionally, this study attempts to pay equal attention to process as well as outcome; the latter has received limited attention in the BDM model.

42 Modest exceptions are Bueno de Mesquita, *The War Trap*; and Zinnes, et al., "Capability, Threat, and the Outbreak of War." The latter uses content analysis to explain the decisions of Austria-Hungary and Germany to go to war in 1914 even when their leaders knew they possessed inferior capability vis-à-vis their adversaries.

43 According to one study, the frequency of major power wars has decreased during the past five centuries. Jack Levy, "Historical Trends in Great Power War, 1495–1975," *International Studies Quarterly*, 26 (June 1982), 278–300. Another ambitious study argues that wars among great powers are becoming obsolete in the same way that social institutions such as slavery and dueling have disappeared. John Mueller, *Retreat from Doomsday: The Obsolescence of Major War* (New York: Basic Books, 1989).

44 A question can be raised whether the criteria on power capability adopted in this study might place Israel weaker than the Arab enemies in overall power capability. Four factors justify the inclusion of this case: (1) Israel held qualitative superiority in aircraft and tanks as well as quantitative parity in many other weapon systems. Historically, the former two

mattered decisively in determining battlefield outcomes in the Middle East; (2) although Egypt and Syria were fighting together, their cooperation was mostly strategic rather than tactical, and therefore did not seriously diminish Israel's relative capability vis-à-vis the opponents; (3) on a majority of indicators – trained personnel, per capita income, or gross national product – Israel held an advantage or was equal to Egypt when the war took place; and (4) Israel's capability cannot be viewed in isolation from the US, as Israeli material strength and strategic calculations heavily relied on the fairly assured US support. One may argue that the Soviet support and commitment to the Arab states were not as strong as the corresponding US support to Israel.

45 Other similar cases are not studied because of the comparative case study method adopted in this book. Six wars are deemed to be sufficient to provide an adequate number of cases across regions and time periods. In chapter 3, the criteria used for the selection of the cases are further elaborated.

2 Explaining war initiation by weaker powers in asymmetric conflicts

1 In the "instrumentalist" view, a rational actor, in order to attain the goals he has defined, chooses the best strategy from a set of options that he may have. In the alternate "proceduralist" conception of rationality, "an actor after properly defining his goals and considering all his alternatives chooses the best one in which psychological and non-logical influences are ignored. The decision would correspond to what an objective observer would consider as the best method to gain the value pursued." Frank C. Zagare, *The Dynamics of Deterrence* (Chicago and London: The University of Chicago Press, 1987), pp. 8–10. The proceduralist conception of rationality assumes the "infinite calculating ability and omniscience of a decision maker," that allow him to "calculate the outcome of an infinite set of alternatives and the expected value of each outcome." Glenn H. Snyder and Paul Diesing, *Conflict among Nations: Bargaining, Decision Making, and System Structure in International Crises* (Princeton: Princeton University Press, 1977), p. 341. In the instrumentalist view, a rational decision does not necessarily have to be as perfect or as omniscient as the proceduralist view of it entails.

2 Ellery Eells, *Rational Decision and Causality* (Cambridge: Cambridge University Press, 1982), pp. 4–5; Richard K. Ashley, "Bayesian Decision Analysis in International Relations Forecasting: The Analysis of Subjective Processes," in Nazli Choucri and Thomas W. Robinson (eds.), *Forecasting in International Relations: Theory, Methods, Problems, Prospects* (San Francisco: W.H. Freeman, 1978), pp. 151–52.

3 Eells, *Rational Decision and Causality*, p. 5; See also Janice Gross Stein and Raymond Tanter, *Rational Decision-Making: Israel's Security Choices, 1967* (Columbus: Ohio State University Press, 1980), ch. 8; Douglas E. Hunter, *Political/Military Applications of Bayesian Analysis: Methodological Issues* (Boulder: Westview Press, 1984).

4 Graham T. Allison, *Essence of Decision: Explaining the Cuban Missile Crisis* (Boston: Little, Brown, 1971), p. 37.

5 A status quo power in this context is a state that does not desire to alter the prevailing state of affairs as the benefits that derive from the continuation of the given situation are in its favor.

6 Steven Rosen, "War Power and the Willingness to Suffer," in Bruce M. Russett (ed.), *Peace, War and Numbers* (Beverly Hills: Sage Publications, 1972), p. 183; Snyder and Diesing, *Conflict among Nations*, p. 190. See also Steven Rosen, "A Model of War and Alliance," in Julian Friedman et al. (eds.), *Alliance in International Politics* (Boston: Allyn and Bacon, 1970), p. 224.

7 For an elaboration of this theme, see Jack Hirshleifer, "The Paradox of Power," UCLA Department of Economics, *Working Paper 582B* (Los Angeles, April 1991). This does not necessarily mean that the weaker side with most cost-tolerance will always win. Indeed, superior force determines most battlefield outcomes. What is pointed out is that if the stakes and interests are asymmetric, a weaker side with higher interest may engage in war and can show more cost-tolerance than the stronger opponent. This is especially true if the weaker side resorts to guerrilla techniques of warfare.

8 Thomas Schelling, *The Strategy of Conflict* (Cambridge, Mass.: Harvard University Press, 1980), p. 24.

9 "Strategic value" refers to the utility attached to the material power content of an object in dispute which has a bearing on a state's future power and bargaining capacity, while "intrinsic value" refers to the utility attached to intangible interests such as prestige and self-respect. Snyder and Diesing, *Conflict among Nations*, pp. 183–84. For the importance of issues in war initiation, see Kalevi J. Holsti, *Peace and War: Armed Conflicts and International Order 1648–1989* (Cambridge: Cambridge University Press, 1991).

10 Although the status quo power may be willing to provide some concessions, it may fear that the other side would not respond with matching concessions, but by greater efforts to extract bigger concessions. Robert Jervis, *Perception and Misperception in International Politics* (Princeton: Princeton University Press, 1976), p. 59.

11 Snyder and Diesing, *Conflict among Nations*, p. 77.

12 Ibid., p. 184.

13 Michael E. Brown, "Deterrence Failures and Deterrence Strategies," P-5842, *Rand Paper Series* (Santa Monica: Rand Corporation, March 1977), p. 2.

14 For the conditions that give rise to preventive wars, see Jack S. Levy, "Declining Power and the Preventive Motivation for War," *World Politics*, 40 (October 1987), 82–107.

15 Richard N. Rosecrance, "Deterrence and Vulnerability in the Pre-nuclear Era," *Adelphi Paper*, 160 (London: Autumn 1980), 24–30.

16 John G. Cross, *The Economics of Bargaining* (New York: Basic Books, 1969), pp. 13 and 45.

17 It is, however, argued that states that are engaged in protracted conflicts

have a higher chance of experiencing crisis more often because of mistrust, constant anticipation of violence, and resulting perceived value threat. Michael Brecher, *Crises in World Politics: Theory and Reality* (Oxford: Pergamon Press, 1993), p. 44.

18 The term "asymmetric conflict" is adapted from Andrew Mack, "Why Big Nations Lose Small Wars: The Politics of Asymmetric Conflict," *World Politics*, 27 (January 1975), 175–200.

19 Carl von Clausewitz, *On War*, Vol.I, trans. Col. J.J Graham (London: Routledge & Kegan Paul, 1962) p. 165; B.H. Liddell Hart, *Strategy*, 2nd edn. (New York: NAL Penguin, 1974), p. 321.

20 This is more in tune with operational strategy as opposed to grand strategy. The latter covers the mobilization and application of industrial, financial, demographic, and social aspects of war planning. For grand strategy see Michael Howard, *The Causes of War*, 2nd edn. (Cambridge, Mass.: Harvard University Press, 1983), p. 101.

21 Great powers tend to enter ongoing inter-state disputes at a higher frequency than minor powers, mainly because these states are enticed by their responsibilities for determining the nature of systemic or regional order. Charles S. Gochman and Zeev Maoz, "Militarized Interstate Disputes, 1816–1976," *Journal of Conflict Resolution*, 28 (December 1984), 585–616.

22 Jervis classifies those weapons that are effective in reducing defensive barriers and fortifications and in facilitating surprise attack as of offensive value, while defensive weapons are those that are useful in holding one's territory against attack. Robert Jervis, "Cooperation under the Security Dilemma," World Politics, 30 (January 1978), 167–214.

23 The three major conceptualizations of power that have been discussed in the literature are: (1) Power as control over resources, (2) power as control over actors, and (3) power as control over outcomes. Jeffrey Hart, "Three Approaches to the Measurement of Power in International Relations," *International Organization*, 30 (Spring 1976), 289–305; Zeev Maoz, "Power, Capabilities, and Paradoxical Conflict Outcomes," *World Politics*, 41 (January 1989), 239–66. International relations theorists commonly use control over resources as synonymous with a nation's power capabilities. For instance, Organski and Knorr treat power as equivalent to the capabilities of nations as measured by population, GNP, and the size of the armed forces. A.F.K. Organski, *World Politics*, 2nd edn. (New York: Alfred A. Knopf, 1968), chs. 6–8; Klaus Knorr, *Military Power and Potential* (Lexington: D.C. Heath, 1970), especially chs. 2 and 3.

24 This conception excludes the "differential exercise of power" by states in specific contexts as applied in force activation models. See James G. March, "The Power of Power," in David Easton (ed.), *Varieties of Political Theory* (New York: Prentice Hall, 1966), pp. 54–61. For holding power see, Frank C. Zagare, "Pathologies of Unilateral Deterrence," in Urs Luterbacher and Michael D. Ward (eds.), *Dynamic Models of International Conflict* (Boulder: Lynne Rienner, 1985), pp. 64–65. Zagare puts it in game theoretic terms; "that the player with holding power has the capability of remaining at an outcome in a sequential game longer than the player without holding power."

25 Kenneth E. Boulding, *Conflict and Defense: A General Theory* (New York: Harper & Row, 1962).

26 According to Wohlstetter, the major powers' capacity for long-distance lift exceeds those of other states whose home base may be closer to the theater of operations. For instance, in the 1960s, on the Thai–Laotian border, the US could lift from 8,500 miles away four times as much as China could from a distance of 450 miles. Faster and bigger cargo ships and aircraft, communication satellites etc. have further increased the ability of big powers to project power capability at a reduced cost. Albert Wohlstetter, "Illusions of Distance," *Foreign Affairs*, 46 (January 1968), 242–55.

27 The Falklands War proved that Britain, although fighting over 10,000 miles away from home waters, was able to supply its troops better than Argentina, which was barely 400 miles off the Islands. This was partly due to Argentina's deficiencies in transportation and communications, especially aircraft carriers, battleships and satellite reconnaissance. In the 1991 Persian Gulf War, the US-led coalition was able to defeat Iraq although the Kuwaiti theater was much closer to Iraq than to the US or its European allies.

28 For this distinction, see Paul Edwards (ed.), *Encyclopedia of Philosophy*, Vol.5 (New York: Macmillan, 1967), p. 60.

29 Sprout and Sprout contend that sufficient conditions are equal to environmental explanations which cannot be confirmed or refuted because history cannot be repeated. Therefore, historical explanations concentrate mostly on "showing how it was possible for a given x to occur; and (if decisions were strategically involved) how it came about that those decisions were taken." Harold and Margaret Sprout, "Explanation and Prediction in International Politics," in James N. Rosenau (ed.), *International Politics and Foreign Policy: A Reader in Research and Theory* (New York: The Free Press, 1961), p. 61.

30 W.B. Gallie, "Explanations in History and the Genetic Sciences," Mind, 64 (April 1955), 160–80. See, for a brief discussion of these three writers' positions, Edwards, *Encyclopedia of Philosophy*, Vol.4, p. 9. See also, Arthur C. Danto, "On Explanations in History," *Philosophy of Science*, 23 (January 1956), 15–30; William Dray, *Laws and Explanations in History* (Oxford: Oxford University Press, 1957); and William Dray, *Philosophy of History* (Englewood Cliffs: Prentice Hall, 1964).

31 For these strategies see, John J. Mearsheimer, *Conventional Deterrence* (Ithaca and London: Cornell University Press, 1983), pp. 33–58.

32 Edward N. Luttwak, *Strategy: The Logic of War and Peace* (Cambridge, Mass.: The Belknap Press of Harvard University Press, 1987), p. 92.

33 Mearsheimer, *Conventional Deterrence*, p. 36.

34 Ibid., p. 29; Clausewitz, *On War*, Vol.III, pp. 131–40.

35 Alexander L. George et al., *The Limits of Coercive Diplomacy: Laos, Cuba, Vietnam* (Boston: Little Brown, 1971), p. 17.

36 Liddell Hart, *Strategy*, p. 320.

37 This is the strategy that the US pursued in both the world wars. Edward N. Luttwak, "The American Style of Warfare and the Military Balance," *Survival*, 21 (March/April 1979), 57–60.

38 The exception to this argument is guerrilla strategies adopted by weaker

NOTES TO PAGES 25–30

challengers. "A highly motivated weak adversary can employ the guerrilla form of attrition strategy in an effort to wear out an opponent who is much stronger militarily but not so highly motivated to continue the war if his losses become excessive, compared to the stakes." George et al., *The Limits of Coercive Diplomacy*, pp. 19–20.

39 For guerrilla strategy, see Walter Laqueur, *Guerrilla: A Historical and Critical Study* (Boston: Little, Brown, 1976); Liddell Hart, *Strategy*, ch. 23; Gerard Chaliand, *Guerrilla Strategies* (Berkeley: University of California Press, 1982).

40 The principal mission of blitzkrieg is destruction of an opponent's army. Mearsheimer, *Conventional Deterrence*, pp. 35–43.

41 Mack, "Why Big Nations Lose Small Wars," p. 181. Jervis cites an example of this nature when many American leaders thought that Japan would never attack the US because it would fail in an all-out war. But they failed to understand that Japan contemplated only a limited war for limited objectives. Robert Jervis, "Deterrence Theory Revisited," *World Politics*, 31 (January 1979), 289–324.

42 Mack, "Why Big Nations Lose Small Wars," p. 117.

43 Robert E. Osgood, *Limited War: The Challenge to American Strategy* (Chicago: University of Chicago Press, 1957), p. 2.

44 Hirshleifer, "The Paradox of Power," p. 2.

45 A potential attacker can assess how risk-acceptant the stronger power is by studying its behavior during previous international crises in which it was involved. Paul Huth, *Extended Deterrence and the Prevention of War* (New Haven and London: Yale University Press, 1988), p. 54.

46 On similar constraints that the US has experienced in small wars, see Eliot A. Cohen, "Constraints on America's Conduct of Small Wars," *International Security*, 9 (Fall 1984), 151–81.

47 Bruce M. Russett, "Further Beyond Deterrence," *Journal of Social Issues*, 34 (1987), 99–104; Paul Huth and Bruce Russett, "Deterrence Failure and Crisis Escalation," *International Studies Quarterly*, 32 (March 1988), 29–45.

48 Richard K. Betts, *Surprise Attack: Lessons for Defense Planning* (Washington DC: Brookings Institution, 1982), p. 5.

49 Alex R. Hybel, *The Logic of Surprise in International Conflict* (Lexington: Lexington Books, 1986), p. 26. Stronger states tend to spurn surprise as they prefer "carefully prepared military operations conducted by the simplest methods at minimal organizational risks." Luttwak, *Strategy: The Logic of War*, p. 15.

50 Clausewitz, *On War*, Vol.I, p. 199.

51 Klaus Knorr, "On Strategic Surprise," *CISA Research Note* 10 (Los Angeles: UCLA, February 1982), p. 3.

52 George H. Quester, *Offense and Defense in the International System* (New York: John Wiley, 1977), p. 3.

53 Ibid. See also James D. Morrow, "A Twist of Truth: A Reexamination of the Effects of Arms Races on the Occurrence of War," *Journal of Conflict Resolution*, 33 (September 1989), 500–29, for an analysis of how transitory advantages and short-term windows of opportunity are exploited by states.

54 It is to be noted that the weaker initiators in asymmetric wars possess

relative advantage only in some categories of weapons prior to war initiation. The relative overall capability, defined in terms of resources, is still in favor of the defender.

55 Boulding, *Conflict and Defense*, p. 259.

56 Defensive weapons on the other hand, allow protecting and securing what one already holds. Jervis, "Cooperation under the Security Dilemma."

57 Robert Axelrod, "The Rational Timing of Surprise," *World Politics*, 31 (January 1979), 228–46.

58 For examples, see Michael D. Intriligator and Dagobert L. Brito, "Can Arms Races Lead to the Outbreak of War?" *Journal of Conflict Resolution*, 28 (March 1984), 63–84.

59 Samuel P. Huntington, "Arms Races: Prerequisites and Results," *Public Policy*, 8 (1958), 41–86.

60 Wars in which the great power ally actually fights with the weaker state in the same theater are excluded from the purview of this study because in such contexts the initiator no longer is weaker in comparison with the defender. In asymmetric war initiations, the great power allies of weaker states are expected not to become involved in actual fighting by committing troops in the battlefield, but to confine themselves to defensive measures such as political and economic support and arms supplies.

61 J. David Singer and Melvin Small, "Alliance Aggregation and the Onset of War, 1885–1945," in J. David Singer (ed.), *Quantitative International Politics: Insights and Evidence* (New York: Free Press, 1968), pp. 247–86.

62 Charles W. Ostrom Jr. and Francis W. Hoole, "Alliances and War Revisited: A Research Note," *International Studies Quarterly*, 22 (June 1978), 215–36.

63 Randolph M. Siverson and Joel King, "Attributes of National Alliance Membership and War Participation, 1815–1965," *American Journal of Political Science*, 24 (February 1980), 1–15.

64 Bruce Bueno de Mesquita and J. David Singer, "Alliance, Capabilities and War: A Review and Synthesis," *Political Science Annual*, 4 (1973), 237–80.

65 Studies find that revolutionary regime changes increase the chances of a state engaging in external conflicts. See Zeev Maoz, "Joining the Club of Nations, Political Development and International Conflict, 1816–1976," *International Studies Quarterly*, 33 (June 1989), 199–231; Stephen M. Walt, "Revolution and War," *World Politics*, 44 (April 1992), 321–68.

66 The existence of such "war hawks" in many societies has been noted by scholars like Schumpeter who argue that the aggressive policies of states can be explained only in part by the real and concrete interests of the people who control a society. Joseph A. Schumpeter, *Imperialism and Social Classes* (New York: Augustus M. Kelley, 1951), p. 84. According to another study, militaristic groups are usually formed through logrolling. They tend to enjoy certain benefits because of their monopoly over information, close ties to the state and certain motivational and organizational advantages deriving from their compact size. Jack Snyder, *Myths of Empire: Domestic Politics and Strategic Ideology* (Ithaca: Cornell University Press, 1991).

67 Brecher, *Crises in World Politics*, p. 47.

68 Arno J. Mayer, "Internal Causes and Purposes of War in Europe, 1870–1956:

A Research Assignment," *Journal of Modern History*, 41 (September 1969), 291–303.
69 Richard N. Rosecrance, *Action and Reaction in World Politics: International Systems in Perspective* (Boston: Little Brown, 1963), pp. 280 and 285.
70 Charles F. Hermann, "Decision Structure and Process Influences on Foreign Policy," in Maurice A East, et al. (eds.), *Why Nations Act: Theoretical Perspectives for Comparative Foreign Policy Studies* (Beverly Hills: Sage Publications, 1978), p. 70; see also Margaret G. Hermann and Charles F. Hermann, "Who Makes Foreign Policy Decisions and How? An Empirical Inquiry," *International Studies Quarterly*, 33 (December 1989), 361–87.
71 Alexander L. George, "The "Operational Code": A Neglected Approach to the Study of Political Leaders and Decision Making," *International Studies Quarterly*, 13 (June 1969), 190–222.
72 Paul Kennedy, *Strategy and Diplomacy: 1870–1945* (London: George Allen & Unwin, 1983), p. 170.
73 For requirements of the method see, Alexander L. George, "Case Studies and Theory Development: The Method of Structured Focused Comparison," in Paul G. Lauren (ed.), *Diplomacy: New Approaches in History, Theory, and Policy* (New York: The Free Press, 1979); Arend Lijphart, "Comparative Politics and Comparative Method," *American Political Science Review*, 65 (September 1971), 682–93; Richard Smoke, *War: Controlling Escalation* (Cambridge, Mass.: Harvard University Press, 1977), Appendix B.
74 The best enunciation of this method is, George, "Case Studies and Theory Development." The method is called focused since it deals with a few crucial aspects of the historical case, in this instance, the war initiation process, and structured because it employs similar general questions in order to facilitate data collection, analysis, and conclusions.
75 Christopher H. Achen and Duncan Snidal, "Rational Deterrence Theory and Comparative Case Studies," *World Politics*, 41 (January 1989), 143–69.
76 Alexander L. George, "Case Studies and Theory Development," Paper Presented at the Second Annual Symposium on Information Processing in Organizations (Carnegie-Mellon University, October 15–16, 1982).

3 The Japanese offensive against Russia, 1904

1 For this type of explanation, see Kanichi Asakawa, *The Russo-Japanese Conflict: Its Causes and Issues* (Port Washington, N.Y.: Kennikat Press, 1970).
2 For instance, see General De Negrier, *Lessons of the Russo-Japanese War* (London: Hugh Rees, 1906); G.A. Ballard, *The Influence of the Sea on the Political History of Japan* (London: John Murray, 1921).
3 See J.N. Westwood, *Russia against Japan, 1904–5; A New Look at the Russo-Japanese War* (Albany: State University of New York Press, 1986), p. 22 for the Army's calculations. The Navy's assessment is cited in Shumpei Okamoto, *The Japanese Oligarchy and the Russo-Japanese War* (New York: Columbia University Press, 1970), p. 101.
4 In 1903, the Russian population was 140 million to Japan's 46 million. Japan's national revenue was estimated at £25 million and that of Russia £208 million. Russia also could borrow easily from abroad for its war efforts,

especially from France. J.N. Westwood, *The Illustrated History of the Russo-Japanese War* (London: Sidgwick & Jackson, 1973), p. 26.

5 Georges Blond, *Admiral Togo*, trans. Edward Hyams (New York: Macmillan, 1960), p. 153.

6 Although Russia's potential for mobilization remained high, there were constraints in bringing in large numbers of troops to the Far East in the short run. Thus when the war broke out, Russia had only 80,000 soldiers stationed in Siberia, Manchuria, and along the Korean border. Christopher Martin, *The Russo-Japanese War* (London: Abelard-Schuman), 1967, p. 30.

7 Seizaburo Sato (personal interview, Tokyo, August 3, 1989). Japan's uneasiness in prolonging the war was evident in its agreeing at the Portsmouth Conference to divide the Sakhalin Islands and drop claims for indemnity. The Japanese were aware of their military and economic disadvantages in fighting a "war of endurance." Alfred L.P. Dennis, *The Anglo-Japanese Alliance* (Berkeley: University of California Publications, 1923), p. 23. Japan also felt the economic pinch as leading international financiers refused to sanction new loans for continued war efforts. Reginald Hargreaves, *Red Sun Rising: The Siege of Port Arthur* (Philadelphia: J.B. Lippincott, 1962), p. 175.

8 On the eve of war, Admiral Togo was well aware of this discrepancy in naval capability. R.V.C. Bodley, *Admiral Togo* (London: Jarrolds Publishers, 1935), pp. 151 and 160.

9 David Walder, *The Short Victorious War: The Russo-Japanese Conflict 1904–5* (London: Hutchinson, 1973), p. 71.

10 Denis and Peggy Warner, *The Tide at Sunrise; A History of the Russo-Japanese War, 1904–1905* (New York: Charter House, 1974), p. 18.

11 A Japanese historian compared Korea's strategic significance to Japan with that of the Low Countries to Britain. Ryochi Tobe (personal communication, Tokyo, September 18, 1989). For Japan's interests and policies in Korea, see Hilary Conroy, *The Japanese Seizure of Korea: 1868–1910, A Study of Realism and Idealism in International Relations* (Philadelphia: University of Pennsylvania Press, 1960).

12 George Alexander Lensen, *Balance of Intrigue, International Rivalry in Korea & Manchuria, 1884–1899*, Vol.II (Tallahassee: University Presses of Florida, 1982), p. 836.

13 The asymmetry in perceived balance of interests was summarized by a *Times* correspondent in these words: "After all, Russia is fighting for its dinner, and Japan for its life." Military Correspondent of *The Times*, *The War in the Far East: 1904–05* (London: John Murray, 1905), p. 32.

14 The Treaty had recognized the independence of Korea, ceded Chinese territories such as Formosa and the Liaotung Peninsula – including Port Arthur – to Japan, and opened four more Chinese cities for trade, and provided a huge war indemnity to be paid by China to the victor. W.G. Beasley, *The Modern History of Japan* (New York: Praeger, 1963), pp. 162–63.

15 Boris A. Romanov, *Russia in Manchuria, 1892–1906*, trans. Susan Wilbur Jones (Ann Arbor: Edwards Brothers, 1956), p. 2.

16 Beasley, *The Modern History of Japan*, p. 166; David J. Dallin, *The Rise of Russia in Asia* (New Haven: Yale University Press, 1949), p. 56.

17 Ibid., p. 75; Abraham Yarmolinsky (ed.), *The Memoirs of Count Witte* (London: William Heinemann, 1921), pp. 116–24; Andrew Malozemoff, *Russian Far Eastern Policy 1881–1904, With Special Emphasis on the Causes of the Russo-Japanese War* (Berkeley: University of California Press, 1958), p. 200.

18 Yarmolinsky, *The Memoirs of Count Witte*, pp. 123–24. Alexeyev passionately believed that Japan was not yet ready for war and that he could extract concessions from Tokyo by maintaining a tough military and diplomatic posture. His view was that "any concessions would lead to other concessions and that a yielding policy would be regarded as a sign of weakness." Martin, *The Russo-Japanese War*, p. 30.

19 Quoted in Dallin, *The Rise of Russia in Asia*, p. 46.

20 Martin, *The Russo-Japanese War*, pp. 25–26.

21 Ibid., p. 32.

22 *The Russo-Japanese War: Reports from the British Officers Attached to the Japanese and Russian Forces in the Field*, Vol.III (London: His Majesty's Stationery Office, 1908), p. 1.

23 Peter Padfield, *The Battleship Era* (London: Rupert Hart Davis, 1972), p. 168.

24 E.B. Potter (ed.), *Sea Power: A Naval History* (Englewood Cliffs: Prentice Hall, 1960), p. 354.

25 Walder, *The Short Victorious War*, p. 53.

26 Romanov, *Russia in Manchuria*, p. 15. The Viceroy to the Far East, Admiral Alexeyev, and his naval commanders reportedly stated: "The plan of operations should be based upon the assumption that it is impossible for our fleet to be beaten." Cited in Hargreaves, *Red Sun Rising*, p. 33. In the Russian leadership's view, although some of the Japanese officers were trained in Britain and Germany, "several of those officers had begun their military careers wearing armor and carrying a battle axe." Westwood, *The Illustrated History*, p. 22.

27 At a conference on December 28, 1903 the Tsar said: "War is unquestionably undesirable. Time is Russia's best ally. Every year strengthens us." The participants concurred with the Tsar, but made no serious efforts to avert war in the short term. Cited in Malozemoff, *Russian Far Eastern Policy*, p. 245.

28 The Baltic Fleet comprised eight battleships and three heavy cruisers while Togo's engaging fleet only had four battleships and eight heavy cruisers. However, the Japanese forces at Tsushima held superiority in light cruisers and torpedo boats. Blond, *Admiral Togo*, p. 213.

29 For the Battle of Tsushima, see Bodley, *Admiral Togo*, pp. 202–3.

30 See report by Major-General J.M. Home, in *The Russo-Japanese War: Reports*, pp. 211–14.

31 Kiyoshi Maekawa (personal interview, Tokyo, August 4, 1989).

32 David Woodward, *The Russians at Sea* (London: William Kimber, 1965), p. 125.

33 George Alexander Lensen (ed.), *Revelations of a Russian Diplomat: The Memoirs of Dimitri I. Abrikossow* (Seattle: University of Washington Press, 1964), p. 91.

34 Potter (ed.), *Sea Power*, p. 356.

35 Cited in William L. Langer, "The Origins of the Russo-Japanese War," in

Carl E. Schorske and Elizabeth Schorske (eds.), *Explorations in Crises: Papers on International History* (Cambridge, Mass.: Belknap Press of the Harvard University Press, 1969), p. 29.

36 General A. Kuropatkin, *The Russian Army and the Japanese War*, Vol. I, trans. Captain A.B. Linsay (New York: E.P. Dutton, 1909), p. 194. The Russian leadership was generally convinced that Japan would simply bear the costs of Russian policies without resistance. The Tsar told the German Emperor in September 1903 that there would be no war in the Far East because he did not wish one. Yarmolinsky, *The Memoirs of Count Witte*, p. 125.

37 Kuropatkin, *The Russian Army*, pp. 121–22 and 134.

38 Martin, *The Russo-Japanese War*, p. 28.

39 Blond, *Admiral Togo*, p. 160.

40 Westwood, *The Illustrated History*, p. 10; Hargreaves, *Red Sun Rising*, p. 11; The naval commanders were doubtful of their ability to completely destroy the Russian Fleet. All they could hope for was to render the fleet ineffective in the first few days of the battle. Ballard, *The Influence of the Sea*, p. 208.

41 Hargreaves, *Red Sun Rising*, p. 12.

42 Blond, *Admiral Togo*, p. 154. Togo was also aware that he had no reserves in case the need arose. Ballard, *The Influence of the Sea*, p. 199.

43 For tactics, see Potter (ed.), *Sea Power*, p. 365.

44 Negrier, *Lessons of the Russo-Japanese War*, p. 44.

45 Westwood, *The Illustrated History*, p. 22. Japan's plans were also based on the superior intelligence network that it had in Moscow and other major world capitals. Japan had spent about 10 percent of its war budget (120 million yen) on gathering intelligence on Russia. Dallin, *The Rise of Russia*, p. 79.

46 Woodward, *The Russians at Sea*, p. 125.

47 Quoted in Westwood, *Russia against Japan*, p. 22.

48 Cited in Okamoto, *The Japanese Oligarchy*, p. 101.

49 Cited in Richard Storry, *The Double Patriots* (Boston: Houghton Mifflin, 1957), p. 18.

50 Cited in Okamoto, *The Japanese Oligarchy*, pp. 101–2.

51 Quoted in Storry, *The Double Patriots*, p. 18.

52 Raymond A. Esthus, *Double Eagle and Rising Sun: The Russians and Japanese at Portsmouth in 1905* (Durham: Duke University Press, 1988), p. 14.

53 Tyler Dennett, *Roosevelt and the Russo-Japanese War* (Gloucester: Peter Smith, 1959), pp. 156–57.

54 Okamoto, *The Japanese Oligarchy*, p. 109.

55 Payson J. Treat, *Diplomatic Relations Between the US and Japan: 1885–1905* (Stanford: Stanford University Press, 1938), p. 238.

56 Cited in Okamoto, *The Japanese Oligarchy*, p. 110.

57 Cited in Ibid., p. 111.

58 Ibid., p. 112.

59 Ibid.

60 John Albert White, *The Diplomacy of the Russo-Japanese War* (Princeton: Princeton University Press, 1964), p. 95; Ryoichi Tobe (personal communication).

61 Beasley, *The Modern History of Japan*, p. 164.

NOTES TO PAGES 53–58

62 Ballard, *The Influence of the Sea*, p. 195.
63 Beasley, *The Modern History of Japan*, pp. 164–65.
64 Ballard, *The Influence of the Sea*, p. 188.
65 Westwood, *The Illustrated History*, p. 26; Anthony J. Watts and Brian G. Gordon, *The Imperial Japanese Navy* (Garden City, N.Y.: Doubleday, 1971), p. x.
66 Kuropatkin, *The Russian Army*, p. 123.
67 Ian H. Nish, *The Origins of the Russo-Japanese War* (London and New York: Longman, 1985), p. 27.
68 Military Correspondent of *The Times, War in the Far East*, p. 6.
69 Malozemoff, *Russian Far Eastern Policy*, pp. 165–66; Nish, *Origins of the Russo-Japanese War*, p. 105. Other stated reasons for no war were the position of Ito and the lack of a powerful ally to provide defensive cover.
70 The Japanese military historians whom I interviewed generally agree that without the defensive alliance with Britain no war would have been possible in 1904. (Personal interviews, Tokyo, August, 1989); See also White, *Diplomacy of the Russo-Japanese War*, p. 96; William L. Langer, *The Diplomacy of Imperialism: 1890–1902*, Vol. II (New York: Alfred A. Knopf, 1935), p. 720.
71 See Dennis, *The Anglo-Japanese Alliance* for the Treaty's provisions.
72 Captain M.D. Kennedy, *Some Aspects of Japan and Her Defense Forces* (London: Kegan Paul, 1928), p. 49.
73 Seizaburo Sato (personal interview).
74 White, *Diplomacy of the Russo-Japanese War*, p. 96.
75 Dallin, *The Rise of Russia*, p. 82; Dennett, *Roosevelt and the Russo-Japanese War*, pp. 27–30.
76 Langer, *Diplomacy of Imperialism*, p. 721.
77 Warner and Warner, *The Tide at Sunrise*, p. 132.
78 Dallin, *The Rise of Russia*, p. 84. The Germans also thought if Russia was humiliated in the Far East, Britain would attempt to form an alliance with them at the height of the Russo-Japanese war and would be willing to pay a high price. Langer, *Diplomacy of Imperialism*, p. 721.
79 Langer "Origins of the Russo-Japanese War," pp. 3–45; André Tardieu, *France and the Alliances: The Struggle for the Balance of Power* (New York: Macmillan, 1908), pp. 18–21.
80 Blond, *Admiral Togo*, p. 146.
81 Dennis, *The Anglo-Japanese Alliance*, p. 4; Frank W. Ikle, "The Triple Intervention, Japan's Lesson in the Diplomacy of Imperialism," *Monumenta Nipponica*, 22 (1967), 122–30.
82 Nish, *Origins of the Russo-Japanese War*, p. 27.
83 Ikle, "The Triple Intervention", pp. 22–30.
84 For the Japanese leadership's deliberations, see Ibid.
85 Cited in White, *Diplomacy of the Russo-Japanese War*, p. 83.
86 Malozemoff, *Russian Far Eastern Policy*, p. 165.
87 Michael Montgomery, *Imperialist Japan: The Yen to Dominate* (London: Christopher Helm, 1987), p. 177.
88 Cited in Langer, *Diplomacy of Imperialism*, p. 720.
89 Okamoto, *The Japanese Oligarchy*, pp. 25 and 96–99; Roger F. Hackett, "Political Modernization and the Meiji Genro," in Robert E. Ward (ed.), *Political*

Development in Modern Japan (Princeton: Princeton University Press, 1968), pp. 65–97.

90 Nish, *Origins of the Russo-Japanese War*, pp. 44–45.

91 White, *Diplomacy of the Russo-Japanese War*, pp. 85–86.

92 Nish, *Origins of the Russo-Japanese War*, p. 246.

93 Lesley Connors, *The Emperor's Advisor: Saionji Kinmochi and Pre-War Japanese Politics* (London: Croom Helm, 1987), p. 13.

94 Ibid.

95 Nish, *Origins of the Russo-Japanese War*, pp. 95–96.

96 E.E.N. Causton, *Militarism and Foreign Policy in Japan* (London: George Allen & Unwin, 1936), p. 39.

97 Ibid., p. 184.

98 Ibid., pp. 105–6.

99 Ibid., pp. 110–12.

100 Delmar M. Brown, *Nationalism in Japan, An Introductory Historical Analysis* (Berkeley: University of California Press, 1955), pp. 132–40.

101 Causton, *Militarism and Foreign Policy*, p. 115.

102 Montgomery, *Imperialist Japan*, pp. 181–82.

103 Ibid., pp. 184–89.

104 These proposals demanded the removal of any restrictions on Japan for the strategic use of Korea, deletion of the article dealing with the neutral zone, recognition of the territorial integrity of both China and Korea, acceptance that Korea was outside the Russian sphere of interest, and the acknowledgement of Japanese rights in Manchuria. White, *Diplomacy of the Russo-Japanese War*, p. 122.

105 Langer, *Diplomacy of Imperialism*, p. 472.

106 Patrick M. Morgan, *Deterrence: A Conceptual Analysis*, 2nd. edn. (Beverly Hills: Sage Publications, 1983), pp. 42–43.

4 The Japanese attack on Pearl Harbor, 1941

1 For instance, see Winston S. Churchill, *The Second World War, Vol. III: The Grand Alliance* (Boston: Houghton Mifflin, 1950), p. 603. In Churchill's words, it was impossible to believe Japan would fight with Britain and the US, and in the end, Russia. "A declaration of war by Japan could not be reconciled with reason ... But governments and peoples do not always take rational decisions. Sometimes they take mad decisions ... I have not hesitated to record repeatedly my disbelief that Japan would go mad." See also Rear Admiral Samuel E. Morison, *History of United States Naval Operations in World War II, Vol.III: The Rising Sun in the Pacific* (Boston: Little, Brown, 1951), p. 132 for the irrationality attribution.

2 At a liaison conference on October 23, 1941, the consensus was that the US power potential was "beyond comparison greater than that of Japan." It was also agreed that the US had built industries for making weapons for use in Europe "which could at any moment be mobilized forthwith for the war against Japan," and that Japan could in no way defeat the US decisively. Shigenori Togo, *The Cause of Japan* (New York: Simon and Schuster, 1956), pp. 125–26.

3 The same liaison conference also agreed that there was no chance of waging separate wars against Britain and the US. Ibid., pp. 125–26. At the Imperial Conference on September 6, 1941, it was stated that a war with the US involved great risks with no assurance of victory. The decision, however, boiled down to the contention that "there will never be a better time than now." Quoted in Nobutake Ike, *Japan's Decision for War, Records of the 1941 Policy Conferences* (Stanford: Stanford University Press, 1967), p. 134.

4 Cited in Paul Kennedy, *The Rise and Fall of the Great Powers: Economic Change and Military Conflict from 1500 to 2000* (New York: Random House, 1987), p. 303.

5 Masanori Ito, *The End of the Imperial Japanese Navy*, trans. Andrew Y. Kuroda and Roger Pineau (New York: Macfadden Books, 1965), pp. 171–72. Despite the overall weakness vis-à-vis its chief adversaries, Japan did achieve qualitative and for a limited period, quantitative advantage in naval strength against the US in the Pacific. For instance, when the attack took place, the US had nine battleships in the Pacific, in addition to four in the Atlantic. The US only retained three aircraft carriers in the Pacific, whereas Japan possessed ten such vessels. E.B. Potter (ed.), *Sea Power in Naval History* (Englewood Cliffs: Prentice Hall, 1960), p. 647. Japan had a total of eleven aircraft carriers to America's eight. However, in overall air power the US held a qualitative and quantitative edge. In December 1941, the US Navy possessed 5,260 aircraft to Japan's 3,202, of which some 1,035 were carrier-type planes.

6 For a discussion of this incompatibility, see Michael A. Barnhart, *Japan Prepares for Total War: The Search for Economic Security 1919–1941* (Ithaca: Cornell University Press, 1987), p. 19.

7 The "Orange" war plans of the US had called for the occupation of Manila Bay and other navigable harbors in the Philippines as well as the mandated islands of Japan while imposing a military and economic blockade. Gerald E. Wheeler, *Prelude to Pearl Harbor: The United States Navy and the Far East 1921–1931* (Columbia: University of Missouri Press, 1963), p. 80.

8 Robert Dallek, *Franklin D. Roosevelt and American Foreign Policy, 1932–1945* (New York: Oxford University Press, 1979), pp. 239 and 272–73.

9 John Mueller, "Pearl Harbor: Military Inconvenience, Political Disaster," *International Security*, 16 (Winter 1991/92) 172–203.

10 For the text, see US Department of State, *Prelude to Infamy: Official Report on the Final Phase of US–Japanese Relations October 17 to December 7, 1941* (Washington DC: The United States News, 1943), pp. 37–38.

11 Togo, *The Cause of Japan*, pp. 125–26. According to a Japanese naval historian, the Hull Note had the effect of "pushing Japan to a corner." Japan had fought a bloody war in China with great human and material sacrifice and it was asked to give up all that, a condition totally unacceptable to the army. Masatake Okumiya (personal interview, Tokyo, August 4, 1989).

12 George contends that the US pursued a "highly ambitious" coercive diplomacy and relied almost exclusively on "sticks" while scantily using "carrots" to make its demands more palatable to Japan. Alexander L. George, *Forceful Persuasion: Coercive Diplomacy as an Alternative to War* (Washington DC, United Institute of Peace Press, 1991), p. 22.

13 Roberta Wohlstetter, *Pearl Harbor: Warning and Decision* (Stanford: Stanford University Press, 1962), pp. 230–31.

14 The Japanese leaders, especially Tojo considered US naval deployments as provocative and specifically directed against the survival of Japan. Robert G.C. Butow, *Tojo and the Coming of the War* (Princeton: Princeton University Press, 1961), p. 190.

15 Cited in Louis Morton, "Japan's Decision for War (1941)," in Kent Roberts Greenfield (ed.), *Command Decisions* (New York: Harcourt, Brace, 1959), p. 73.

16 Ibid., p. 87.

17 Mitsuo Fuchida and Masatake Okumiya, *Midway: The Battle that Doomed Japan* (Annapolis: United States Naval Institute, 1955), pp. 20–21.

18 Yoichi Hirama, "Interception-Attrition Strategy: The Sun against the Eagle," *Journal of the Pacific Society* (January 1989), 9–21.

19 Herbert Feis, *The Road to Pearl Harbor* (New York: Atheneum, 1964), p. 270; These leaders seemed to consciously or unconsciously remind themselves of the lessons from the Russo-Japanese War of 1904–5. In that war, despite the larger territorial size and aggregate power capability of Russia, Japan could make early military successes by employing surprise and new tactical concepts. The war was concluded in Japan's favor following the timely intervention of the then US President, Theodore Roosevelt. For evidence of this learning, see Ike, *Japan's Decision for War*, pp. xxv–xxvi. For the Japanese decision-making in 1904, see ch. 3 of the present volume.

20 Cited in Paul S. Dull, *The Battle History of the Imperial Japanese Navy, 1941–1945* (Annapolis: Naval Institute Press, 1978), p. 7.

21 Ibid.; Gordon W. Prange, *At Dawn we Slept: The Untold Story of Pearl Harbor* (New York: McGraw Hill, 1981), p. 14; Fujiwara Akira, "The Role of the Japanese Army," in Dorothy Borg and Shumpei Okamoto (eds.), *Pearl Harbor as History: Japanese–American Relations 1931–1941* (New York: Columbia University Press, 1973), p. 195.

22 Wohlstetter, *Pearl Harbor: Warning and Decision*, p. 342.

23 Ibid., p. 343.

24 Morton, "Japan's Decision for War (1941)," p. 74; Admiral Tomioka Sadatoshi, an important official in the Japanese Naval Staff, summarized the strategic calculations in these words:

> Before and at the beginning of war we all believed in the concept of limited war ... and anticipated the course of the war as follows: Firstly, to attain overwhelming supremacy over the enemy forces in the early stages and create a strategic equilibrium against the Allies; then to seek a favorable opportunity to enter into negotiations with our enemies for a compromise peace, keeping enough potential to continue the war ..."

Quoted in Ikeda Kiyoshi, "Japanese Strategy and the Pacific War, 1941–5," in Ian Nish (ed.), *Anglo-Japanese Alienation 1919–1952* (Cambridge: Cambridge University Press, 1982), p. 144.

25 Morton, "Japan's Decision for War (1941)," p. 87.

26 Masuo Kato, *The Lost War: A Japanese Reporter's Inside Story* (New York: Alfred A. Knopf, 1946), p. 56.

27 Charles Bateson, *The War with Japan: A Concise History* (London: Barrie and Rockliff, 1968), p. 39.

196

28 Kiyoshi, "Japanese Strategy and the Pacific War, 1941–5," p. 144.
29 Ito, *The End of the Imperial Japanese Navy*, p. 14; Yamamoto reportedly told Kanoye: "If you tell me that it is necessary that we fight, then in the first six months to a year of war against the US and England, I will run wild, and I will show you an uninterrupted succession of victories; I must tell you that, should the war be prolonged for two or three years, I have no confidence in our ultimate victory." Cited in Wohlstetter, *Pearl Harbor: Warning and Decision*, p. 350.
30 Bateson, *The War with Japan*, p. 33.
31 Fuchida and Okumiya, *Midway: The Battle that Doomed Japan*, p. 34.
32 Bateson, *The War with Japan*, p. 41; Kennedy, *The Rise and Fall of the Great Powers*, p. 301.
33 George Quester, *Offense and Defense in the International System* (New York: John Wiley, 1977), p. 148.
34 James H. Belote and William M. Belote, *The Titans of the Seas: The Development and Operations of Japanese and American Carrier Task Forces During World War II* (New York: Harper & Row, 1975), pp. 19–20.
35 Ibid., p. 20.
36 Ian Nish, *Japanese Foreign Policy 1869–1942: Kasumigaseki to Miyakezaka* (London: Routledge and Kegan Paul), 1977, p. 167.
37 Fuchida and Okumiya, *Midway: The Battle that Doomed Japan*, p. 12.
38 Ito, *The End of the Imperial Japanese Navy*, p. 18.
39 Belote and Belote, *The Titans of the Seas*, p. 26.
40 The Japanese Navy possessed the tactical capability to score a higher hit rate than other carrier-based forces of the time. Unlike the British and American practice of using one or two carriers in a single operation, the Japanese Navy adopted the tactic of using six fleet carriers at one time. The carrier task force also had attempted a long-distance expedition of 3,500 nautical miles, a feat no other such force had tried in the past. Masatake Okumiya, "Some Background to Remember Pearl Harbor," Unpublished Ms. (Tokyo: December 1989).
41 Belote and Belote, *The Titans of the Seas*, pp. 23–24; Kiyoshi Maekawa, (personal interview, Tokyo, August 4, 1989); Bateson, *The War with Japan*, p. 41.
42 Ito, *The End of the Imperial Japanese Navy*, pp. 7–10; Hosaya Chihiro, "Britain and the United States in Japan's View of the International System, 1919–1937," in Ian Nish (ed.), *Anglo-Japanese Alienation 1919–1952*, (Cambridge: Cambridge University Press, 1982), p. 10.
43 Nish, *Japanese Foreign Policy 1869–1942*, pp. 204–7; Stephen E. Pelz, *Race to Pearl Harbor: The Failure of the Second London Naval Conference and the Onset of World War II* (Cambridge, Mass.: Harvard University Press, 1974), p. 14.
44 Ibid., p. 32; Ito, *The End of the Imperial Japanese Navy*, p. 11.
45 Cited in Morton, "Japan's Decision for War (1941)," p. 66.
46 F.C. Jones, *Japan's New Order in East Asia: Its Rise and Fall 1937–45* (London: Oxford University Press, 1954), p. 83.
47 Bateson, *The War with Japan*, p. 39.
48 Kennedy, *The Rise and Fall of the Great Powers*, p. 301.

49 Morton, "Japan's Decision for War (1941)," p. 82. During the 1930s when Japan built naval systems up to the treaty limits, the US lagged behind in naval acquisition. Japan was able to acquire a total tonnage closer to 80 percent of that of the US. However, because of domestic pressures, especially following the passage of the Winson Bill in 1934, President Roosevelt decided to embark on an accelerated naval building program. Pelz, *Race to Pearl Harbor*, p. 25.

50 James B. Crowley, "A New Asian Order: Some Notes on Pre-war Japanese Nationalism," in Bernard S. Silberman and H.D. Harootunian (eds.), *Japan in Crisis: Essays on Taisho Democracy* (Princeton: Princeton University Press, 1974), p. 293; Ryoichi Tobe, (personal communication, Tokyo, September 18, 1989). A military historian summarized the Japanese leadership's thinking in Clausewitzian terms: "A small state which is involved in a contest with a very superior power, and foresees that each year its position will become worse," should "make use of the time when the situation is farthest from worse," if it considers war to be inevitable. The small state in this position is advised to attack. Captain M.D. Kennedy, *Some Aspects of Japan and Her Defence Forces* (London: Kegan Paul, 1928), p. 137.

51 Ike, *Japan's Decision for War*, p. 233.

52 Quoted in Togo, *The Cause of Japan*, p. 47.

53 The Statesman's Year Book (London: Macmillan, 1941), p. 510; Belote and Belote, *The Titans of the Seas*, p. 27.

54 Ike, *Japan's Decision for War*, pp. 130–31.

55 Johanna Menzel Meskill, *Hitler and Japan: The Hollow Alliance* (New York: Atherton Press, 1966), p. 8; Jones, *Japan's New Order in East Asia*, pp. 102–3; and Frank William Ikle, *German–Japanese Relations 1936–1940* (New York: Bookman Associates 1956), pp. 34–39.

56 Ryoichi Tobe (personal communication); Jones, *Japan's New Order in East Asia*, pp. 200–1.

57 For the negotiations, see Meskill, *Hitler and Japan*, pp. 10–12; Delmar M. Brown, *Nationalism in Japan, An Introductory Historical Analysis* (Berkeley: University of California Press, 1955), p. 218.

58 Japan expected that through the alliance Germany would provide Tokyo with long-term and short-term economic and technological assistance in the form of machine tools, armaments, and critical raw materials and help produce synthetic goods so as to lessen its external dependence for strategic raw materials. Meskill, *Hitler and Japan*, pp. 21 and 143.

59 Kato, *The Lost War*, p. 43; Ernst L. Presseisen, *Germany and Japan, A Study in Totalitarian Diplomacy 1933–1941* (The Hague: Martinus Nijhoff 1958), pp. 257 and 259. In the strategic calculations of Hitler, American neutrality could be prolonged until Britain was defeated. A surprise Japanese attack on British possessions in South East Asia, especially in Singapore, would result in a quick victory for Japan so that the US would not have the time to enter the war in the Pacific. If the US entered prematurely, the Axis powers would be able to conclude the war rapidly. David J. Dallin, *Soviet Russia and the Far East* (New Haven: Yale University Press, 1948), p. 161.

60 William L. Langer and S. Everett Gleason, *The Undeclared War: 1940–1941* (New York: Harper & Brothers, 1953), p. 30.

61 Nish, *Japanese Foreign Policy 1869–1942*, p. 246; Jones *Japan's New Order in East Asia*, p. 324.

62 Quoted in Ibid., p. 325.

63 A limited agreement delineating respective military spheres of the three Axis powers was signed only on January 18, 1942. Even this agreement failed to provide either an integrated operational plan or a common approach to strategic goals. Meskill, *Hitler and Japan*, pp. 51–52 and 59–60.

64 "Liaison Conference Decision Plan, November 11, 1941," cited in Meskill, *Hitler and Japan*, pp. 52–53.

65 Langer and Gleason, *The Undeclared War*, p. 355.

66 Ibid., p. 356; Stalin was interested in the Pact because it would allow him to focus all his attention on a possible war with Germany. Dallin, *Soviet Russia and the Far East*, pp. 153 and 163.

67 At the 34th Liaison Conference, Matsuoka vehemently argued for an attack on Russia without delay as once Germany defeated Russia, "we won't get anywhere diplomatically. If we attack the Soviets quickly, the United States won't come in." Ike, *Japan's Decision for War*, p. 65.

68 George Alexander Lensen, *The Strange Neutrality: Soviet-Japanese Relations during the Second World War 1941–1945* (Tallahassee: The Diplomatic Press, 1972), pp. 30–31 and 35–36. The Soviets observed neutrality until August 8, 1945, for a period of three and a half years, when they declared war on Japan. Dallin, *Soviet Russia and the Far East*, p. 173.

69 Ike, *Japan's Decision for War*, p. 194.

70 Bateson, *The War with Japan*, p. 21.

71 Yale Candee Maxon, *Control of Japanese Foreign Policy: A Study of Civil–Military Rivalry 1930–1945* (Berkeley and Los Angeles: University of California Press, 1957), pp. 72–90.

72 Ibid., p. 92.

73 Ibid., p. 100; Butow, *Tojo and the Coming of the War*, p. 36.

74 W.G. Beasley, *The Modern History of Japan* (New York: Praeger, 1963), p. 261; Richard Storry, *The Double Patriots, A Study of Japanese Nationalism* (London: Chatto and Windus, 1957), p. 70.

75 Ibid., 196; Jones, *Japan's New Order in East Asia*, pp. 14–17.

76 Butow, *Tojo and the Coming of the War*, pp. 80–81; Maxon, *Control of Japanese Foreign Policy*, pp. 108–12.

77 Ben-Ami Shillony, *Revolt in Japan: The Young Officers and the February 26, 1936 Incident* (Princeton: Princeton University Press, 1973), pp. 209–10; Toshikazu Kase, *Journey to the Missouri* (New Haven: Yale University Press, 1950), pp. 33–34.

78 Ibid., pp. 39–40. Yonai's departure "inaugurated a period of complete eclipse of civil authority." Maxon, *Control of Japanese Foreign Policy*, p. 149. It has been argued that the Yonai Cabinet "might have been able to get Japan firmly on the 'middle course' had not the spectacular German victories of May and June 1940 powerfully revived sentiment in favor of close alliance with the Axis." Storry, *The Double Patriots*, p. 260.

79 Until Kanoye's arrival, the Prime Minister and the Foreign Minister had acted as a restraint on the army's plans. The new cabinet agreed on a

foreign policy course similar to what the army field officers had long been clamoring for. Maxon, *Control of Japanese Foreign Policy*, p. 149.

80 Langer and Gleason, *The Undeclared War*, pp. 4–5.
81 Kase, *Journey to the Missouri*, p. 41.
82 Barnhart, *Japan Prepares for Total War*, p. 241.
83 Kato, *The Lost War*, pp. 48–51.
84 Ibid., p. 55. In Tojo's conception, "to break through the pressing international political situation, Japan must also employ diplomatic maneuvers, but history clearly showed that diplomacy, unless backed by force, would produce no effect whatsoever." Butow, *Tojo and the Coming of the War*, p. 46.
85 Jones, *Japan's New Order in East Asia*, p. 293.
86 Richard E. Lauterbach, "Secret Jap War Plans," *Life Magazine* (March 4, 1946), 18; George Morgenstern, *Pearl Harbor: The Story of the Secret War* (New York: Devin-Adair, 1947), p. 17; Fuchida and Okumiya, *Midway: The Battle that Doomed Japan*, p. 5.
87 Cited in Akira, "The Role of the Japanese Army," p. 189.
88 Ibid., p. 190.
89 Ibid., pp. 189–90.
90 Morton, "Japan's Decision for War (1941)," p. 66.
91 Cited in Prange, *At Dawn We Slept*, p. 15.
92 Cited in Ike, *Japan's Decision for War*, pp. 51 and 56–57.
93 Cited in Ibid., pp. 77–78; 106.
94 Cited in Ibid., p. 133.

5 The Chinese intervention in Korea, 1950

1 According to estimates, the PLA had sent nearly 350,000 men into North Korea between October 14 and October 25, 1950 to the complete surprise of US military command. Edwin P. Hoyt, *The Day the Chinese Attacked, 1950: The Story of the Failure of America's China Policy* (New York: McGraw Hill, 1990), p. 91.
2 The PLA strength in 1950 was estimated at about five million, divided into two: The Field Army and the Garrison Army. The former, comprising between two and three million, were mainly veterans of the Civil War and the latter, ex-Kumingtang troops. The quality of Garrison troops was reported to be low. John Gittings, *The Role of The Chinese Army* (New York: Oxford University Press, 1967), pp. 76–78. The US/UN enjoyed air, naval, and tank superiority. In October 1950, the US Navy possessed fifteen carriers and deployed 500 tanks in the Korean theater. The Chinese Air Force had an estimated 650 aircraft although many of them were of low quality. Harry G. Summers Jr., *Korean War Almanac* (New York: Facts on File, 1990), pp. 42, 50 and 83. Lacking modern tanks and artillery, China relied on arms such as mortars, light machine guns, and hand grenades. During the early stages China had sent only about 270,000 to 340,000 troops against a far better equipped UN total of 440,000. Communications and transportation also posed problems for the Chinese as they were vulnerable to US attack. Allen S. Whiting, *China Crosses the Yalu: The Decision to Enter the Korean War* (Stanford: Stanford University Press, 1962), pp. 122–23.

3 At a Politburo meeting held on October 1, 1950 Mao Tse-tung agreed with the opponents of intervention who argued that China was about to fight a country that emerged as the most powerful nation after World War II. The meeting noted the several times greater ability of the US to produce all key industrial goods compared with China and the overwhelming nuclear and conventional forces that it possessed. Several leaders argued that despite China's superiority in raw troop strength, a large number of the forces was scattered throughout the large country. Their weapons were mostly captured from the Kumingtang (KMT) and the retreating Japanese forces. After four years of civil war, the PLA remained battle fatigued and was still confronting the remnants of the KMT forces and local bandits. The regime was yet to establish firm grass-root control. Hao Yufan and Zhai Zhihai, "China's Decision to Enter the Korean War: History Revisited," *China Quarterly*, 121 (March 1990), 94–115.

4 "Mao's Dispatch of Chinese Troops to Korea: Forty-Six Telegrams July–October 1950," *Chinese Historians*, 5 (Spring 1992) 63–86.

5 For the US atomic threats and the Chinese consideration of them, see Rosemary J. Foot, "Nuclear Coercion and the Ending of the Korean Conflict," *International Security*, 13 (Winter 1988/89), 92–112; Roger Dingman, "Atomic Diplomacy During the Korean War," *International Security*, 13 (Winter 1988/89), 50–91.

6 According to Zhou En-lai, while Mao "hoped for a good outcome, he prepared for a bad outcome, even to the extent of reckoning that the US might use the atomic bomb against China." Quoted in Mark A. Ryan, *Chinese Attitudes Toward Nuclear Weapons: China and the United States During the Korean War* (Armonk, N.Y.: M.E. Sharpe), 1989, p. 30.

7 Summers, *Korean War Almanac*, p. 260.

8 Dingman, "Atomic Diplomacy During the Korean War."

9 On September 1, Truman expressed the hope that China would not interfere in the UN effort to establish peace in Korea and promised to withdraw the 7th Fleet from Formosa once the war was over. A day before that, Acheson had said that the US harbored no aggressive intentions toward China. *New York Times* (September 1, 1950), p. 1. For the US strategy of deterrence and reassurance, see Walter A. Zelman, "Chinese Intervention in the Korean War: A Bilateral Failure of Deterrence," *Security Studies Paper* 11 (University of California, Los Angeles, 1967).

10 Rosemary Foot, *The Wrong War: American Policy and the Dimensions of the Korean Conflict, 1950–1953* (Ithaca: Cornell University Press, 1985), p. 82.

11 John W. Spanier, *The Truman–MacArthur Controversy and the Korean War* (Cambridge, Mass.: The Belknap Press of Harvard University Press, 1959), p. 97.

12 Edgar O'Ballance, *Korea: 1950–1953* (Handen: Archen Books, 1969), p. 62.

13 Hoyt, *The Day the Chinese Attacked*, p. 89.

14 Cited in Foot, *The Wrong War*, p. 81. Similarly a CIA report on October 12, 1950 concluded that a Chinese intervention was highly unlikely and that "barring a Soviet decision for global war, such action is not probable in 1950." Cited in Joseph C. Goulden, *Korea: The Untold Story of the War* (New York: Times Books, 1982), pp. 276–77.

15 *Substance of Statements Made at the Wake Island Conference, October 15, 1950* (Washington DC: Government Printing Office, 1951), p. 5.
16 Ibid.
17 *New York Times* (September 11, 1950), p. 1.
18 James L. Stokesbury, *A Short History of the Korean War* (New York: William Morrow, 1988), p. 97.
19 Spanier, *The Truman–MacArthur Controversy*, pp. 125 and 130.
20 Hoyt, *The Day the Chinese Attacked*, p. 91.
21 Goulden, *Korea: The Untold Story of the War*, p. 312.
22 The relatively easy landing at Inchon and collapse of the North Korean Army gave MacArthur increased leverage in choosing further military advancements. J. Lawton Collins, *War in Peacetime: The History and Lessons of Korea* (Boston: Houghton Mifflin, 1969), pp. 141–42.
23 For the influence of Berlin on US thinking, see Russell D. Buhite, *Soviet–American Relations in Asia 1945–1954* (Norman: University of Oklahoma Press, 1981), p. 233.
24 Spanier, *The Truman–MacArthur Controversy*, p. 98.
25 *New York Times* (November 8, 1950), p. 1.
26 For the text of this draft resolution, see *Department of State Bulletin*, 23 (November 27, 1950), p. 853.
27 *New York Times* (November 16, 1950), p. 1.
28 Harry G. Summers Jr., *On Strategy: A Critical Analysis of Vietnam War* (Novato: Presidio Press, 1982), pp. 57–58.
29 Spanier, *The Truman–MacArthur Controversy*, p. 82.
30 Bernard Brodie, *War and Politics* (New York: Macmillan, 1973), p. 63; Callum A. MacDonald, *Korea: the War before Vietnam* (Houndmills: Macmillan, 1986), p. 201.
31 Spanier, *The Truman–MacArthur Controversy*, p. 9. The European Allies, especially Britain, feared that escalation of the war into mainland China would force the US to commit major segments of its troops to East Asia, leaving Europe vulnerable to a possible Soviet attack. They were concerned that the Soviets would not sit idle if China was attacked. Ibid., p. 165.
32 William W. Whitson, *The Chinese High Command: A History of Communist Military Politics, 1927–71* (New York: Praeger, 1973), p. 94.
33 Hoyt, *The Day the Chinese Attacked*, pp. 85–86.
34 Jonathan D. Pollack, "The Korean War and Sino-American Relations," in Harry Harding and Yuan Ming (eds.) *Sino-American Relations 1945–1955: A Joint Reassessment of a Critical Decade* (Wilmington: Scholarly Resources, 1989), p. 224.
35 Whitson, *The Chinese High Command*, p. 94; Shen Zhonghong (ed.), *The History of the Anti-America Supporting Korean War* (Peking: Chinese Military Academy, 1990), p. 9.
36 Michael Schaller, *Douglas MacArthur, The Far Eastern General* (New York: Oxford University Press, 1989), p. 202.
37 Statement contained in Mao's telegram on 13 October, 1950 to Zhou En-lai who was in the USSR. "Mao's Dispatch of Chinese Troops to Korea,", p. 72.
38 Chen Xiaolu, "China's Policy Toward the United States, 1949–1955," in Harry Harding and Yuan Ming (eds.), *Sino-American Relations 1945–1955: A*

Joint Re-assessment of a Critical Decade (Wilmington: Scholarly Resources, 1989), p. 190. Zhou's statement is in *Selected Works of Zhou Enlai*, Vol.II (Peking: Foreign Languages Press, 1981), p. 51.

39 Joseph Camilleri, *Chinese Foreign Policy, The Maoist Era and its Aftermath* (Seattle: University of Washington Press, 1980), p. 36.

40 Richard Whelan, *Drawing the Line: The Korean War, 1950–1953* (Boston: Little, Brown, 1990), p. 217.

41 Chai Cheng-Wen and Zhao Yong-Tian, *Panmunjom Negotiations* (Peking: PLA Publishing Agency, 1989) p. 73.

42 Chow Ching-Wen, *Ten Years of Storm: The True Story of the Communist Regime in China* (New York: Holt, Rinehart and Winston, 1960), p. 116.

43 David Rees, *Korea: The Limited War* (New York: St. Martin's Press, 1964), p. 113.

44 David Allan Mayers, *Cracking the Monolith: US Policy against the Sino-Soviet Alliance, 1949–1955* (Baton Rouge: Louisiana State University Press, 1986), p. 91.

45 Barton J. Bernstein, "The Policy of Risk: Crossing the 38th Parallel and Marching to the Yalu," *Foreign Service Journal*, 54 (March 1977), 16–22 and 29.

46 *Memoirs of a Chinese Marshal – The Autobiographical Notes of Peng Dehuai* (1898–1974), trans. Zheng Longpu (Peking: Foreign Languages Press, 1984), p. 473.

47 Spanier, *The Truman–MacArthur Controversy*, p. 87; Camilleri, *Chinese Foreign Policy*, p. 35.

48 In Zhou En-lai's words:

> With the decisive duel between China and the US imperialists being inevitable, the question is where to do it ... Korea as a battleground chosen by the imperialists is favorable to us ... Looking at three battlefronts, it is easy to understand that it would be much more difficult to wage a war against America in Vietnam, not to mention on the offshore islands, than here [Korea]. Here we have the most favorable terrain, the closest communication to China, the most convenient material and manpower backup ... and the most convenient way for us to get indirect Soviet support.

Zhou's Speech to CPV Conference, cited in Yufan and Zhihai, "China's Decision to Enter the Korean War."

49 The military leaders had apparently convinced their men that their superior tactics, doctrine, and higher morale could defeat the well-equipped opponent in a short war. Alexander L. George, *The Chinese Communist Army in Action, The Korean War and its Aftermath* (New York: Columbia University Press, 1967), p. 7.

50 Pollack, "The Korean War and Sino–American Relations," p. 220.

51 *Memoirs of a Chinese Marshal*, pp. 479–82.

52 "Mao's Dispatch of Chinese Troops to Korea," p. 67.

53 Russell Spurr, *Enter the Dragon: China's Undeclared War against the US in Korea 1950–51* (New York: Newmarket Press, 1988), p. 69.

54 Quoted in Ibid., p. 82.

55 Ye Yu-Meng, *On the Spot Reports of Dispatching Troops to Korea* (Peking: Ji-Nan Press, 1991), p. 44.

56 Schaller, *Douglas MacArthur, The Far Eastern General*, p. 202.

57 Camilleri, *Chinese Foreign Policy*, p. 38.
58 Yu-Meng, *On the Spot Reports of Dispatching Troops*, pp. 228 and 270.
59 Schaller, *Douglas MacArthur, The Far Eastern General*, p. 248; Summers, *Korean War Almanac*, p. 83. It is possible that the Chinese leaders were afraid of massive aircraft losses at the hands of a superior US air force. The MiG-15 had only limited range which might also have restricted their offensive use.
60 Hi Di (personal interview, Peking, August 8, 1992).
61 "Mao's Dispatch of Chinese Troops to Korea," p. 80.
62 The plan was to lure the American troops to northern areas, where the Chinese troops would conceal themselves for surprise attack. Hoyt, *The Day the Chinese Attacked*, pp. 93–94.
63 Manpower was a key element of the Chinese capability. In some instances, only one in five soldiers had a weapon and they were instructed to use grenades until they could capture a rifle from the enemy. Ibid., p. 92.
64 K.M. Panikkar, *In Two Chinas: Memoirs of a Diplomat* (London: George Allen & Unwin, 1955), p. 108.
65 Yu-Meng, *On the Spot Reports of Dispatching Troops*, p. 44.
66 "How to Understand the United States," *Current Affairs Journal*, 1 (November 5, 1950), cited in Whiting, *China Crosses the Yalu*, p. 142.
67 Li Xiangwen (personal interview, Peking, August 4, 1992); Du Ping, *In the Headquarters of the Volunteer Force* (Peking: PLA Publishing House, 1989), pp. 19–20.
68 *Selected Military Writings of Mao Tse-tung* (Peking: Foreign Languages Press, 1967), pp. 142–46.
69 Ibid., pp. 105–14.
70 Zhu Chun (personal interview, Peking, August 6, 1992).
71 For the offensive–defensive approach of the PLA, see Whitson, *The Chinese High Command*, p. 488.
72 Chinese forces employed this tactic vigorously in the second stage of the campaign that began in November 1950. *Memoirs of a Chinese Marshal*, pp. 475–77.
73 Roy E. Appleman, *Disaster in Korea: The Chinese Confront MacArthur* (College Station: Texas A&M University Press, 1989), p. 17.
74 Li Xiangwen (personal interview, Peking, August 4, 1992).
75 Melvin Gurtov and Byong-Moo Hwang, *China under Threat: The Politics of Strategy and Diplomacy* (Baltimore and London: The Johns Hopkins University Press, 1980), p. 33.
76 For the demobilization plans, see Ibid., p. 30; Yufan and Zhihai, "China's Decision to Enter the Korean War."
77 Appleman, *Disaster in Korea*, p. 17; During the final years of the Civil War, the PLA had captured about 60,000 pieces of heavy and light artillery, 582 tanks, 361 armored cars, 250,000 machine guns and several thousand other small arms. Gittings, *The Role of The Chinese Army*, p. 133.
78 Paul H.B. Godwin, *The Chinese Communist Armed Forces* (Maxwell Air Force Base, Ala: Air University Press, 1988), pp. 81 and 95.
79 Whitson, *The Chinese High Command*, pp. 461–62.
80 Du Ping, *In the Headquarters of the Volunteer Force*, pp. 18–20.
81 Yu-Meng, *On the Spot Reports of Dispatching Troops*, p. 44.

82 Speech at the Tenth Plenum of the Eighth Central Committee, September 24, 1962, quoted in Stuart Schram (ed.), *Chairman Mao Talks to the People, Talks and Letters: 1956–1971* (New York: Pantheon Books, 1974), p. 191.

83 Cited in Gurtov and Hwang, *China under Threat*, p. 46.

84 Cited in He Di, "The Most Respected Enemy: Mao Zedong's Perception of the United States," Paper Presented at the Conference on China's Foreign Policy (Washington, DC, Woodrow Wilson Center, July 7–9, 1992), pp. 18–19.

85 Khrushchev, who wrote about this meeting, does not suggest the precise nature of Soviet support, except that Stalin refused to take part in the war directly. *Khrushchev Remembers, The Glasnost Tapes,* trans. and eds. Jerrold L. Schecter and Vyacheslav V. Luchkov (Boston: Little, Brown 1990), p. 147. In the earlier published memoirs, Khrushchev discusses the meeting and suggests that initially Stalin and Zhou agreed on the futility of China's intervention. However, just before Zhou left Sochi, Stalin changed his mind and gave his concurrence. Khrushchev also mentions that Mao dispatched the Soviet leader many battle reports that Peng had sent to him from the field. *Khrushchev Remembers,* trans. and ed. Strobe Talbott (Boston: Little, Brown 1970), pp. 371–72.

86 Yufan and Zhihai, "China's Decision to Enter the Korean War." These authors make their case based on extensive interviews with Chinese decision-makers of the time.

87 "Mao's Dispatch of Chinese Troops to Korea," p. 68.

88 Panikkar, *In Two Chinas*, p. 117.

89 *Memoirs of a Chinese Marshal*, p. 473.

90 Quoted in Spurr, *Enter the Dragon*, p. 62. An article appeared in a Peking journal in November 1950 that also echoed the deterrent effect of Soviet nuclear weapons. It said: "The atomic bomb is no longer monopolized by the US. The Soviet Union has it too. If the US dares to use the atomic bomb she naturally will get the retaliation deserved ..." "How to Understand the United States," *Current Affairs Journal*, I (November 5, 1950), cited in Whiting, *China Crosses the Yalu*, p. 142.

91 The decision to withdraw advisers and pilots from the front line, eight days after the North Korean invasion, showed Moscow's desire to minimize its involvement in the war. Peter Lowe, *The Origins of the Korean War* (London: Longman, 1986), pp. 156–57.

92 Mayers, *Cracking the Monolith*, p. 90.

93 Gittings, *The Role of The Chinese Army*, p. 22.

94 Jurgen Domes, *Peng Te-huai, The Man and the Image* (London: C. Hurst, 1985), p. 60.

95 Cited in Gurtov and Hwang, *China under Threat*, p. 31.

96 Whitson, *The Chinese High Command*, p. 460.

97 Xiaolu, "China's Policy Toward the United States, 1949–1955," p. 190.

98 Steven M. Goldstein, "Sino-American Relations, 1948–1950: Lost Chance or No Chance?" in Harry Harding and Yuan Ming (eds.), *Sino-American Relations 1945–1955: A Joint Reassessment of a Critical Decade*, p. 128.

99 Hong Xue-Zhi, *Reminiscences of the War to Resist US Aggression and Aid Korea (1950–1953)* (Peking: PLA Literature Press, 1991), p. 26.

100 *Memoirs of Nie Rongzhen* (Peking: Liberation Army Publishing House), p. 738, quoted in Pollack, "The Korean War and Sino-American Relations," p. 217.
101 Cited in Whiting, *China Crosses the Yalu*, p. 64; Du Ping, *In the Headquarters of the Volunteer Force*, pp. 12–13.
102 Cited in Yufan and Zhihai, "China's Decision to Enter the Korean War"; Du Ping, *In the Headquarters of the Volunteer Force*, p. 17.
103 On the opposition, see Gurtov and Hwang, *China under Threat*, p. 55; James C. Hsiung, *Ideology and Practice: The Evolution of Chinese Communism* (New York: Praeger, 1970), pp. 172–73.
104 *Memoirs of Nie Rongzhen*, pp. 739–40, cited in Pollack, "The Korean War and Sino-American Relations," p. 218.
105 Cited in Lawrence Stephen Weiss, *Storm Around the Cradle: The Korean War and the Early Years of the People's Republic of China, 1949–1953* (Ph.D. Dissertation, New York: Columbia University, 1981), pp. 80–82; See also Ching-Wen, *Ten Years of Storm*, p. 116; "Red Guard Paper, February 1967," *Far Eastern Economic Review* (October 2, 1969), p. 25.
106 Yufan and Zhihai, "China's Decision to Enter the Korean War."

6 The Pakistani offensive in Kashmir, 1965

1 Following the 1947–48 War, India held nearly two-thirds of Kashmir (henceforth Jammu and Kashmir), and Pakistan most of the remaining portions (henceforth "Azad" or "Free" Kashmir). During the 1962 Sino-Indian War, China occupied parts of the territory in the Ladakh area. The Vale of Kashmir, including the capital, Srinagar, remained under Indian control.
2 For the operation and the war, see Russell Brines, *The Indo-Pakistani Conflict* (London: Pall Mall Press, 1968), pp. 9–10; Sumit Ganguly, *The Origins of War in South Asia: Indo-Pakistani Conflicts Since 1947* (Boulder: Westview Press, 1986), ch. 3.
3 Pakistan's Army Chief in 1965, General Musa, had recognized that India held a numerical superiority, although Pakistan possessed some qualitative advantages in tanks and aircraft. In his estimate, India held a 3:1 superiority in land forces. "The ratio in her favor was about 5:4 in East Pakistan, approximately 5:2 in West Pakistan and 5:1 in Kashmir." Mohammad Musa, *My Version: India–Pakistan War 1965* (New Delhi: ABC Publishing House, 1983), pp. 3 and 14–15.
4 International Institute for Strategic Studies, *The Military Balance 1965–66* (London: 1965), pp. 28 and 34.
5 *The Times of India* (Bombay: April 29, 1965), pp. 1 and 9.
6 See for the origins of the dispute, Michael Brecher, *The Struggle for Kashmir* (New York: Oxford University Press, 1953); Sisir Gupta, *Kashmir: A Study in India–Pakistan Relations* (Bombay: Asia Publishing House, 1966); Brines, *The Indo-Pakistani Conflict*, chs. 2–5.
7 In Bhutto's words: "If a Muslim majority area can remain a part of India, then the raison d'être of Pakistan collapses ... Pakistan is incomplete without Jammu and Kashmir both territorially and ideologically." Zulfikar

Ali Bhutto, *The Myth of Independence* (London: Oxford University Press, 1969), p. 180.

8 New Year's Message, *The Hindu* (Madras: January 2, 1952), cited in Brines, *The Indo-Pakistani Conflict*, p. 13.

9 Former Indian Air Force Chief, Arjan Singh, points out that New Delhi had just started the defense modernization program and was not sure of the strength of Pakistan's newly acquired Patton tanks and Sabre aircraft (personal interview, New Delhi, July 18, 1989).

10 S.N. Prasad (personal interview, New Delhi, July 18, 1989).

11 B.C. Chakravarthy (personal interview, New Delhi, July 18, 1989); Leo Heiman, "Lessons from the War in Kashmir," *Military Review* 46 (February 1966), 22–29.

12 Ganguly, *The Origins of War in South Asia*, p. 90; "The Army was given sufficient time to inflict more attrition on the Pakistani forces but not enough to launch a more punishing offensive." Brines, *The Indo-Pakistani Conflict*, p. 347.

13 Jasjit Singh (personal interview, New Delhi, July 21, 1989).

14 For the major Indian steps in integrating the state, see Brines, *The Indo-Pakistani Conflict*, p. 98.

15 Ibid., p. 238.

16 Ibid., p. 11.

17 As proven later on, this expectation did not materialize, as the Kashmiri people refused to support the invading guerrillas and regular Pakistani troops.

18 Abdul Ali Malik, "Operation Gibraltar: A General's View," *Muslim* (October 14, 1986); Musa, *My Version*, p. 2.

19 Salmaan Taseer, *Bhutto: A Political Biography* (New Delhi: Vikas Publishing House, 1980), p. 61.

20 Quoted in Ibid., p. 62. In Bhutto's conception, continued hostilities would disturb the status quo, which would be in the interests of Pakistan.

21 Mohammed Asghar Khan, *The First Round: Indo-Pakistan War 1965* (London: Islamic Information Services, 1979), p. 76.

22 Cited in Stephen P. Cohen, *The Pakistan Army* (Berkeley: University of California Press, 1984), p. 66. The widespread civil unrest in the Indian Kashmir, following the Hazrat Bal Incident, was viewed by Bhutto and his supporters as providing an opportune moment for military action.

> The spontaneity of the riots in Srinagar seemed to indicate seething discontent in the state. Bhutto digested this and deduced that if this was the prevalent feeling, the aspirations of the populations could be ignited into a full-scale anti-Indian insurgency. If these currents could be properly channeled into an insurrection, the Indian Government would be forced to reconsider its fossilized position on the future of Kashmir. (Taseer, *Bhutto: A Political Biography*, p. 59)

23 Musa, *My Version*, pp. 35–36; Amjad Ali Khan Chaudhry, *September '65: Before and After* (Lahore: Ferozsons, 1977), p. 47.

24 Herbert Feldman, *From Crisis to Crisis, Pakistan 1962–1969* (London: Oxford University Press, 1972), p. 141.

25 Anwar H. Sayed, *The Discourse and Politics of Zulfikar Ali Bhutto* (New York:

St. Martin's Press, 1992) p. 50. As a result of this belief, when the Indian offensive on Punjab occurred, the Pakistani Army was caught by surprise. Many soldiers in Lahore were engaging in morning exercise. Mohammed Yusuf (personal interview, Islamabad, July 25, 1989); Pakistan also had removed mines and fences on the Lahore/Sialkot front as per the Kutch agreements and had sent many troops on leave. Basheer Ahmed (personal interview, Islamabad, July 26, 1989).

26 Ehsm ul-Haq Malik (personal interview, Karachi, July 28, 1989). A leading Pakistani military analyst argues that the Indian deterrent threat was simply overlooked. A.R. Siddiqui, "September: Time for Critical Self-Assessment," *Defence Journal* (Karachi), 9 (1983), 1–7. During the course of the war, Shastri again threatened Pakistan with major counter-attacks if it did not withdraw its troops back to the cease-fire line. According to one retired Pakistani military commander, this unequivocal statement of intent was ignored by the Pakistani leadership as bluff. Riazul Karim Khan, "Higher Conduct of 1965 Indo-Pak War," *Defence Journal*, 10 (1984), 7–14.

27 M. Attiqur Rahman (personal communications, Lahore, September 22, 1989).

28 Basheer Ahmed (personal interview); Edgar O'Ballance, "The 1965 War in Retrospect," *Defence Journal*, 7 (1978), 15–19.

29 A.R. Siddiqi, "The War Analyzed," *Defence Journal*, 1 (1975), 1–12.

30 Brines, *The Indo-Pakistani Conflict*, p. 130.

31 M.H. Askari (personal interview, Karachi, July 27, 1989).

32 The leadership viewed Shastri's retaliatory warning as a bluff, intended to quell domestic opposition for allowing arbitration on the Kutch dispute. Pervaiz Iqbal Cheema (personal interview, Islamabad, July 25, 1989).

33 For the lessons of Rann of Kutch skirmishes, see William J. Barnds, *India, Pakistan and the Great Powers* (New York: Praeger, 1972), pp. 198–200. The author's interviews in Pakistan confirmed this general belief among the top military hierarchy at that time. According to Agha Shahi, a former Foreign Minister, after the Rann of Kutch episode there was a pronounced tilt in the Pakistani military's thinking regarding the usefulness of a limited, controlled offensive in order to alter the Kashmir imbroglio (personal interview, Islamabad, July 25, 1989).

34 Asghar Khan, *The First Round*, p. 74.

35 Brines, *The Indo-Pakistani Conflict*, p. 9.

36 Ibid., p. 76.

37 Sayed, *The Discourse and Politics of Zulfikar Ali Bhutto*, p. 48.

38 Mohammed Yusuf (personal interview).

39 To one analyst, this belief was due to the militarization of political life in Pakistan and the overemphasis on Kashmir in the domestic politics of the country that gave the armed forces exaggerated importance and power. M.V. Naqvi (personal interview, Karachi, July 27, 1989). The fighting capacity of one Muslim Pakistani soldier was claimed to be equivalent to five Hindu soldiers. Stephen P. Cohen, "Arms and Politics in Bangladesh, India and Pakistan," *Special Studies*, 49 (New York: Council on International Studies, State University of New York at Buffalo, 1973), p. 26.

40 For the army's new strategic and tactical concepts, see Chaudhry, *September '65: Before and After*, pp. 21–22.
41 Ibid., p. 24.
42 Ibid.
43 Cohen, *The Pakistan Army*, p. 145; General Musa also points out that in 1965 the Pakistani strategic doctrine was based on offense–defense. Musa, *My Version*, p. 14.
44 Feldman, *From Crisis to Crisis*, p. 147; B.M. Kaul, *Confrontation with Pakistan* (Delhi: Vikas Publications, 1971), p. 66.
45 With the introduction of this policy, tensions between the two countries mounted. Barnds, *India, Pakistan and the Great Powers*, p. 194. The United Nations Military Observer Group for India and Pakistan (UNMOGIP) reported a "disturbing increase in the number of incidents involving violations of the CFL [cease-fire line] since the beginning of 1965." By mid-June 1965, 377 border violations had been confirmed for the year, of which 218 were committed by Pakistan and 159 by India. United Nations, Security Council, *Report by the Secretary General on the Current Situation in Kashmir with Particular Reference to the Cease-fire Agreement, The Cease-fire Line and the Functioning of UNMOGIP*, S/6651 (September 3, 1965).
46 Dilip Mukerjee, *Zulfikar Ali Bhutto, Quest for Power* (Delhi: Vikas Publishing House, 1972), p. 46.
47 Cohen, *The Pakistan Army*, p. 145.
48 A commentary in a leading Pakistani defense journal summarizes the military leadership's thinking in 1965:

> After four years of arms inflow from the US, the armed forces were beginning to experience a new sense of strength. . . Life looked like an endless adventure with armor, medium and heavy artillery and modern jet fighters coming in. An army in such a frame of mind must find a catharsis in action: India had been there like always to provide the opportunity almost on demand. (*Defence Journal*, 4, 1978, 1–10.)

49 Attiqur Rahman (personal communication); John Fricker, *Battle for Pakistan: The Air War of 1965* (Shepperton: Ian Allan, 1979), pp. 11 and 13.
50 Basheer Ahmed (personal interview); Brines, *The Indo-Pakistani Conflict*, pp. 11–12.
51 Zulfikar Ali Bhutto, interviewed by Kuldip Nayar, *Sunday Magazine* (Calcutta: July 10–16, 1983), reprinted in *Strategic Digest* (New Delhi: July 1984), 745–46.
52 Mohammad Ayub Khan, *Friends Not Masters: A Political Autobiography* (Oxford: Oxford University Press, 1967), p. 122; Ayub Khan, "The Pakistan–American Alliance: Stresses and Strains," *Foreign Affairs*, 42 (January 1964), 195–209.
53 *Sunday Times* (October 20, 1963), cited in G.W. Choudhury, *Pakistan's Relations with India 1947–1966* (London: Pall Mall Press, 1968), p. 270.
54 Ibid.
55 Speech at the National Assembly of Pakistan, July 17, 1963, in Zulfikar Ali Bhutto, *Foreign Policy of Pakistan: A Compendium of Speeches made in the National Assembly of Pakistan 1962–64* (Karachi: Pakistan Institute of International Affairs, 1964), pp. 73–74.

56 Cited in Lorne J. Kavic, *India's Quest for Security: Defence Policies, 1947–1965* (Berkeley: University of California Press, 1967), pp. 192–93.

57 Raju G.C. Thomas, *The Defence of India: A Budgetary Perspective of Strategy and Politics* (Delhi: Macmillan, 1978), p. 3; and Raju G.C. Thomas, *Indian Security Policy* (Princeton: Princeton University Press, 1986), p. 186.

58 Brines, *The Indo-Pakistani Conflict*, p. 11. India was expected to take about eighteen months to attain its authorized ground strength. International Institute for Strategic Studies, *The Military Balance, 1965–66*, p. 34.

59 Ehsm ul-Haq Malik (personal interview).

60 *Dawn*, (Karachi: June 18, 1963), quoted in S.M. Burke, *Pakistan's Foreign Policy: An Historical Analysis* (London: Oxford University Press, 1973), p. 293.

61 Yacov Verzberger, *The Enduring Entente, Sino-Pakistani Relations 1960–1980* (New York: Praeger, 1983), p. 9.

62 In this agreement China acceded nearly 750 sq. miles of territory to Pakistan.

63 Lars Blinkenberg, *India–Pakistan, The History of Unsolved Conflicts* (Copenhagen: Dansk Udenrigspolitisk Instituts, 1972), p. 242.

64 *Asian Recorder* (March 18–24, 1964), p. 5729.

65 Speech in the National Assembly, July 17, 1963, in Bhutto, *Foreign Policy of Pakistan*, p. 75.

66 Bhabani Sen Gupta, *The Fulcrum of Asia: Relations among China, India, Pakistan and the USSR* (New York: Pegasus, 1970), p. 195. It is generally believed that during meetings in March 1965 and subsequent occasions, the Chinese leaders gave assurances that they would provide diplomatic support to Pakistan in a war with India and military aid if the Pakistani position on the front worsened. Arthur A. Stahnke, "Diplomatic Triangle: China's Policies Toward India and Pakistan in the 1960s," in Jerome A. Cohen (ed.), *The Dynamics of China's Foreign Relations* (Cambridge, Mass.: Harvard University Press, 1970), p. 27.

67 Brig. A.R. Siddiqi (personal interview, Karachi, July 27, 1989); The nature of China's assistance in the event of war was never publicly announced. Despite this ambivalence, it seemed the Pakistani leadership believed that Chinese support would be forthcoming in the event of an India–Pakistan war. China did in fact make some limited moves when the tide of the war began to turn against Pakistan. On September 16, 1965, China accused India of establishing border camps on the Tibetan side of Sikkim and demanded their immediate dismantlement. However, on September 22 China announced that India had complied with its demands. Cited in Vertzberger, *The Enduring Entente*, p. 37.

68 Choudhury, *Pakistan's Relations with India*, pp. 277–78; Burke, *Pakistan's Foreign Policy*, p. 349.

69 Shirin Tahir-Kheli, *The United States and Pakistan: The Evolution of an Influence Relationship* (New York: Praeger, 1982), p. 21.

70 Askari (personal interview).

71 United Nations, *Security Council Official Records*, 1091st Meeting (14 February 1964), p. 12.

72 Tahir-Kheli, *The United States and Pakistan*, p. 20.

73 The US decision during the war to impose an embargo on arms supply came as a surprise to Pakistani leaders. Clearly, they were not expecting such a severe response from the US. Siddiqi (personal interview). The US interest in the strategic relationship with Pakistan had waned somewhat by the early 1960s. With the advent of satellite monitoring systems, the Kennedy Administration downgraded Pakistan's importance as a staging ground for intelligence operations on the Soviet Union. Tahir-Kheli, *The United States and Pakistan*, p. 9.

74 Askari (personal interview).

75 Richard Sisson, "Politics and the Military in Pakistan," in John P. Lovell (ed.), *The Military and Politics in Five Developing Nations* (Kensington: Center for Research in Social Systems, 1970).

76 Lawrence Ziring, *The Ayub Khan Era: Politics in Pakistan 1958–1969* (Syracuse: Syracuse University Press, 1971), pp. 53 and 62.

77 Sayed, *The Discourse and Politics of Zulfikar Ali Bhutto*, p. 28.

78 Speech at Lahore, December 20, 1970, cited in Taseer, *Bhutto: A Political Biography*, p. 65.

79 Bhutto successfully convinced Ayub Khan that Pakistan's exclusive reliance on the US was against its interests and that an alignment with China would bring important dividends in terms of neutralizing India's power position in the region. Verzberger, *The Enduring Entente*, pp. 10–14.

80 Taseer, *Bhutto: A Political Biography*, p. 59.

81 Ziring, *The Ayub Khan Era*, p. 50.

82 Ibid.

83 Stanley A. Kochanek, *Interest Groups and Development: Business and Politics in Pakistan* (Delhi: Oxford University Press, 1983), pp. 53–54.

84 Taseer, *Bhutto: A Political Biography*, p. 60.

85 Attiqur Rahman (personal communication). General Musa acknowledges that he attended one of the meetings that formulated the strategy for the offensive. Musa, *My Version*, pp. 9–10.

86 S.G. Mehdi (personal interview, Karachi, July 27, 1989).

87 Habibullah Khan Khattak, "A General's Version: Rejoinder to *My Version*," *Defence Journal*, 9 (1983), 9–17.

88 Quoted in Taseer, *Bhutto: A Political Biography*, p. 60.

89 Asghar Khan, *The First Round*, p. 6.

90 Cited in Musa, *My Version*, p. 4.

91 *Mehdi Papers*, Serial 3 (Karachi: 1987), p. 37.

92 Louis D. Hayes, *Politics in Pakistan: The Struggle for Legitimacy* (Boulder: Westview Press, 1984), pp. 97–98. According to Hayes, the elections encouraged the Ayub Government to adopt a more assertive posture toward the Kashmir question.

93 Shireen M. Mazari, "Kashmir Factor in Pakistan's Politics – I: The Years 1947–65," *Muslim* (October 21, 1986).

94 The younger officers especially wanted war, and were later critical of Ayub for not making use of the opportunity. Naqvi (personal interview); Cohen, *The Pakistan Army*, pp. 112 and 139.

95 National Assembly of Pakistan, *Debates, Official Report* (Karachi: Government Printing Press, November 21, 1962), p. 10, cited in Tahir-Kheli, *The*

United States and Pakistan, p. 11. A Pakistani defense specialist suggests that Ayub was very susceptible to American pressures at that time. Until 1962, Ayub was the closest ally of the US in the region, which changed after the Sino-Indian war. Ayub also had no other allies to turn to as rapprochement with China or the USSR was not considered as a serious option. Siddiqi (personal interview); Choudhury, *Pakistan's Relations with India*, p. 132.

96 Tahir-Kheli, *The United States and Pakistan*, p. 16.

97 Ayub Khan, *Friends, Not Masters*, p. 141.

98 It is possible that the Pakistani leadership was afraid of a complete rupture of relations with the US which were already under strain following the inauguration of the Kennedy Administration. During Ayub Khan's visit to Washington in July 1961, the US Administration, in an effort to allay the Pakistani fears, promised one squadron of F-104 jet fighters. Tahir-Kheli, *The United States and Pakistan*, p. 10. Between 1954 and 1965, Pakistan had received grants of over $630 million for purchase of weapons, $619 million in defense support assistance, and $55 million in equipment. Stephen P. Cohen, "US Weapons and South Asia: A Policy Analysis," *Pacific Affairs*, 49 (Spring 1976), 49–69.

99 Malik (personal interview).

7 The Egyptian offensive in the Sinai, 1973

1 Although Egypt was fighting along with Syria, it may well be argued that the cooperation between them was at the strategic and not at the tactical level and therefore, to a large extent they were waging two separate wars in two different theaters.

2 In Egyptian Chief of Staff General Saad el Shazly's appraisal, Israel held an overall 2:1 military superiority. Walter Laqueur, *Confrontation: The Middle East War and World Politics* (London: Abacus, 1974), p. 40. According to the Egyptian War Minister in 1973, General Ahmad Ismail, Israel held four major advantages: air superiority, technological capability, rigorous training, and an assured US supply of weapons. Interview with Mohamad Heikal, *Al-Ahram* (November 18, 1973), cited in John W. Amos, *Arab-Israeli Military/Political Relations: Arab Perceptions and the Politics of Escalation* (New York: Pergamon Press, 1979), p. 142. To Chief of Operations, Field Marshal Al Gamasi, Israel held superiority in aircraft and tanks even when the Egyptian capabilities in these two areas were added to that of Syria (personal communication, Cairo, December 14, 1990). To President Sadat's National Security Adviser, Hafez Ismail, the Egyptian decision-makers were conscious of Israel's better internal lines of communications, ability to rapidly shift troops from the Syrian front to the Sinai, and the geographical advantage accruing from the possession of Sinai, a 200-mile long buffer zone (personal interview, Cairo, September 17, 1990).

3 For a comparison of the military power of Israel and Egypt, see Geoffrey Kemp, "Israel and Egypt: Military Force Posture 1967–1972," in Frank B. Horton et. al. (eds.), *Comparative Defense Policy* (Baltimore and London: The Johns Hopkins University Press, 1974), pp. 392–405. Egypt had a total of 1.1

million men in uniform in 1973, of which the army commanded half a million. Half of the army consisted of National Guard units, with limited training and inferior equipment, who were generally assigned to domestic duties. Trevor N. Dupuy, *Elusive Victory: The Arab–Israeli Wars, 1947–1974* (New York: Harper & Row, 1978), p. 401.

4 Kemp, "Israel and Egypt," p. 393. Specifically, in air power, its 127 Phantoms and 170 Skyhawks allowed Israel's numerically inferior fleet to carry almost twice the tonnage of the combined aircraft capabilities of Egypt, Syria, Jordan, Iraq, and Libya. The longer range of its aircraft allowed Israel to reach far deeper into Arab territory than could the Arabs into Israel. According to one analyst, the superiority in equipment, command and control, training, and manpower assured Israeli fighters of a more than 10:1 kill ratio in air combat. Nadav Safran, *Israel: the Embattled Ally* (Cambridge, Mass.: Harvard University Press, 1978), p. 275. Israel also had 2,200 tanks, equipped with 105m guns which were superior to the comparable guns on most of its opponent's tanks. Ibid.

5 The exact timing of the Israeli decision to go nuclear or how many weapons it had manufactured by 1973 are matters of speculation. Israel had most likely decided to build a nuclear weapon capability in the aftermath of the 1967 War and might have built its first bomb between 1969 and 1973. Moreover, leaders such as Moshe Dayan had hinted at the Israeli nuclear capability and made ambiguous nuclear threats from 1970 to 1973. Peter Pry, *Israel's Nuclear Arsenal* (Boulder: Westview Press, 1984), pp. 19–32; Uri Bar-Joseph, "The Hidden Debate: The Formation of Nuclear Doctrines in the Middle East," *Journal of Strategic Studies*, 5 (June 1982), 205–27.

6 Chaim Herzog, *The War of Atonement* (London: Weidenfeld and Nicolson, 1975), p. 8.

7 Rogers made his initiative in November 1969 in which he had outlined among other things, a timetable for the withdrawal of Israeli forces from Egyptian territory, an end to the state of war between the two countries, and an extension of the right of navigation through the Suez Canal to all states including Israel. Israel rejected the plan immediately, followed by Egypt and the Soviet Union. William B. Quandt, *Decade of Decisions, American Policy Toward the Arab–Israeli Conflict, 1967–1976* (Berkeley: University of California Press, 1977), pp. 89–92.

In his interim peace initiative, announced on February 4, 1971, Sadat said that provided Israel agreed to a partial withdrawal of troops from the East Bank of the Suez Canal and a timetable for full implementation of Security Council Resolution 262, Egypt was willing to reopen the Suez Canal for international navigation. *New Middle East* (March 1971), 32–35, cited in Ibid., p. 135; Anwar el-Sadat, *In Search of Identity, an Autobiography* (New York: Harper & Row, 1977), p. 219.

8 These proposals were accepted by Egypt after making its own additions, while Tel Aviv rejected them by stating: "Israel will not withdraw to the pre-June 5, 1967 lines," although it was willing to negotiate with Egypt without any preconditions. Quandt, *Decade of Decisions*, pp. 135–36.

9 For these negotiations, see Henry Kissinger, *Years of Upheaval* (Boston: Little, Brown, 1982), pp. 210–16 and 223–27.

10 Amos Perlmutter, "Israel's Fourth War, October 1973: Political and Military Misperceptions," *Orbis*, 19 (Summer 1975), 434–60.

11 Michael I. Handel, "Perception, Deception and Surprise: The Case of the Yom Kippur War," *Jerusalem Papers on Peace Problems*, 19 (1976), 23 and 49.

12 Chaim Herzog, *Arab–Israeli Wars* (New York: Vintage Books, 1982), p. 227.

13 Laqueur, *Confrontation*, p. 37; Israel could neither translate its military victory into political victory nor impose its will on the vast Arab population.

14 Kissinger, *Years of Upheaval*, p. 221.

15 Michael Brecher, *Decisions in Crisis, Israel, 1967 and 1973* (Berkeley: University of California Press, 1980), pp. 67–68. Brecher contends that an exception to this general belief among the leaders was Deputy Prime Minister Yigal Allon who was concerned that mounting Arab frustrations could result in war. The Israeli leaders in general expected that Israel's victory in the 1967 pre-emptive attack was so decisive that it would act as a sufficient deterrent against any offensives by the Arab states in the foreseeable future. Perlmutter, "Israel's Fourth War, October 1973," p. 447.

16 Prime Minister Meir made these proposals to Egypt, Syria, and Jordan in October 1969. Prior to this, she had declared the extension of Israeli law into the occupied Golan Heights. A hardened Israeli position was again manifested when the Meir Government announced the construction of additional settlements in the occupied territories. Dan Tschirgi, *The American Search for Mideast Peace* (New York: Praeger, 1989), p. 63.

17 Safran, *Israel: the Embattled Ally*, p. 277.

18 Laqueur, *Confrontation*, p. 85.

19 Saadia Amiel, "Defensive Technologies for Small States: A Perspective," in Louis Williams (ed.), *Military Aspects of the Israeli–Arab Conflict* (Tel Aviv: University Publishing Projects, 1975), p. 16. The Israeli leaders had already decided not to mobilize in the event of another military maneuver by Egypt due to its high cost and the fear of an inadvertent break out of war. Michael I. Handel, "The Yom Kippur War and the Inevitability of Surprise," *International Studies Quarterly*, 21 (September 1977), 461–502.

20 Edgar O'Ballance, *No Victor, No Vanquished: The Yom Kippur War* (San Rafael, Calif.: Presidio Press, 1978), p. 50.

21 Herzog, *Arab–Israeli Wars*, p. 227; General Bar-Lev told Brecher, the Israeli conception was that Egypt would not initiate a war without attaining superior air power, essential for in-depth attack and the dislocation of the Israeli Air Force. Brecher, *Decisions in Crisis*, p. 53. The Egyptians knew they could not neutralize Israel's superiority in the air itself. They compensated for this by deploying ground-to-air missiles. Handel, "Perception, Deception and Surprise." pp. 49–50.

22 Ibid., p. 51.

23 Cited in O'Ballance, *No Victor, No Vanquished*, p. 51.

24 Handel, "The Yom Kippur War and the Inevitability of Surprise."

25 Kissinger, *Years of Upheaval*, p. 206. To Kissinger the likely initiator of war would be Israel, as the Arab states were disunited and without the leadership necessary to launch a coordinated military offensive. Marvin Kalb and Bernard Kalb, *Kissinger* (New York: Dell Publishing, 1974), p. 515.

26 Some top advisers of President Sadat whom the author interviewed in

Cairo asserted that US Secretary of State Henry Kissinger hinted to visiting Egyptian National Security Advisor Hafez Ismail in 1973 that unless the situation on the ground changed, no peace initiative was possible. Sadat viewed this as a signal that a military move would attract US attention to settle the dispute. Tahseen Basheer (personal interview, Cairo, September 19, 1990); Mustapha Khalil (personal interview, Cairo, September 16, 1990). Sadat alludes to this claim in his autobiography by saying that Kissinger's message conveyed through Ismail was that the US could not do anything to change the status quo as long as Egypt was the defeated side. Sadat, *In Search of Identity*, p. 238. Heikal also points out that Sadat received reports from several sources of hints that Kissinger had made to the effect that some level of "heating up" in the region was necessary for the US to help make any positive changes in the status quo. Mohamed Heikal, *Autumn of Fury: The Assassination of Sadat* (New York: Random House, 1983), pp. 49–50.

27 Hafez Ismail (personal interview).
28 Mohamed Heikal, *The Road to Ramadan* (New York: Ballantine Books, 1975), pp.263–64.
29 Al Gamasi (personal communication).
30 Saad el Shazly, *The Crossing of the Suez* (San Francisco: American Mideast Research, 1980), pp. 24–25.
31 Khalil (personal interview).
32 Shazly, *The Crossing of the Suez*, pp. 25–26.
33 O'Ballance, *No Victor, No Vanquished*, p. 147.
34 In actual operations, these expectations proved correct as during the first two days of the war the Egyptian and Syrian Armies gained all the advantages of strategic surprise without tactically engaging the enemy forces. Laqueur, *Confrontation*, p. 112; Field Marshal Al Gamasi confirms that Egypt had effectively learned the importance of surprise from the 1967 Israeli operations. Al Gamasi (personal communication).
35 Basheer (personal interview).
36 Yaacov Bar-Siman-Tov, *The Israeli–Egyptian War of Attrition, 1969–1970* (New York: Columbia University Press, 1980), p. 111.
37 O'Ballance, *No Victor, No Vanquished*, p. 13.
38 Anwar el-Sadat, interviewed by Mohamed Heikal, in *Al-Ahram* (November 18, 1973), quoted in Amos, *Arab–Israeli Military/Political Relations*, p. 142.
39 Basheer (personal interview).
40 Shimon Shamir, "Arab Military Lessons from the October War," in Louis Williams (ed.), *Military Aspects of the Israeli–Arab Conflict*, p. 175.
41 Al Gamasi (personal communication); Basheer (personal interview).
42 Bar-Joseph, "The Hidden Debate."
43 Ali Dessouki (personal interview, Cairo, September 15, 1990).
44 Heikal, *The Road to Ramadan*, p. 6.
45 For the operations, see Laqueur, *Confrontation*, p. 88.
46 *Al-Ahram* (November 18, 1973), cited in Amos, *Arab–Israeli Military/Political Relations*, pp. 142–43.
47 Heikal, *The Road to Ramadan*, p. 18.
48 Al Gamasi (personal communication); Heikal, *The Road to Ramadan*, p. 264.

49 Heikal, *The Road to Ramadan*, p. 10.

50 Shazly, *The Crossing of the Suez*, p. 18.

51 The Egyptians had learned from the 1967 War that the Israelis would concentrate heavily on air power in any future war. The Egyptian military, therefore, focused on acquiring anti-aircraft SAM missiles together with fighter planes with the objective of neutralizing and minimizing the impact of Israeli air power. Al Gamasi (personal communication).

52 Riad N. El-Rayyes and Dunia Nahas (eds.), *The October War Documents, Personalities, Analyses and Maps* (Beirut: An-nahar Press Services, 1973), pp. 5–6; O'Ballance, *No Victor, No Vanquished*, p. 24.

53 Herzog, *The War of Atonement*, pp. 24–25; The supply of Scuds seems to have provided Sadat with the incentive to believe that Moscow was now ready to support his limited war plans. Alvin Z. Rubinstein, *Red Star on the Nile, The Soviet–Egyptian Influence Relationship Since the June War* (Princeton: Princeton University Press, 1977), p. 257.

54 Heikal, *Autumn of Fury*, p. 46.

55 See Rubinstein, *Red Star on the Nile*, pp. 227–28 and 251 for Soviet–Egyptian deliberations on the resumption of arms supply. Under the new arms agreement, the Soviets had offered Egypt one squadron of MiG-23s, one brigade of R-17E surface-to-surface Scud missiles, about 200 BMP mechanized infantry combat vehicles, about fifty Sagger anti-tank guided weapons, one brigade of SAM-6s, four MIG-25 reconnaissance aircraft, and an electronic reconnaissance and jamming squadron which was earlier withdrawn from Egypt. Shazly, *The Crossing of the Suez*, p. 198.

56 Anwar el-Sadat interviewed by Arnaud de Borchgrave in *Newsweek* (9 April 1973), p. 49.

57 Heikal, *The Road to Ramadan*, p. 183. The level of arms supply between December 1972 and June 1973 was higher than all of the preceding years.

58 Mohamed Heikal, *Sphinx and the Commissar: The Rise and Fall of Soviet Influence in the Arab World* (London: Collins, 1978), p. 254.

59 John Bullock, *The Making of a War: The Middle East from 1967 to 1973* (London: Longman, 1974), p. 187.

60 Basheer (personal interview). According to Heikal, the Soviet military must have concurred with Brezhnev in making it possible for Egypt to "embark on a limited war." The Russians "were not instructing the Arabs to fight, but they were providing them with sufficient arms to make the idea of fighting extremely tempting." Heikal, *Sphinx and the Commissar*, p. 254.

61 Shazly, *The Crossing of the Suez*, p. 172.

62 Heikal, *The Road to Ramadan*, p. 25.

63 Cited in Ibid., pp. 16–17.

64 Ibid., p. 210.

65 el-Sadat, *In Search of Identity*, p. 229.

66 Shazly, *The Crossing of the Suez*, p. 100.

67 Kissinger, *Years of Upheaval*, p. 527–28. It has been contended that the US did not want Israel to achieve a resounding victory as in 1967 so as to humiliate the Arabs, while the Russians did not want a decisive Arab victory which would have attracted US intervention. Heikal, *Sphinx and the Commissar*, p. 258.

68 Heikal, *The Road to Ramadan*, p. 10.
69 Raymond A. Hinnebusch, *Egyptian Politics under Sadat, The Post-Populist Development of an Authoritarian-Modernizing State* (Cambridge: Cambridge University Press, 1985), p. 10. The Egyptian foreign policy making has also been described as "leader–staff type," with the President acting as more or less an authoritarian decision-maker. Ali E. Hillal Dessouki, "The Primacy of Economics: The Foreign Policy of Egypt," in Bahgat Korany and Ali Dissouki (eds.), *The Foreign Policies of Arab States* (Boulder: Westview Press, 1984), pp. 119–41.
70 Shazly, *The Crossing of the Suez*, p. 180.
71 Hinnebusch, *Egyptian Politics under Sadat*, p. 128.
72 *Arab World Weekly* (November 4, 1972), cited in Amos *Arab–Israeli Military/Political Relations*, p. 139; Shazly, *The Crossing of the Suez*, pp. 27–28.
73 Rubinstein, *Red Star on the Nile*, p. 216.
74 Amos Perlmutter, *Egypt the Praetorian State* (New Brunswick, N.J.: Transaction Books, 1974), p. 200.
75 R. Michael Burrell and Abbas R. Kelidar, "Egypt: The Dilemmas of a Nation – 1970–1977" *The Washington Papers* Vol.5 (Beverly Hills: Sage Publications, 1977), p. 14; Laqueur, *Confrontation*, p. 11.
76 Ghali Shoukri, *Egypt: Portrait of a President 1971–1981: Sadat's Road to Jerusalem* (London: Zed Press, 1981), p. 154; (personal interview, Cairo, September, 1990).
77 Burrell and Kelidar, "Egypt: The Dilemmas of a Nation."
78 Ibid.
79 Hinnebusch, *Egyptian Politics under Sadat*, p. 125; Sadat seems to have feared that impatience on the part of educated people might spread to the military and its morale would be affected. Mustapha El Sayed (personal interview, Cairo: September 15, 1990). In a coup attempt in November 1982 nearly one hundred officers of the armored corps were arrested. O'Ballance, *No Victor, No Vanquished*, p. 4.
80 The bulk of the military preferred to follow Chief of Staff Sadek who was "more than pleased to combine with Sadat to replace Fawzi as Minister of War." Hinnebusch, *Egyptian Politics under Sadat*, pp. 126–27.
81 Ibid., p. 127.
82 Ali Dissouki (personal interview).
83 After several declarations throughout 1971 of his intent to go to war, in November Sadat and his regime appeared to have mobilized for war. They reimposed the blackout and reactivated the "battle committees." In addition, Sadat moved his office to the armed forces headquarters, while escalating the rhetoric on the impending war. David Hirst and Irene Beeson, *Sadat* (London: Faber & Faber, 1981), p. 124.
84 *Speeches by President Anwar el-Sadat, September 1970–March 1971* (Cairo: Ministry of Information, n.d.), p. 116.
85 Address to the Nation's Council, Radio Cairo (February 4, 1971), in Raphael Israeli, *The Public Diary of President Sadat, Part One, The Road to War (October 1970–October 1973)* (Leiden: E.J. Brill, 1978), p. 31.
86 *Al-Ahram* (June 6, 1971), cited in Hirst and Beeson, *Sadat*, p. 122.
87 In this speech, Sadat said: "I shall not let the year of 1971 go by without this

war being decided, lest I would be granting Israel a time-spell, because for Israel, the ideal situation is 'no peace and no war,' while she is holding the Canal shore without incurring casualties, and watching for an internal explosion to occur [in Egypt]." Address to the 9th Convention of the Palestinian National Council, Radio Cairo (July 7, 1971), in Israeli, *The Public Diary of President Sadat*, p. 93.

88 Excerpts from Sadat's interview in *Le Monde*, reprinted in *New York Times* (January 23, 1975), p. 4.

89 Cited in Shoukri, *Egypt: Portrait of a President*, p. 90; According to Basheer, if Egypt had received necessary air cover, such as the Scud missiles, Sadat would have gone to war in 1971. Basheer (personal interview).

90 Shazly, *The Crossing of the Suez*, pp. 28–29. Although Egypt had about 800,000 troops, over 58 percent of them were not field troops, ready for front line fighting. Ibid., p. 22.

91 The Insight Team of the London *Sunday Times, The Yom Kippur War* (Garden City, N.Y.: Doubleday, 1974), p. 34.

92 Heikal, *The Road to Ramadan*, p. 156; Senior officials whom I interviewed in Cairo confirmed that the Soviet insistence on Egypt accepting the status quo for as long as possible and their objection to launching an offensive were the major factors that prohibited Sadat going to war (personal interviews, Cairo, September 1990). The Soviet opposition also gave added strength to the opponents of limited war in the Egyptian high command who argued for more time to absorb Soviet-made weaponry; Rubinstein, *Red Star on the Nile*, p. 163. Sadat suggests that he would not have been able to launch the offensive based on the strategy that he had laid down as long as the Soviets were present in Egypt; el-Sadat, *In Search of Identity*, p. 230.

8 The Argentine invasion of the Falklands/Malvinas, 1982

1 About 75 percent of the Argentine Army and over 50 percent of both its navy and air force consisted of conscripts, with training periods of twelve to fourteen months. International Institute for Strategic Studies, *The Military Balance 1981–82* (London: IISS, 1981), pp. 92–93. Additionally, Argentina had not fought a war since the nineteenth century and its air force had never been battle tested. Ruben O. Moro, *The History of the South Atlantic Conflict, The War for the Malvinas* (New York: Praeger), 1989, p. 20.

2 Arthur Gavson and Desmond Rice, *The Sinking of the Belgrano* (London: Secker & Warburg, 1984), p. 40.

3 This constraint was especially felt after the sinking of the Argentine cruiser *General Belgrano*, when the military leadership decided to keep its naval surface forces within the twelve-mile zone as they feared that Britain's superior nuclear-powered submarines would destroy their limited number of naval vessels. William J. Ruhe, "Submarine Lessons," in Bruce W. Watson and Peter M. Dunn (eds.), *Military Lessons of the Falklands War: Views from the United States* (Boulder: Westview Press, 1984), p. 9.

4 James L. George, "Large Versus Small Carriers," in Watson and Dunn (eds.), op. cit., p. 16. Argentina had six French-made Super Etendards, a number of A-4 Skyhawks, French Mirages, and Israeli Daggers, a few

Canberra bombers, and some domestically built Pucara counter-insurgency aircraft. Operating from the home bases, 400 miles was the maximum range of most of these aircraft. Norman Friedman, "Surface Combatant Lessons," in Watson and Dunn (eds.), op. cit., p. 22. Due to these constraints, the Argentine fighter aircraft could only fly fewer sorties, and could carry considerably less amount of ammunition with them, in order to prolong their airborne capability. Moro, *The History of the South Atlantic Conflict*, p. 80.

5 Earl H. Tilford, "Air Power Lessons," in Watson and Dunn (eds.) *Military Lessons of the Falklands War*, pp. 38 and 44.

6 General Jose Goyert (personal interview, Buenos Aires, May 24, 1990).

7 On the recommendations of this Committee, the UN General Assembly passed Resolution 2065 in December 1965, urging both parties to engage in negotiations to find a peaceful solution.

8 Lawrence Freedman and Virginia Gamba-Stonehouse, *Signals of War: The Falklands Conflict of 1982* (London: Faber & Faber, 1990), p. 8.

9 In May 1972, Britain allowed Argentina to build a temporary airstrip at Port Stanley, the capital of the territory. The British position underwent some major changes to the extent that by January 1974 it was proposing a condominium arrangement. In addition, Britain dispatched the Shackleton mission to the Islands to study the economic potential of the territory. For the negotiations, see Douglas Kinney, *National Interest/National Honor, The Diplomacy of the Falklands Crisis* (New York: Praeger, 1989), pp. 48–52; Freedman and Gamba-Stonehouse, *Signals of War*, pp. 8–9.

10 Ibid., p. 9.

11 The Commission would include representatives from the Falklands Islands Legislative Council. This agreement, however, was not acceptable to the Argentine regime which was already working on a timetable for an invasion. For the final round of negotiations, see Franks Committee, *Falklands Islands Review Report of a Committee of Privy Councillors*, Cmnd 8787 (London: HMSO, 1983) (henceforth the Franks Committee Report), pp. 39–40; and Max Hastings and Simon Jenkins, *The Battle for the Falklands* (New York: W.W. Norton, 1983), pp. 50–51.

12 Gerald W. Hopple, "Intelligence and Warning Lessons," in Watson and Dunn (eds.), *Military Lessons of the Falklands War*, p. 104; Lawrence Freedman, *Britain and the Falklands War* (Oxford: Basil Blackwell, 1988), p. 2. In psychological terms, the British decision-making prior to the war has been described as one of "collective defensive avoidance." Richard Ned Lebow, "Miscalculation in the South Atlantic: The Origins of the Falklands War," in Robert Jervis, et al. (eds.), *Psychology and Deterrence* (Baltimore: The Johns Hopkins University Press, 1985), p. 103.

13 Hopple, "Intelligence and Warning Lessons,", p. 106.

14 The Franks Committee Report, p. 19.

15 Virginia Gamba, *The Falklands/Malvinas War, A Model for North–South Crisis Prevention* (Boston: Allen & Unwin, 1987), pp. 108–9.

16 Freedman and Gamba-Stonehouse, *Signals of War*, pp. 19–21; Peter Beck, *The Falklands Islands as an International Problem* (London and New York: Routledge, 1988), p. 126.

17 Peter Calvert, *The Falklands Crisis: The Rights and Wrongs* (London: Frances Pinter, 1982), pp. 57–58.
18 Gavson and Rice, *The Sinking of the Belgrano*, p. 21.
19 Nicanor Costa Mendez, "Beyond Deterrence: The Malvinas–Falklands Case," *Journal of Social Issues*, 43 (1987), 119–22.
20 Hastings and Jenkins, *The Battle for the Falklands*, p. 32.
21 Lt. Col. Alberto Morales and Admiral Jorge Busser (personal interviews, Buenos Aires, May 24 and May 26, 1990).
22 Busser and General Garcia Enciso (personal interview, Buenos Aires, May 26, 1990).
23 Jimmy Burns, *The Land that Lost its Heroes: The Falklands, the Post War and Alfonsin* (London: Bloomsbury Publishing, 1987), pp. 30–31; Beck, *The Falklands Islands as an International Problem*, p. 6.
24 *Informe Rattenbach* (Buenos Aires: Editiones Espartaco, Serie Documentos Historicos, 1988), p. 190. When the Junta met on March 26, 1982, it had three options on the table for consideration. The first was to pursue negotiations, which it rejected as Britain need not concede sovereignty in the near future. The second option was to bring the issue before the UN Security Council for immediate action, the prospects of success for which were considered remote as the Council may not convene for this purpose. The third was to use force for the recovery of the Islands. This was accepted as the best choice, the one that could "force Britain back to the negotiating table while giving Argentina the upper hand." Moro, *The History of the South Atlantic Conflict*, p. 2.
25 Costa Mendez, "Beyond Deterrence", p. 121.
26 Nicanor Costa Mendez (personal interview, Buenos Aires, May 22, 1990).
27 Moro, *The History of the South Atlantic Conflict*, p. 2.
28 Calvert, *The Falklands Crisis*, p. 86.
29 George H. Quester, "The Falklands and the Malvinas: Strategy and Arms Control," *ACIS Working Paper* 46 (Los Angeles: UCLA Center for International and Strategic Affairs, May 1984). The Argentine expectation of a no-war situation was further evident in the military not providing sufficient winter blankets to the troops that were sent to the Islands, indispensable for a long entrenched presence there. Roberto Russell (personal interview, Buenos Aires, May 21, 1990).
30 For a brief summary of the Commission report, see Gavson and Rice, *The Sinking of the Belgrano*, p. 136.
31 Alejandro Dabat and Luis Lorenzano, *Argentina, the Malvinas and the End of Military Rule*, trans. Ralph Johnson (London: Verso Editions, 1982), p. 101.
32 During this period, Argentina's relations with Chile had deteriorated, mainly because of its repudiation of the 1972 Treaty under which Argentina had ceded a group of islands in the Beagle Channel to that country.
33 Tilford, "Air Power Lessons,", p. 47.
34 *Informe Rattenbach*, pp. 186–87 and 201–2; Morales (personal interview).
35 The armed forces, especially the navy, were more interested in preserving their corporate interests than the national interest. The navy commanders knew that any lost hardware could not be replaced easily, and would thus imperil their chance of survival as an important branch of the Argentine

armed forces. Carlos Escude (personal interview, Buenos Aires, May 25, 1990). The Rattenbach Commission Report blamed the Junta for withdrawing the navy from the combat prematurely and allowing the air force to fight its own war, and thereby not engaging in any joint air–sea assaults. Quoted in Gavson and Rice, *The Sinking of the Belgrano*, p. 136.

36 For this incident, see Moro, *The History of the South Atlantic Conflict*, p. 15; Hastings and Jenkins, *The Battle for the Falklands*, pp. 54–55.

37 Goyert (personal interviews).

38 Morales (personal interviews).

39 Busser (personal interviews).

40 Moro, *The History of the South Atlantic Conflict*, p. 68.

41 Costa Mendez (personal interviews).

42 Ibid.

43 Gamba, *The Falklands/Malvinas War*, p. 34.

44 Cited in Robert E. Looney, *The Political Economy of Latin American Defense Expenditures, Case Studies of Venezuela and Argentina* (Lexington: Lexington Books, 1986), p. 213.

45 For these estimates, see Paul H. Lewis, *The Crisis of Argentine Capitalism* (Chapel Hill: The University of North Carolina Press, 1990), p. 454.

46 Burns, *The Land that Lost its Heroes*, pp. 17–18; *World Armaments and Disarmament, SIPRI Yearbook 1982* (London: Taylor and Francis, 1982), p. 207.

47 Dabat and Lorenzano, *Argentina, the Malvinas and the End of Military Rule*, pp. 93–94.

48 Only five of the twelve Super Etendards had been delivered when the invasion took place. Moro, *The History of the South Atlantic Conflict*, pp. 68 and 80.

49 Costa Mendez (personal interviews).

50 Jose Moria Vasquez (personal interview, Buenos Aires, May 23, 1990).

51 Alexander Haig claims that in National Security Council (NSC) meetings, Kirkpatrick opposed his arguments for supporting Britain by saying that the condemnation of Argentina "would buy the United States a hundred years of animosity in Latin America." Alexander M. Haig, Jr., *Caveat, Realism, Reagan, and Foreign Policy* (New York: Macmillan, 1984), p. 269.

52 Jeane J. Kirkpatrick, "My Falklands War and Theirs," *The National Interest*, 18 (Winter 1989/90), 11–20.

53 Moro, *The History of the South Atlantic Conflict*, p. 34; Enders later clarified that the "hands off policy" was only in regard to the dispute and that the US wanted the Anglo-Argentine negotiations to continue. Freedman and Gamba-Stonehouse, *Signals of War*, p. 33.

54 The *Sunday Times* of London Insight Team, *War in the Falklands: the Full Story* (New York: Harper & Row, 1982), p. 62.

55 Cited in Ibid., p. 63; Burns, *The Land that Lost its Heroes*, p. 34.

56 Dabat and Lorenzano, *Argentina, the Malvinas and the End of Military Rule*, p. 78.

57 Burns, *The Land that Lost its Heroes*, p. 34.

58 Moro, *The History of the South Atlantic Conflict*, p. 33.

59 Anthony Barnett, *Iron Britannia* (London: Allison and Busby, 1982), p. 113; *The Guardian* (June 1, 1982), p. 2.

60 Kirkpatrick, "My Falklands War and Theirs," p. 14.

61 *Washington Post* (April 13, 1983), p. A27.

62 Costa Mendez (personal interviews). The Argentines also expected diplomatic support from the USSR, especially by way of a veto of any UN Security Council resolutions that might condemn their invasion. Argentina's grain sale to the USSR, despite a US embargo, and Moscow's historic support for decolonization, were the reasons behind this expectation. Lawrence Freedman, "The War of the Falkland Islands, 1982," *Foreign Affairs*, 61 (Fall 1982), 196–210.

63 Statement by Costa Mendez in *Informe Rattenbach*, pp. 91–92.

64 Looney, *The Political Economy of Latin American Defense Expenditures*, pp. 243–44.

65 Lewis, *The Crisis of Argentine Capitalism*, p. 476.

66 For the Junta's economic policies and the repercussions, see William C. Smith, "Reflections on the Political Economy of Authoritarian Rule and Capitalist Reorganization in Contemporary Argentina," in Philip O'Brien and Paul Cammack (eds.), *Generals in Retreat, The Crisis of Military Rule in Latin America* (Manchester: Manchester University Press, 1985), pp. 51–61.

67 Ibid., pp. 58–59; Hastings and Jenkins, *The Battle for the Falklands*, p. 47.

68 In the final quarter of 1981, the Argentine GNP fell by 11.4 percent, industrial production by 23 percent, and real wages by 20 percent. Cited in Smith, "Reflections on the Political Economy," pp. 60–61.

69 Cited in John Simpson and Jana Bennett, *The Disappeared: Voices from a Secret War* (London: Robson Books, 1985), p. 305.

70 Dabat and Lorenzano, *Argentina, the Malvinas and the End of Military Rule*, p. 76; Carlos J. Moneta, "The Malvinas Conflict: Some Elements for an Analysis of the Argentine Military Regime's Decision-Making Process, 1976–82," *Millennium: Journal of International Studies*, 13 (Winter 1984), 311–23.

71 Guillermo A. Makin, "The Military in Argentine Politics: 1880–1982," *Millennium: Journal of International Studies*, 12 (Spring 1983), 49–68.

72 Hastings and Jenkins, *The Battle for the Falklands*, p. 31.

73 Simpson and Bennett, *The Disappeared*, pp. 309–10; Oscar R. Cordoso et al., *Falklands – The Secret Plot* (East Molesey, Surrey: Preston Editions, 1987), ch. I; Andres Miguel Fontana, *Political Decision Making by a Military Corporation: Argentina 1976–1983*, (Ph.D. Dissertation, Austin: The University of Texas, 1987), p. 123.

74 *Sunday Times* Insight Team, *War in the Falklands*, p. 28; Freedman and Gamba-Stonehouse, *Signals of War*, pp. 6–7.

75 Dabat and Lorenzano, *Argentina, the Malvinas and the End of Military Rule*, p. 92.

76 Calvert, *The Falklands Crisis*, p. 54.

77 Gamba, *The Falklands/Malvinas War*, p. 98.

78 On January 2, 1976, the Foreign Minister, Arauz Castex told the British Ambassador in Buenos Aires that Argentina and Britain were "rapidly moving towards a head on collision... In the end he could only see one course open to Argentina irrespective of what Government might be in

power... His Government could accept no responsibility for such a disastrous outcome." Quoted in the Franks Committee Report, p. 10.

79 For the incident, see Simpson and Bennett, *The Disappeared*, p. 306; and Kinney, *National Interest/National Honor*, p. 54. The British Joint Intelligence Committee, after studying the incident, concluded that the objective of the Argentine Navy was to "assert Argentine sovereignty over the Falkland Islands and their surrounding waters, in order to bring pressure to bear on the British Government to negotiate." In the Committee's assessment, the Argentine military commanders were opposed to a full-fledged military invasion and that all that the Argentine Government was interested in was to follow a policy of "continued pin-pricks." The Franks Committee Report, pp. 12–13.

80 Ibid., p. 15; Kinney, *National Interest/National Honor*, p. 56.

81 Simpson and Bennett, *The Disappeared*, p. 309; Hastings and Jenkins, *The Battle for the Falklands*, p. 36; The Franks Committee Report, p.18.

82 The Franks Committee Report, p. 18.

Conclusion

1 These authors have argued that initiators can challenge deterrence through strategies such as "limited probes" or "controlled pressure." Alexander L. George and Richard Smoke, *Deterrence in American Foreign Policy: Theory and Practice* (New York: Columbia University Press, 1974), pp. 521–22.

2 In his view, deterrence can be obtained if the defender holds sufficient capability to deny battlefield success to an attacker. John J. Mearsheimer, *Conventional Deterrence* (Ithaca and London: Cornell University Press, 1983), ch. 2.

3 In 1981 Waltz argued that the "gradual spread of nuclear weapons is better than no spread and better than rapid spread." In his view, nuclear weapons may make defense and deterrence easier and the costs of war higher for potential initiators. The likelihood of war will decrease if the new nuclear states are able to signal convincing deterrent messages. Kenneth N. Waltz, "The Spread of Nuclear Weapons: More May be Better," *Adelphi Papers*, 171 (Autumn 1981). Nearly a decade later Waltz repeated the virtues of nuclear weapons by contending that they dissuade states more often from going to war than conventional weapons and that they are a "tremendous force for peace and afford nations that possess them the possibility of security at reasonable cost." Kenneth Waltz, "Nuclear Myths and Political Realities," *American Political Science Review*, 84 (September 1990), 731–45.

BIBLIOGRAPHY

General Theory

Achen, Christopher H. and Duncan Snidal. "Rational Deterrence: Theory and Comparative Case Studies." *World Politics* 41 (January 1989), 143–69.

Allison, Graham T. *Essence of Decision: Explaining the Cuban Missile Crisis.* Boston: Little, Brown, 1971.

Ashley, Richard K. "Bayesian Decision Analysis in International Relations Forecasting: The Analysis of Subjective Processes." *In Forecasting in International Relations: Theory, Methods, Problems, Prospects,* eds. Nazli Choucri and Thomas W. Robinson. San Francisco: W.H. Freeman, 1978.

Axelrod, Robert. "The Rational Timing of Surprise." *World Politics* 31 (January 1979), 228–46.

Betts, Richard K. *Surprise Attack: Lessons for Defense Planning.* Washington DC: Brookings Institution, 1982.

Boulding, Kenneth E. *Conflict and Defense: A General Theory.* New York: Harper & Row, 1962.

Brecher, Michael. *Crises in World Politics: Theory and Reality.* Oxford: Pergamon Press, 1993.

Brown, Michael E. "Deterrence Failures and Deterrence Strategies." *Rand Paper Series* P-5842. Santa Monica: Rand Corporation (March 1977).

Bueno de Mesquita, Bruce. *The War Trap.* New Haven and London: Yale University Press, 1981.

Bueno de Mesquita, Bruce and J. David Singer. "Alliance, Capabilities and War: A Review and Synthesis." *Political Science Annual* 4 (1973), 237–80.

Chaliand, Gerard. *Guerrilla Strategies.* Berkeley: University of California Press, 1982.

Choucri, Nazli and Robert C. North. *Nations in Conflict.* San Francisco: W.H. Freeman, 1974.

Claude, Inis, L. *Power and International Relations.* New York: Random House, 1964.

Clausewitz, Carl von. *On War.* Vols.I and III. Trans. Col. J.J. Graham. London: Routledge & Kegan Paul, 1962.

Cohen, Eliot A. "Constraints on America's Conduct of Small Wars." *International Security* 9 (Fall 1984), 151–81.

Cross, John, G. *The Economics of Bargaining.* New York: Basic Books, 1969.

Danto, Arthur C. "On Explanations in History." *Philosophy of Science* 23 (January 1956), 15–30.

Diehl, Paul F. "Arms Races to War: Testing Some Empirical Linkages." *Sociological Quarterly* 26 (1985), 331–49.

Dray, William. *Laws and Explanations in History.* Oxford: Oxford University Press, 1957.

Philosophy of History. Englewood Cliffs: Prentice Hall, 1964.

Edwards, Paul, ed. *Encyclopedia of Philosophy.* Vols.4 and 5. New York: Macmillan, 1967.

Eells, Ellery. *Rational Decision and Causality.* Cambridge: Cambridge University Press, 1982.

Ferris, Wayne H. *The Power Capabilities of Nation States.* Lexington: Lexington Books, 1973.

Gallie, W.B. "Explanations in History and the Genetic Sciences." *Mind* 64 (April 1955), 160–80.

George, Alexander L. "The Operational Code: A Neglected Approach to the Study of Political Leaders and Decision Making." *International Studies Quarterly* 13 (June 1969), 190–222.

"Case Studies and Theory Development: The Method of Structured, Focused Comparison." In *Diplomacy: New Approaches in History, Theory and Policy*, ed. Paul G. Lauren. New York: Free Press, 1979.

"Case Studies and Theory Development." Paper Presented at the Second Annual Symposium on Information Processing in Organization. Carnegie-Mellon University, October 15–16, 1982.

George, Alexander L, David K. Hall, and William E. Simons, eds. *The Limits of Coercive Diplomacy: Laos, Cuba, Vietnam.* Boston: Little Brown, 1971.

George, Alexander L. and Richard Smoke. *Deterrence in American Foreign Policy: Theory and Practice.* New York: Columbia University Press, 1974.

"Deterrence and Foreign Policy." *World Politics* 41 (January 1989), 170–82.

Gilpin, Robert. *War and Change in World Politics.* Cambridge: Cambridge University Press, 1981.

Gochman, Charles S. and Zeev Maoz. "Militarized Interstate Disputes, 1816–1976." *Journal of Conflict Resolution* 28 (December 1984), 585–616.

Haas, Ernst B. "The Balance of Power: Prescription, Concept or Propaganda?" *World Politics* 5 (July 1953), 442–77.

Hart, Jeffrey. "Three Approaches to the Measurement of Power in International Relations." *International Organization* 30 (Spring 1976), 289–305.

Hermann, Charles F. "Decision Structure and Process Influences on Foreign Policy." In *Why Nations Act: Theoretical Perspectives for Comparative Foreign Policy Studies*, eds. Maurice A. East, Stephen A. Salmore, and Charles F. Hermann. Beverly Hills: Sage Publications, 1978.

Hermann, Margaret G. and Charles F. Hermann. "Who Makes Foreign Policy Decisions and How? An Empirical Enquiry." *International Studies Quarterly* 33 (December 1989), 361–87.

Hirshleifer, Jack. "The Paradox of Power." UCLA Department of Economics. *Working Paper 582B* (Los Angeles: April 1991).

Hoffmann, Stanley. "Balance of Power." In *International Encyclopedia of the Social Sciences*, Vol.I, ed. David L. Sills. New York: Macmillan and Free Press, 1968.

Holsti, Kalevi J. *Peace and War: Armed Conflicts and International Order 1648–1989.* Cambridge: Cambridge University Press, 1991.

Howard, Michael. *The Causes of War.* 2nd edn. Cambridge, Mass.: Harvard University Press, 1983.

Hunter, Douglas E. *Political/Military Applications of Bayesian Analysis: Methodological Issues.* Boulder: Westview Press, 1984.

Huntington, Samuel P. "Arms Races: Prerequisites and Results." *Public Policy* 8 (1958), 41–86.

Huth, Paul. *Extended Deterrence and the Prevention of War.* New Haven and London: Yale University Press, 1988.

Huth, Paul and Bruce Russett. "What Makes Deterrence Work? Cases from 1900 to 1980." *World Politics* 36 (July 1984), 496–526.

"Deterrence Failure and Crisis Escalation." *International Studies Quarterly* 32 (March 1988), 29–45.

"General Deterrence between Enduring Rivals." *American Political Science Review* 87 (March 1993), 61–73.

Hybel, Alex. R. *The Logic of Surprise in International Conflict.* Lexington: Lexington Books, 1986.

Intriligator, Michael D. and Dagobert L. Brito. "Can Arms Races Lead to the Outbreak of War?" *Journal of Conflict Resolution* 28 (March 1984), 63–84.

James, Patrick. *Crisis and War.* Kingston and Montreal: McGill–Queens University Press, 1988.

Jervis, Robert. *Perception and Misperception in International Politics.* Princeton: Princeton University Press, 1976.

"Cooperation under the Security Dilemma." *World Politics* 30 (January 1978), 167–214.

"Deterrence Theory Revisited." *World Politics* 31 (January 1979), 289–324.

Jervis, Robert, Richard Ned Lebow, and Janice Gross Stein, eds. *Psychology and Deterrence.* Baltimore and London: The Johns Hopkins University Press, 1985.

Kahn, Herman. *On Thermonuclear War.* Princeton: Princeton University Press, 1961.

Kaufman, William W. "The Requirements of Deterrence." In *Military Policy and National Security,* ed. William W. Kaufman. Princeton: Princeton University Press, 1956.

Kennedy, Paul. *Strategy and Diplomacy: 1870–1945.* London: George Allen & Unwin, 1983.

Knorr, Klaus. *Military Power and Potential.* Lexington: D.C. Heath, 1970.

The Power of Nations: The Political Economy of International Relations. New York: Basic Books, 1975.

"On Strategic Surprise." *CISA Research Note* 10 (Los Angeles: UCLA, February 1982).

Laffin, John. *Brassey's Battles.* London: Brassey's, 1986.

Laqueur, Walter. *Guerrilla: A Historical and Critical Study.* Boston: Little, Brown, 1976.

Lebow, Richard Ned. *Between Peace and War: The Nature of International Crisis.* Baltimore and London: The Johns Hopkins University Press, 1981.

Lebow, Richard Ned and Janice Gross Stein. "Beyond Deterrence." *Journal of Social Issues* 43 (1987), 5–71.

Levy, Jack S. "Historical Trends in Great Power War, 1495–1975." *International Studies Quarterly* 26 (June 1982), 278–300.

"Declining Power and the Preventive Motivation for War." *World Politics* 40 (October 1987), 82–107.

"Review Article: When Do Deterrent Threats Work?" *British Journal of Political Science* 18 (October 1988), 485–512.

Liddell Hart, B.H. *Strategy*. 2nd edn. New York: NAL Penguin, 1974.

Lijphart, Arend. "Comparative Politics and Comparative Method." *American Political Science Review* 65 (September 1971), 682–93.

Liska, George. *International Equilibrium: A Theoretical Essay on the Politics and Organization of Security*. Cambridge, Mass.: Harvard University Press, 1957.

Luttwak, Edward N. *The Grand Strategy of the Roman Empire: From the First Century A.D. to the Third*. Baltimore and London: The Johns Hopkins University Press, 1976.

"The American Style of Warfare and the Military Balance." *Survival* 21 (March/April 1979), 57–60.

Strategy: The Logic of War and Peace: Cambridge, Mass.: The Belknap Press of Harvard University Press, 1987.

Mack, Andrew. "Why Big Nations Lose Small Wars: The Politics of Asymmetric Conflict." *World Politics* 27 (January 1975), 175–200.

Mandelbaum, Michael. *The Fate of Nations*. Cambridge: Cambridge University Press, 1988.

Maoz, Zeev. "Power, Capabilities, and Paradoxical Conflict Outcomes." *World Politics* 41 (January 1989), 239–66.

"Joining the Club of Nations, Political Development and International Conflict, 1816–1976." *International Studies Quarterly* 33 (June 1989), 199–231.

March, James G. "The Power of Power." In *Varieties of Political Theory*, ed. David Easton. New York: Prentice Hall, 1966.

Mayer, Arno J. "Internal Causes and Purposes of War in Europe, 1870–1956: A Research Assignment." *Journal of Modern History* 41 (September 1969), 291–303.

Mearsheimer, John J. *Conventional Deterrence*. Ithaca and London: Cornell University Press, 1983.

Morgan, Patrick M. *Deterrence: A Conceptual Analysis*. 2nd edn. Beverly Hills: Sage Publications, 1983.

Morrow, James D. "Moving Forward in Time: Paths toward a Dynamic Utility Theory of Crisis Decisions." In *Dynamic Models of International Conflict*, eds. Urs Luterbacher and Michael D. Ward. Boulder: Lynne Rienner, 1985.

"A Twist of Truth: A Reexamination of the Effects of Arms Races on the Occurrences of War." *Journal of Conflict Resolution* 33 (September 1989), 500–29.

Mueller, John. *Retreat from Doomsday: The Obsolescence of Major War*. New York: Basic Books, 1989.

Nye, Joseph S. "Old Wars and Future Wars: Causation and Prevention." *Journal of Interdisciplinary History* 18 (Spring 1988), 581–90.

Organski, A.F.K. *World Politics*. 2nd edn. New York: Alfred A. Knopf, 1968.

Organski, A.F.K. and Jacek Kugler. *The War Ledger*. Chicago and London: University of Chicago Press, 1980.

Osgood, Robert E. *Limited War: The Challenge to American Strategy*. Chicago: University of Chicago Press, 1957.

Ostrom, Charles W. Jr. and Francis W. Hoole. "Alliances and War Revisited: A Research Note." *International Studies Quarterly* 22 (June 1978), 215–36.

Quester, George, H. *Offense and Defense in the International System*. New York: John Wiley, 1977.

Rosecrance, Richard N. *Action and Reaction in World Politics: International Systems in Perspective*. Boston: Little, Brown, 1963.

"Deterrence and Vulnerability in the Pre-nuclear Era." *Adelphi Paper* 160 (London: Autumn 1980), 24–30.

Rosen, Steven. "A Model of War and Alliance." In *Alliance in International Politics*, eds. Julian Friedman, Christopher Bladen, and Steven Rosen. Boston: Allyn and Bacon, 1970.

'War Power and the Willingness to Suffer." In *Peace, War and Numbers*, ed. Bruce M. Russett. Beverly Hills: Sage Publications, 1972.

Russett, Bruce M. "Further Beyond Deterrence." *Journal of Social Issues* 34 (1987), 99–104.

Schelling, Thomas. *The Strategy of Conflict*. Cambridge, Mass.: Harvard University Press, 1980.

Schumpeter, Joseph A. *Imperialism and Social Classes*. New York: Augustus M. Kelley, 1951.

Singer, J. David. ed. *The Correlates of War, Vol.I: Research Origins and Rationale*. New York: The Free Press, 1979.

Singer, J. David, Stuart Bremer, and John Stuckey, eds. "Capability Distribution, Uncertainty, and Major Power War." In *Peace, War and Numbers*, ed. Bruce Russett. Beverly Hills: Sage Publications, 1972.

Singer, J. David and Melvin Small. "Alliance Aggregation and the Onset of War, 1885–1945." In *Quantitative International Politics: Insights and Evidence*, ed. J. David Singer. New York: Free Press, 1968.

Siverson, Randolph M. and Joel King. "Attributes of National Alliance Membership and War Participation, 1815–1965." *American Journal of Political Science* 24 (February 1980), 1–15.

Siverson, Randolph M. and Michael P. Sullivan. "The Distribution of Power and the Onset of War." *Journal of Conflict Resolution* 27 (September 1983), 473–94.

Smoke, Richard. *War: Controlling Escalation*. Cambridge, Mass.: Harvard University Press, 1977.

Snyder, Glenn H. "Deterrence and Power." *Journal of Conflict Resolution* 4 (June 1960), 163–81.

Deterrence and Defense: Toward a Theory of National Security. Princeton: Princeton University Press, 1961.

Snyder, Glenn H. and Paul Diesing. *Conflict among Nations: Bargaining, Decision Making, and System Structure in International Crises*. Princeton: Princeton University Press, 1977.

Snyder, Jack. *Myths of Empire: Domestic Politics and Strategic Ideology*. Ithaca: Cornell University Press, 1991.

228

Sprout, Harold and Margaret Sprout. "Explanation and Prediction in International Politics." In *International Politics and Foreign Policy: A Reader in Research and Theory*, ed. James N. Rosenau. New York: The Free Press, 1961.

Stein, Janice Gross and Raymond Tanter. *Rational Decision-Making: Israel's Security Choices, 1967*. Columbus: Ohio State University Press, 1980.

Steinbruner, John. "Beyond Rational Deterrence: The Struggle for New Conceptions." *World Politics* 28 (January 1976), 223–45.

Taylor, A.J.P. *The Origins of the Second World War*. 2nd edn. Greenwich, Conn.: Fawcett Publications, 1961.

Thompson, William R. *On Global War: Historical-Structural Approaches to World Politics*. Columbia: University of South Carolina Press, 1988.

Vasquez, John A. "The Steps to War: Toward a Scientific Explanation of Correlates of War Findings." *World Politics* 40 (October 1987), 108–45.

The War Puzzle. Cambridge: Cambridge University Press, 1993.

Wallace, Michael D. "Armaments and Escalation: Two Competing Hypotheses." *International Studies Quarterly* 26 (March 1982), 37–56.

Walt, Stephen M. "Alliance Formation and the Balance of World Power." *International Security* 9 (Spring 1985), 3–43.

"Revolution and War." *World Politics* 44 (April 1992), 321–68.

Waltz, Kenneth N. *Theory of International Politics*. New York: Random House, 1979.

"The Spread of Nuclear Weapons: More May be Better." *Adelphi Papers* 171 (Autumn 1981).

"Nuclear Myths and Political Realities." *American Political Science Review* 84 (September 1990), 731–45.

Weede, Erich. "Overwhelming Preponderance as a Pacifying Condition among Contiguous Asian Dyads, 1950–69." *Journal of Conflict Resolution* 20 (September 1976), 395–411.

Wohlstetter, Albert. "Illusions of Distance." *Foreign Affairs*. 46 (January 1968), 242–55.

Zagare, Frank C. "Pathologies of Unilateral Deterrence." In *Dynamic Models of International Conflict*, eds. Urs Luterbacher and Michael D. Ward. Boulder: Lynne Rienner, 1985.

The Dynamics of Deterrence. Chicago and London: The University of Chicago Press, 1987.

Zinnes, Dina A., Robert C. North, and H.E. Koch. "Capability, Threat, and the Outbreak of War." In *International Politics and Foreign Policy: A Reader in Research and Theory*, ed. James N. Rosenau. New York: Free Press, 1961.

The Russo-Japanese War

Asakwa, Kanichi. *The Russo-Japanese Conflict: Its Causes and Issues*. Port Washington, N.Y.: Kennikat Press, 1970.

Ballard, G.A. *The Influence of the Sea on the Political History of Japan*. London: John Murray, 1921.

Beasley, W.G. *The Modern History of Japan*. New York: Praeger, 1963.

Blond, Georges. *Admiral Togo*. Trans. Edward Hyams. New York: Macmillan, 1960.

Bodley, R.V.C. *Admiral Togo*. London: Jarrolds Publishers, 1935.

Brown, Delmar M. *Nationalism in Japan: An Introductory Historical Analysis*. Berkeley: University of California Press, 1955.

Causton, E.E.N. *Militarism and Foreign Policy in Japan*. London: George Allen & Unwin, 1936.

Connors, Lesley. *The Emperor's Advisor: Saionji Kinmochi and Pre-War Japanese Politics*. London: Croom Helm, 1987.

Conroy, Hilary. *The Japanese Seizure of Korea: 1868–1910, A Study of Realism and Idealism in International Relations*. Philadelphia: University of Pennsylvania Press, 1960.

Dallin, David J. *The Rise of Russia in Asia*. New Haven: Yale University Press, 1949.

Dennett, Tyler. *Roosevelt and the Russo-Japanese War*. Gloucester: Peter Smith, 1959.

Dennis, Alfred L.P. *The Anglo-Japanese Alliance*. Berkeley: University of California Publications, 1923.

Esthus, Raymond A. *Double Eagle and Rising Sun: The Russians and Japanese at Portsmouth in 1905*. Durham: Duke University Press, 1988.

Hackett, Roger F. "Political Modernization and the Meiji Genro." In *Political Development in Modern Japan*, ed. Robert E. Ward. Princeton: Princeton University Press, 1968.

Hargreaves, Reginald. *Red Sun Rising: The Siege of Port Arthur*. Philadelphia: J.B. Lippincott, 1962.

Ikle, Frank W. "The Triple Intervention, Japan's Lesson in the Diplomacy of Imperialism." *Monumenta Nipponica* 22 (1967), 122–30.

Kennedy, Captain M.D. *Some Aspects of Japan and Her Defense Forces*. London: Kegan Paul, 1928.

Kuropatkin, General A. *The Russian Army and the Japanese War*, Vol.I. Trans. Captain A.B. Linsay. New York: E.P. Dutton, 1909.

Langer, William L. *The Diplomacy of Imperialism: 1890–1902*, Vol.II. New York and London: Alfred A. Knopf, 1935.

"The Origins of the Russo-Japanese War." In *Explorations in Crises: Papers on International History*, eds. Carl E. Schorske and Elizabeth Schorske. Cambridge, Mass.: Belknap Press of the Harvard University Press, 1969.

Lensen, George Alexander, ed. *Revelations of a Russian Diplomat: The Memoirs of Dimitri I. Abrikossow*. Seattle: University of Washington Press, 1964.

Balance of Intrigue: International Rivalry in Korea & Manchuria, 1884–1899. Vol.II. Tallahassee: University Presses of Florida, 1982.

Malozemoff, Andrew. *Russian Far Eastern Policy, 1881–1904, With Special Emphasis on the Causes of the Russo-Japanese War*. Berkeley: University of California Press, 1958.

Martin, Christopher. *The Russo-Japanese War*. London: Abelard-Schuman, 1967.

Military Correspondent of *The Times*. *The War in the Far East: 1904–05*. London: John Murray, 1905.

Montgomery, Michael. *Imperialist Japan: The Yen to Dominate*. London: Christopher Helm, 1987.

Negrier, General De. *Lessons of the Russo-Japanese War*. London: Hugh Rees, 1906.

Nish, Ian H. *The Origins of the Russo-Japanese War*. London and New York: Longman, 1985.

Okamato, Shumpei. *The Japanese Oligarchy and the Russo-Japanese War*. New York: Columbia University Press, 1970.

Padfield, Peter. *The Battleship Era*. London: Rupert Hart Davis, 1972.

Potter E.B., ed. *Sea Power: A Naval History*. Englewood Cliffs: Prentice Hall, 1960.

Romanov, Boris A. *Russia in Manchuria, 1892–1906*. Trans. Susan Wilbur Jones. Ann Arbor: Edwards Brothers, 1956.

Storry, Richard. *The Double Patriots*. Boston: Houghton Mifflin, 1957.

Tardieu, André. *France and the Alliances: The Struggle for the Balance of Power*. New York: Macmillan, 1908.

The Russo-Japanese War: Reports from the British Officers Attached to the Japanese and Russian Forces in the Field, Vol.III. London: His Majesty's Stationery Office, 1908.

Treat, Payson. *Diplomatic Relations between the U.S. and Japan: 1885–1905*. Stanford: Stanford University Press, 1938.

Walder, David. *The Short Victorious War: The Russo-Japanese Conflict 1904–5*. London: Hutchinson, 1973.

Warner, Denis and Peggy Warner. *The Tide at Sunrise: A History of the Russo-Japanese War, 1904–1905*. New York, Charter House, 1974.

Watts, Anthony J. and Brian G. Gordon. *The Imperial Japanese Navy*. Garden City, N.Y.: Doubleday, 1971.

Westwood J.N. *The Illustrated History of the Russo-Japanese War*. London: Sidgwick & Jackson, 1973.

Russia against Japan, 1904–5: A New Look at the Russo-Japanese War. Albany: State University of New York Press, 1986.

White, John Albert. *The Diplomacy of the Russo-Japanese War*. Princeton: Princeton University Press, 1964.

Woodward, David. *The Russians at Sea*. London: William Kimber, 1965.

Yarmolinsky, Abraham, ed. *The Memoirs of Count Witte*. London: William Heinemann, 1921.

Pearl Harbor

Akira, Fujiwara. "The Role of the Japanese Army." In *Pearl Harbor as History: Japanese–American Relations 1931–1941*, eds. Dorothy Borg and Shumpei Okamoto. New York: Columbia University Press, 1973.

Barnhart, Michael A. *Japan Prepares for Total War: The Search for Economic Security, 1919–1941*. Ithaca: Cornell University Press, 1987.

Bateson, Charles. *The War with Japan: A Concise History*. London: Barrie and Rockliff, 1968.

Beasley, W.G. *The Modern History of Japan*. New York: Praeger, 1963.

Belote, James H. and William M. Belote. *The Titans of the Seas: The Development and Operations of Japanese and American Carrier Task Forces during World War II*. New York: Harper & Row, 1975.

Brown, Delmar M. *Nationalism in Japan, An Introductory Historical Analysis*. Berkeley: University of California Press, 1955.

Butow, Robert G.C. *Tojo and the Coming of the War*. Princeton: Princeton University Press, 1961.

Chihiro, Hosaya. "Britain and the United States in Japan's View of the International System, 1919–1937." In *Anglo-Japanese Alienation 1919–1952*, ed. Ian Nish. Cambridge: Cambridge University Press, 1982.

Churchill, Winston S. *The Second World War, Vol.III: The Grand Alliance*. Boston: Houghton Mifflin, 1950.

Crowley, James B. "A New Asian Order: Some Notes on Pre-War Japanese Nationalism." In *Japan in Crisis: Essays on Taisho Democracy*, eds. Bernard S. Silberman and H.D. Harootunian. Princeton: Princeton University Press, 1974.

Dallek, Robert. *Franklin D. Roosevelt and American Foreign Policy, 1932–1945*. New York: Oxford University Press, 1979.

Dallin, David J. *Soviet Russia and the Far East*. New Haven: Yale University Press, 1948.

Dull, Paul S. *The Battle History of the Imperial Japanese Navy, 1941–1945*. Annapolis: Naval Institute Press, 1978.

Feis, Herbert. *The Road to Pearl Harbor*. New York: Atheneum, 1964.

Fuchida, Mitsuo and Masatake Okumiya. *Midway: The Battle that Doomed Japan*. Annapolis: United States Naval Institute, 1955.

George, Alexander L. *Forceful Persuasion: Coercive Diplomacy as an Alternative to War*. Washington DC: United States Institute of Peace Press, 1991.

Hirama, Yoichi. "Interception–Attrition Strategy: The Sun against the Eagle." *Journal of the Pacific Society* (January 1989), 9–21.

Ike, Nobutake. *Japan's Decision for War, Records of the 1941 Policy Conferences*. Stanford: Stanford University Press, 1967.

Ikle, Frank William. *German–Japanese Relations 1936–1940*. New York: Bookman Associates, 1956.

Ito, Masanori. *The End of the Imperial Japanese Navy*. Trans. Andrew Y. Kuroda and Roger Pineau. New York: Macfadden Books, 1965.

Jones, F.C. *Japan's New Order in East Asia: Its Rise and Fall 1937–45*. London: Oxford University Press, 1954.

Kase, Toshikazu. *Journey to the Missouri*. New Haven: Yale University Press, 1950.

Kato, Masuo. *The Lost War: A Japanese Reporter's Inside Story*. New York: Alfred A. Knopf, 1946.

Kennedy, Captain M.D. *Some Aspects of Japan and Her Defence Forces*. London: Kegan Paul, 1928.

Kennedy, Paul. *The Rise and Fall of the Great Powers: Economic Change and Military Conflict from 1500 to 2000*. New York: Random House, 1987.

Kiyoshi, Ikeda. "Japanese Strategy and the Pacific War, 1941–5." In *Anglo-Japanese Alienation 1919–1952*, ed. Ian Nish. Cambridge: Cambridge University Press, 1982.

Langer, William L. and S. Everett Gleason. *The Undeclared War: 1940–1941*. New York: Harper & Brothers, 1953.

Lauterbach, Richard E. "Secret Jap War Plans." *Life Magazine* (March 4, 1946), 18.

Lensen, George Alexander. *The Strange Neutrality: Soviet–Japanese Relations during the Second World War 1941–1945*. Tallahassee: The Diplomatic Press, 1972.

Maxon, Yale Candee. *Control of Japanese Foreign Policy: A Study of Civil–Military Rivalry 1930–1945*. Berkeley and Los Angeles: University of California Press, 1957.

Meskill, Johanna Menzel. *Hitler and Japan: The Hollow Alliance*. New York: Atherton Press, 1966.

Morgenstern, George. *Pearl Harbor: The Story of the Secret War*. New York: Devin-Adair, 1947.

Morison, Rear Admiral Samuel E. *History of United States Naval Operations in World War II, Vol.III: The Rising Sun in the Pacific*. Boston: Little, Brown, 1951.

Morton, Louis. "Japan's Decision for War (1941)." In *Command Decisions*, ed. Kent Roberts Greenfield. New York: Harcourt, Brace, 1959.

Mueller, John. "Pearl Harbor: Military Inconvenience, Political Disaster." *International Security* 16 (Winter 1991/92), 172–203.

Nish, Ian. *Japanese Foreign Policy 1869–1942: Kasumigaseki to Miyakezaka*. London: Routledge & Kegan Paul, 1977.

Okumiya, Masatake. "Some Background to Remember Pearl Harbor." Unpublished Ms. (Tokyo: December 1989).

Pelz, Stephen E. *Race to Pearl Harbor: The Failure of the Second London Naval Conference and the Onset of World War II*. Cambridge, Mass.: Harvard University Press, 1974.

Potter, E.B., ed. *Sea Power in Naval History*. Englewood Cliffs: Prentice Hall, 1960.

Prange, Gordon W. *At Dawn We Slept: The Untold Story of Pearl Harbor*. New York: McGraw Hill, 1981.

Presseisen, Ernst L. *Germany and Japan: A Study in Totalitarian Diplomacy 1933–1941*. The Hague: Martinus Nijhoff, 1958.

Quester, George. *Offense and Defense in the International System*. New York: John Wiley, 1977.

Shillony, Ben-Ami. *Revolt in Japan: The Young Officers and the February 26, 1936 Incident*. Princeton: Princeton University Press, 1973.

Storry, Richard. *The Double Patriots: A Study of Japanese Nationalism*. London: Chatto and Windus, 1957.

The Statesman's Year Book. London: Macmillan, 1941.

Togo, Shigenori. *The Cause of Japan*. New York: Simon and Schuster, 1956.

US Department of State: *Prelude to Infamy: Official Report on the Final Phase of U.S.–Japanese Relations, October 17 to December 7, 1941*. Washington DC: The United States News, 1943.

Wheeler, Gerald E. *Prelude to Pearl Harbor: The United States Navy and the Far East 1921–1931*. Columbia: University of Missouri Press, 1963.

Wohlstetter, Roberta. *Pearl Harbor: Warning and Decision*. Stanford: Stanford University Press, 1962.

The Korean War

Appleman, Roy E. *Disaster in Korea: The Chinese Confront MacArthur*. College Station: Texas A&M University Press, 1989.

Bernstein, Barton J. "The Policy of Risk: Crossing the 38th Parallel and Marching to the Yalu." *Foreign Service Journal* 54 (March 1977), 16–22 and 29.

Brodie, Bernard. *War and Politics*. New York: Macmillan, 1973.

Buhite, Russell D. *Soviet–American Relations in Asia 1945–1954*. Norman: University of Oklahoma Press, 1981.

Camilleri, Joseph. *Chinese Foreign Policy: The Maoist Era and its Aftermath.* Seattle: University of Washington Press, 1980.

Cheng-Wen, Chai and Zhao Yong-Tian. *Panmunjom Negotiations*. Peking: PLA Publishing Agency, 1989.

Ching-Wen, Chow. *Ten Years of Storm: The True Story of the Communist Regime in China*. New York: Holt, Rinehart and Winston, 1960.

Collins, J. Lawton. *War in Peacetime: The History and Lessons of Korea*. Boston: Houghton Mifflin, 1969.

Department of State Bulletin 23 (November 27, 1950)

Di, He. "The Most Respected Enemy: Mao Zedong's Perception of the United States," Paper Presented at the Conference on China's Foreign Policy, Washington DC, Woodrow Wilson Center, July 7–9, 1992.

Dingman, Roger. "Atomic Diplomacy during the Korean War." *International Security* 13 (Winter 1988/89), 50–91.

Domes, Jurgen. *Peng Te-huai, The Man and the Image*. London: C. Hurst, 1985.

Foot, Rosemary. *The Wrong War: American Policy and the Dimensions of the Korean Conflict, 1950–1953*. Ithaca: Cornell University Press, 1985.

"Nuclear Coercion and the Ending of the Korean Conflict." *International Security* 13 (Winter 1988/89), 92–112.

George, Alexander L. *The Chinese Communist Army in Action: The Korean War and Its Aftermath*. New York: Columbia University Press, 1967.

Gittings, John. *The Role of the Chinese Army*. New York: Oxford University Press, 1967.

Godwin, Paul H.B. *The Chinese Communist Armed Forces*. Maxwell Air Force Base, Ala: Air University Press, 1988.

Goldstein, Steven M. "Sino-American Relations, 1948–1950: Lost Chance or No Chance?" In *Sino–American Relations 1945–1955: A Joint Reassessment of a Critical Decade*, eds. Harry Harding and Yuan Ming. Wilmington: Scholarly Resources, 1989.

Goulden, Joseph C. *Korea: The Untold Story of the War*. New York: Times Books, 1982.

Gurtov, Melvin and Byong-Moo Hwang. *China under Threat: The Politics of Strategy and Diplomacy*. Baltimore and London: The Johns Hopkins University Press, 1980.

Hastings, Max. *The Korean War*. London: Michael Joseph, 1987.

Hoyt, Edwin P. *The Day the Chinese Attacked, 1950: The Story of the Failure of America's China Policy*. New York: McGraw Hill, 1990.

Hsiung, James C. *Ideology and Practice: The Evolution of Chinese Communism.* New York: Praeger, 1970.

Khrushchev Remembers. Trans. and ed. Strobe Talbott. Boston: Little, Brown, 1970.

Khrushchev Remembers, The Glasnost Tapes. Trans. and eds. Jerrold L. Schecter and Vyacheslaw V. Luchkov. Boston: Little, Brown, 1990.

Lowe, Peter. *The Origins of the Korean War*. London: Longman 1986.

MacDonald, Callum A. *Korea: The War Before Vietnam*. Houndmills: Macmillan, 1986.

"Mao's Dispatch of Chinese Troops to Korea: Forty-six Telegrams, July–October 1950." *Chinese Historians* 5 (Spring 1992) 63–86.

Mayers, David Allen. *Cracking the Monolith: U.S. Policy Against the Sino-Soviet Alliance, 1949–1955*. Baton Rouge: Louisiana State University Press, 1986.

Memoirs of A Chinese Marshal – The Autobiographical Notes of Peng Dehuai (1898–1974). Trans. Zheng Longpu. Peking: Foreign Languages Press, 1984.

O'Ballance, Edgar. *Korea: 1950–1953*. Handen: Archen Books, 1969.

Panikkar, K.M. *In Two Chinas: Memoirs of a Diplomat*. London: George Allen & Unwin, 1955.

Ping, Du. *In the Headquarters of the Volunteer Force*. Peking: PLA Publishing House, 1989.

Pollack, Jonathan D. "The Korean War and Sino-American Relations." In *Sino–American Relations 1945–1955: A Joint Reassessment of a Critical Decade*, eds. Harry Harding and Yuan Ming. Wilmington: Scholarly Resources, 1989.

"Red Guard Paper, February 1967." *Far Eastern Economic Review* (October 2, 1969), 25.

Rees, David. *Korea: The Limited War*. New York: St. Martin's Press, 1964.

Ryan, Mark A. *Chinese Attitudes Toward Nuclear Weapons: China and the United States During the Korean War*. Armonk, N.Y.: M.E. Sharpe, 1989.

Schaller, Michael. *Douglas MacArthur, The Far Eastern General*. New York: Oxford University Press, 1989.

Schram, Stuart, ed. *Chairman Mao Talks to the People, Talks and Letters: 1956–1971*. New York: Pantheon Books, 1974.

Selected Military Writings of Mao Tse-tung. Peking: Foreign Languages Press, 1967.

Selected Works of Zhou Enlai, Vol.II. Peking: Foreign Languages Press, 1981.

Spanier, John W. *The Truman–MacArthur Controversy and the Korean War*. Cambridge, Mass.: The Belknap Press of Harvard University Press, 1959.

Spurr, Russell. *Enter the Dragon: China's Undeclared War against the U.S. in Korea 1950–51*. New York: Newmarket Press, 1988.

Stokesbury, James L. *A Short History of the Korean War*. New York: William Morrow, 1988.

Substance of Statements Made at the Wake Island Conference on October 15, 1950. Washington DC: Government Printing Office, 1951.

Summers, Harry G. Jr. *On Strategy: A Critical Analysis of Vietnam War*: Novato: Presidio Press, 1982.

Korean War Almanac. New York: Facts on File, 1990.

Weiss, Lawrence Stephen. *Storm Around the Cradle: The Korean War and the Early Years of the People's Republic of China, 1949–1953*. Ph.D. Dissertation, New York: Columbia University, 1981.

Whelan, Richard. *Drawing the Line: The Korean War, 1950–1953*. Boston: Little, Brown, 1990.

Whiting, Allen S. *China Crosses the Yalu: The Decision to Enter the Korean War*. Stanford: Stanford University Press, 1962.

Whitson, William W. *The Chinese High Command: A History of Communist Military Politics, 1927–71.* New York: Praeger, 1973.

Xiaolu, Chen. "China's Policy Toward the United States, 1949– 1955." In *Sino-American Relations 1945–1955: A Joint Reassessment of a Critical Decade,* eds. Harry Harding and Yuan Ming. Wilmington: Scholarly Resources, 1989.

Xue-Zhi, Hong. *Reminiscences of the War to Resist U.S. Aggression and Aid Korea (1950–1953).* Peking: PLA Literature Press, 1991.

Yufan, Hao and Zhai Zhihai. "China's Decision to Enter the Korean War: History Revisited." *China Quarterly* 121 (March 1990), 94–115.

Yu-Meng, Ye. *On the Spot Reports of Dispatching Troops to Korea.* Peking: Ji-Nan Press, 1991.

Zelman, Walter A. "Chinese Intervention in the Korean War: A Bilateral Failure of Deterrence." *Security Studies Paper* 11. Los Angeles: University of California, 1967.

Zhonghong, Shen, ed. *The History of the Anti-America Supporting Korean War.* Peking: Chinese Military Academy, 1990.

The India–Pakistan War

Barnds, William J. *India, Pakistan and the Great Powers.* New York: Praeger, 1972.

Bhutto, Zulfikar Ali. *Foreign Policy of Pakistan: A Compendium of Speeches Made in the National Assembly of Pakistan 1962–64.* Karachi: Pakistan Institute of International Affairs, 1964.

The Myth of Independence. London: Oxford University Press, 1969.

Blinkenberg, Lars. *India–Pakistan: The History of Unresolved Conflicts.* Copenhagen: Dansk Udenrigspolitisk Instituts, 1972.

Brecher, Michael. *The Struggle for Kashmir.* New York: Oxford University Press, 1953.

Brines, Russell. *The Indo-Pakistani Conflict.* London: Pall Mall Press, 1968.

Burke, S.M. *Pakistan's Foreign Policy: A Historical Analysis.* London: Oxford University Press, 1973.

Chaudhry, Amjad Ali Khan. *September '65: Before and After.* Lahore: Ferozsons, 1977.

Choudhury, G.W. *Pakistan's Relations with India 1947–1966.* London: Pall Mall Press, 1968.

Cohen, Stephen P. "Arms and Politics in Bangladesh, India and Pakistan." *Special Studies* 49. New York: Council on International Studies, State University of New York at Buffalo, 1973.

"U.S. Weapons and South Asia: A Policy Analysis." *Pacific Affairs* 49 (Spring 1976), 49–69.

The Pakistan Army. Berkeley: University of California Press, 1984

Defence Journal 4 (Karachi: 1978), 1–10.

Feldman, Herbert. *From Crisis to Crisis: Pakistan 1962–1969.* London: Oxford University Press, 1972.

Fricker, John. *Battle for Pakistan: The Air War of 1965.* Shepperton: Ian Allan, 1979.

Ganguly, Sumit. *The Origins of War in South Asia: Indo-Pakistani Conflicts Since 1947*. Boulder: Westview Press, 1986.

Gupta, Sisir. *Kashmir: A Study in India–Pakistan Relations*. Bombay: Asia Publishing House, 1966.

Hayes, Louis D. *Politics in Pakistan: The Struggle for Legitimacy*. Boulder: Westview Press, 1984.

Heiman, Leo. "Lessons form the War in Kashmir." *Military Review* 46 (February 1966), 22–29.

International Institute for Strategic Studies. *The Military Balance 1965–66*. London: 1965.

Kaul, B.M. *Confrontation with Pakistan*. Delhi: Vikas Publications, 1971.

Kavic, Lorne J. *India's Quest for Security: Defence Policies, 1947–1965*. Berkeley: University of California Press, 1967.

Khan, Mohammed Asghar. *The First Round: Indo-Pakistan War 1965*. London: Islamic Information Services, 1979.

Khan, Mohammad Ayub. "The Pakistan–American Alliance: Stresses and Strains." *Foreign Affairs* 42 (January 1964), 195–209.

Friends: Not Masters: A Political Autobiography. Oxford: Oxford University Press, 1967.

Khan, Riazul Karim. "Higher Conduct of 1965 Indo-Pak War." *Defence Journal* (Karachi) 10 (1984), 7–14.

Khattak, Habibullah Khan. "A General's Version: Rejoinder to *My Version*." *Defence Journal* 9 (1983), 9–17.

Kochanek, Stanley A. *Interest Groups and Development: Business and Politics in Pakistan*. Delhi: Oxford University Press, 1983.

Malik, Abdul Ali. "Operation Gibraltar: A General's View." *Muslim* (October 14, 1986).

Mazari, Shireen M. "Kashmir Factor in Pakistan's Politics – I; The Years 1947–65." *Muslim* (October 21, 1986).

Mehdi Papers. Serial 3 (Karachi: 1987).

Mukerjee, Dilip. *Zulfikar Ali Bhutto: Quest for Power*. Delhi: Vikas Publishing House, 1972.

Musa, General Mohammad. *My Version: India-Pakistan War 1965*. New Delhi: ABC Publishing House, 1983.

Nayar, Kuldip. "Pakistan Provoked the 1965 War." *Sunday Magazine* (July 10–16, 1983), reprinted in *Strategic Digest* (July 1984), 745–46.

O'Ballance, Edgar. "The 1965 War in Retrospect." *Defence Journal*. 7 (1978), 15–19.

Sayed, Anwar H. *The Discourse and Politics of Zulfikar Ali Bhutto*. New York: St. Martin's Press, 1992.

Sen Gupta, Bhabani. *The Fulcrum of Asia: Relations among China, India, Pakistan, and the U.S.S.R.* New York: Pegasus, 1970.

Sidiqui, A.R. "The War Analyzed." *Defence Journal* 1 (1975), 1–12.

"September: Time for Critical Self-Assessment." *Defence Journal* 9 (1983), 1–7.

Sisson, Richard. "Politics and the Military in Pakistan." In *The Military and Politics in Five Developing Nations*, ed. John P. Lovell. Kensington: Center for Research in Social Systems, 1970.

Stahnke, Arthur A. "Diplomatic Triangle: China's Policy Towards India and Pakistan in the 1960s." In *The Dynamics of China's Foreign Relations*, ed. Jerome A. Cohen. Cambridge, Mass.: Harvard University Press, 1970.

Tahir-Kheli, Shirin. *The United States and Pakistan: The Evolution of An Influence Relationship*. New York: Praeger, 1982.

Taseer, Salmaan. *Bhutto: A Political Biography*. New Delhi: Vikas Publishing House, 1980.

Thomas, Raju. G.C. *The Defence of India: A Budgetary Perspective of Strategy and Politics*. Delhi: Macmillan, 1978.

Indian Security Policy. Princeton: Princeton University Press, 1986.

United Nations. *Security Council Official Records* 1091st Meeting (14 February, 1964).

United Nations Security Council. *Report by the Secretary General on the Current Situation in Kashmir with Particular Reference to the Cease-fire Agreement, The Cease-fire Line and the Functioning of UNMOGIP* S/6651 (September 3, 1965).

Verzberger, Yacov. *The Enduring Entente: Sino-Pakistani Relations 1960–1980*. New York: Praeger, 1983.

Wriggins, Howard. "The Balancing Process in Pakistan's Foreign Policy." In *Pakistan: The Long View*, eds. Lawrence Ziring, Ralph Braibanti, and W. Howard Wriggins. Durham: Duke University Press, 1977.

Ziring Lawrence. *The Ayub Khan Era: Politics in Pakistan 1958–1969*. Syracuse: Syracuse University Press, 1971.

The Middle East War

Amiel, Saadia. "Defensive Technologies for Small States: A Perspective." In *Military Aspects of the Israeli–Arab Conflict*, ed. Louis Williams. Tel Aviv: University Publishing Projects, 1975.

Amos, John W. *Arab–Israeli Military/Political Relations: Arab Perceptions and the Politics of Escalation*. New York: Pergamon Press, 1979.

Bar-Joseph, Uri. "The Hidden Debate: The Formation of Nuclear Doctrines in the Middle East." *Journal of Strategic Studies* 5 (June 1982), 205–27.

Bar-Siman-Tov, Yaacov. *The Israeli–Egyptian War of Attrition, 1969–1970*. New York: Columbia University Press, 1980.

de Borchgrave, Arnaud. "The Battle is Now Inevitable." *Newsweek* (9 April 1973), 44–45 and 49.

Brecher, Michael. *Decisions in Crisis: Israel, 1967 and 1973*. Berkeley: University of California Press, 1980.

Bullock, John. *The Making of a War: The Middle East from 1967 to 1973*. London: Longman, 1974.

Burrell, R. Michael and Abbas R. Kelidar. "Egypt: The Dilemmas of a Nation – 1970–1977." *The Washington Papers*, Vol.5. Beverly Hills: Sage Publications, 1977.

Dessouki, Ali E. Hillal. "The Primacy of Economics: The Foreign Policy of Egypt." In *The Foreign Policies of Arab States*, eds. Bahgat Korany and Ali Dissouki. Boulder: Westview Press, 1984.

Dupuy, Trevor N. *Elusive Victory: The Arab–Israeli Wars, 1947–1974*. New York: Harper & Row, 1978.

El-Rayyes, Riad N. and Dunia Nahas, eds. *The October War; Documents, Personalities, Analyses and Maps*. Beirut: An-nahar Press Services, 1973.

Handel, Michael I. "Perception, Deception and Surprise: The Case of the Yom Kippur War." *Jerusalem Papers on Peace Problems* 19 (1976).

"The Yom Kippur War and the Inevitability of Surprise." *International Studies Quarterly* 21 (September 1977), 461–502.

Heikal, Mohamed. *The Road to Ramadan*. New York: Ballantine Books, 1975.

Sphinx and the Commissar: The Rise and Fall of Soviet Influence in the Arab World. London: Collins, 1978.

Autumn of Fury: The Assassination of Sadat. New York: Random House, 1983.

Herzog, Chaim. *The War of Atonement*. London: Weidenfeld and Nicolson, 1975.

Arab–Israeli Wars. New York: Vintage Books, 1982.

Hinnebusch, Raymond A. *Egyptian Politics under Sadat: The Post-Populist Development of an Authoritarian-Modernizing State*. Cambridge: Cambridge University Press, 1985.

Hirst, David and Irene Beeson. *Sadat*. London: Faber & Faber, 1981.

The Insight Team of the London *Sunday Times*. *The Yom Kippur War*. Garden City N.Y.: Doubleday, 1974.

Israeli, Raphael. *The Public Diary of President Sadat, Part One, The Road to War (October 1970–October 1973)*. Leiden: E.J. Brill, 1978.

Kalb, Marvin, and Bernard Kalb. *Kissinger*. New York: Dell Publishing, 1974.

Kemp, Geoffrey. "Israel and Egypt: Military Force Posture 1967– 1972." In *Comparative Defense Policy*, eds. Frank B. Horton, Anthony C. Rogerson, and Edward L. Warner. Baltimore and London: The Johns Hopkins University Press, 1974.

Kissinger, Henry. *Years of Upheaval*. Boston: Little Brown, 1982.

Laqueur, Walter. *Confrontation: The Middle East War and World Politics*. London: Abacus, 1974.

O'Ballance, Edgar. *No Victor, No Vanquished: The Yom Kippur War*. San Rafael, Calif.: Presidio Press, 1978.

Perlmutter, Amos. *Egypt the Praetorian State*. New Brunswick, N.J.: Transaction Books, 1974.

"Israel's Fourth War, October 1973: Political and Military Misperceptions." *Orbis* 19 (Summer 1975), 434–60.

Pry, Peter. *Israel's Nuclear Arsenal*. Boulder: Westview Press, 1984.

Quandt, William B. *Decade of Decisions: American Policy Toward the Arab–Israeli Conflict, 1967–1976*. Berkeley: University of California Press, 1977.

Rubinstein, Alvin Z. *Red Star on the Nile: The Soviet–Egyptian Influence Relationship Since the June War*. Princeton: Princeton University Press, 1977.

el-Sadat, Anwar. *In Search of Identity: An Autobiography*. New York: Harper & Row, 1977.

Safran, Nadav. *Israel, the Embattled Ally*. Cambridge, Mass.: Harvard University Press, 1978.

Shamir, Shimon. "Arab Military Lessons from the October War." In *Military Aspects of the Israeli–Arab Conflicts*, ed. Louis Williams. Tel Aviv: University Publishing Projects, 1975.

el Shazly, Saad. *The Crossing of the Suez*. San Francisco: American Mideast Research, 1980.

Shoukri, Ghali. *Egypt: Portrait of a President 1971–1981: Sadat's Road to Jerusalem.* London: Zed Press, 1981.

Speeches by President Anwar el-Sadat, September 1970–March 1971. Cairo: Ministry of Information, n.d.

Tschirgi, Dan. *The American Search for Mideast Peace.* New York: Praeger, 1989.

The Falklands War

Barnett, Anthony. *Iron Britannia.* London: Allison and Busby, 1982.

Beck, Peter. *The Falklands Islands as an International Problem.* London and New York: Routledge, 1988.

Burns, Jimmy. *The Land that Lost Its Heroes: The Falklands, the Post-War and Alfonsin.* London: Bloomsbury Publishing, 1987.

Calvert, Peter. *The Falklands Crisis: The Rights and Wrongs.* London: Frances Pinter, 1982.

Cordoso, Oscar R., Ricardo Kirschbaum, and Edvordo Van der Kooy. *Falklands – The Secret Plot.* East Molesey Surrey: Preston Editions, 1987.

Costa Mendez, Nicanor. "Beyond Deterrence: The Malvinas–Falklands Case." *Journal of Social Issues* 43 (1987), 119–22.

Dabat, Alejandro and Luis Lorenzano. *Argentina: The Malvinas and the End of Military Rule.* Trans. Ralph Johnson. London: Verso Editions, 1982.

Fontana, Andres Miguel. *Political Decision Making by a Military Corporation: Argentina 1976–1983.* Ph.D. Dissertation; Austin: University of Texas, 1987.

Franks Committee. *Falklands Islands Review Report of a Committee of Privy Counsellors.* Chairman, Rt. Hon. The Lord Franks. Cmnd 8787. London: HMSO, 1983.

Freedman, Lawrence. "The War of the Falklands Islands, 1982." *Foreign Affairs* 61 (Fall 1982), 196–210.

Britain and the Falklands War. Oxford: Basil Blackwell, 1988.

Freedman, Lawrence and Virginia Gamba-Stonehouse. *Signals of War: The Falklands Conflict of 1982.* London: Faber & Faber, 1990.

Friedman, Norman. "Surface Combatant Lessons." In *Military Lessons of the Falklands War: Views from the United States,* eds. Bruce W. Watson and Peter M. Dunn. Boulder: Westview Press, 1984.

Gamba, Virginia. *The Falklands/Malvinas War: A Model for North–South Crisis Prevention.* Boston: Allen & Unwin, 1987.

Gavson, Arthur and Desmond Rice. *The Sinking of the Belgrano.* London: Secker & Warburg, 1984.

George, James L. "Large Versus Small Carriers." In *Military Lessons of the Falklands War: Views from the United States,* eds. Bruce W. Watson and Peter M. Dunn. Boulder: Westview Press, 1984.

Haig, Alexander M. Jr. *Caveat, Realism, Reagan, and Foreign Policy.* New York: Macmillan, 1984.

Hastings, Max and Simon Jenkins. *The Battle for the Falklands.* New York: W.W. Norton, 1983.

Hopple, Gerald W. "Intelligence and Warning Lessons." In *Military Lessons of the Falklands War: Views from the United States,* eds. Bruce W. Watson and Peter M. Dunn. Boulder: Westview Press, 1984.

Informe Rattenbach. Buenos Aires: Editiones Espartaco, Serie Documentos Historicos, 1988.

International Institute for Strategic Studies. The *Military Balance 1981–82.* London: ISS, 1981.

Kinney, Douglas. *National Interest/National Honor: The Diplomacy of the Falklands Crisis.* New York: Praeger, 1989.

Kirkpatrick, Jeane J. "My Falklands War and Theirs." *The National Interest* 18 (Winter 1989/90), 11–20.

Lebow, Richard Ned. "Miscalculation in the South Atlantic: The Origins of the Falklands War." In *Psychology and Deterrence,* eds. Robert Jervis, Richard Ned Lebow, and Janice Gross Stein. Baltimore: The Johns Hopkins University Press, 1985.

Lewis, Paul H. *The Crisis of Argentine Capitalism.* Chapel Hill: The University of North Carolina Press, 1990.

Looney, Robert E. *The Political Economy of Latin American Defense Expenditures: Case Studies of Venezuela and Argentina.* Lexington: Lexington Books, 1986.

Makin, Guillermo A. "The Military in Argentine Politics: 1880–1982." *Millennium: Journal of International Studies* 12 (Spring 1983), 49–68.

Moneta, Carlos J. "The Malvinas Conflict: Some Elements for an Analysis of the Argentine Military Regime's Decision Making Process, 1976–82." *Millennium: Journal of International Studies* 13 (Winter 1984), 311–23.

Moro, Ruben O. *The History of the South Atlantic Conflict, The War for the Malvinas.* New York: Praeger, 1989.

Quester, George H. "The Falklands and the Malvinas: Strategy and Arms Control." *ACIS Working Paper* 46. Los Angeles: UCLA Center for International and Strategic Affairs, May 1984.

Ruhe, William J. "Submarine Lessons." In *Military Lessons of the Falklands War: Views from the United States,* eds. Bruce W. Watson and Peter M. Dunn. Boulder: Westview Press, 1984.

Simpson, John and Jana Bennett. *The Disappeared: Voices from a Secret War.* London: Robson Books, 1985.

Smith, William C. "Reflections on the Political Economy of Authoritarian Rule and Capitalist Reorganization in Contemporary Argentina." In *Generals in Retreat: The Crisis of Military Rule in Latin America,* eds. Philip O'Brien and Paul Cammack. Manchester: Manchester University Press, 1985.

The *Sunday Times* of London Insight Team. *War in the Falklands: The Full Story.* New York: Harper & Row, 1982.

Tilford, Earl H. "Air Power Lessons." In *Military Lessons of the Falklands War: Views from the United States,* eds. Bruce W. Watson and Peter M. Dunn. Boulder: Westview Press, 1984.

World Armaments and Disarmament, SIPRI Yearbook 1982. London: Taylor and Francis, 1982.

INDEX

243

Hart, Liddell, 21, 25
Hassan, Abdel Kader, 140, 172
He Long, 101
hegemonic leadership, 4
Heikal, Mohammed, 134, 136–39
Hermann, Charles F., 34
Hirota, Koki, 80
Hitler, Adolph, 75, 76, 198n
HMS *Endurance*, 153, 154
Hoole, Francis W., 31
Hoshino, Naoki, 81
Hull Note, 66–67
Humphrey-Kennedy Amendment, 158
Huntington, Samuel P., 31
Hussein, Saddam, 174

Imperial Conference (1941), 83
Imperial Way Group (Kodo-ha), 79, 80
Inchon landing, 90, 93, 202n
independent variables, 35
India, 25, 179n
    Second Kashmir War (1965), 107–25; air
        power, 107; capabilities, 107–108,
        116–17, 206n; deterrent threat, 108–9,
        208n; policies towards Kashmir, 110;
        strategy, 109–110; and super powers,
        119
    war with China, 117, 122, 123
Indonesia, 179n
initiator, 3–5, 7, 8, 10, 11, 13
    defined, 17, 20
interest groups, 35
international system, 4, 15
intrinsic value, 17, 19, 184n
Iraq, ix, 4, 176
Irou, Karou, 59
Ismail, Ahmad, 136, 140, 212n
Ismail, Hafez, 127, 132, 138, 140, 212, 215n
Israel, 3, 25, 26
    Middle East War (1973), 126–145; air
        force, 126, 128–29, 213n–14n, 216n;
        army, 129; reserves, 133; capabilities,
        126, 129, 133, 212n–13n; deterrent
        efforts, 128; nuclear capability, 126,
        133, 213n; perceptions of Egypt,
        129–30; strategy, 128–30, 214n,
        weakness of, 129, 130
Italy, 75
    Pyrrus' attack on, 3
Ito, Hirobumi, 57–61 (*passim*)

Japan 3, 13, 26
    Pearl Harbor Atttack (1941)
    air power, 71–72, 195n; alliance
        relationships, 74–78, 84, 198n–99n;
        army, 73, 79; capabilities, 64, 70–74,
        195n, 198n; conflict with the US,
        64–65; dependence on US, 64–65;

domestic changes, 78–85; factions, 79,
    80; irrationality attribution, 64, 194n;
    learning from Russo-Japanese War,
    69, 196n; navy, 68, 70–74, 80, 83,
    197n; 1941, 134–135, 159n, 164n–165n;
    previous war plans, 82–83; strategy,
    67–70, 84, 168, 196n–97n; and time
    pressure, 68
Russo Japanese War (1904), 41–63;
    alliance relationships, 55–58, 193n
    (*see also* Anglo-Japanese Treaty);
    armored cruisers, 42; army, 41–42, 54,
    189n; decision makers, 50–51, army,
    58–63; domestic changes, 58–62;
    intellegence gathering, 192n; and
    Korea, 43; and militarism, 59–62;
    navy, 41, 42, 50, 53–55, 191n;
    offensive capability, 42, 53–55,
    189n–90n; strategy, 49–53, 62–63,
    192n; tactics, 50; and time pressure,
    53; "war scare," 54, 57
Jarring Mission (1971), 127

Kanoye, Prince Fumimaro, 51, 80, 81, 82,
    199n
Kashmir, 3, 13, 172, 206n, 207n
    Azad Kashmir, 107, 111, 122, 206n
    dispute, 108–10, 206n
Kato, Kanji, 72
Katsura, Taro, 58, 60–61
Kennedy, John F., 123
Khan, Liaquat Ali, 121
Khan, Mohammed Asghar, 11, 111, 113
Khan, Mohammed Ayub, 112, 113, 115–16,
    120–23, 212n
Khrushchev, Nikita, 205n
King, Joel, 32
Kirkpatrick, Jeane, 157–59, 221n
Kissinger, Henry, 127, 138, 158,
    214n–15n
Knorr, Klaus, 6
Kodama, Gentaro, 52, 58, 60
Kogetsukai (Anti-Russian national
    league), 59
Kokumin Domeikai, 59
Kolpino Steel Works, 42
Komura, Jutaro, 58, 59, 60
Konoe, Atsumaro, 59, 60
Korea, 3, 13, 43, 45, 46, 48, 49, 56, 57
Korean War, (1950–53) (*see also* Peoples'
    Republic of China and United States
    of America), 3, 13, 86–106, 168–69
Kumingtang (KMT), 94, 103, 201n
Kuropatkin, Alexie, 45, 48
Kuwait, ix, 3, 174

Lami Dozo, Basilio, 162, 164
Lamsdorff, Vladimir, 45, 54, 57